Destination

Grammar &
Vocabulary

Malcolm Mann
Steve Taylore-Knowles

MACMILLAN

Macmillan Education
4 Crinan Street
London N1 9XW
A division of Macmillan Publishers Limited
Companies and representatives throughout the world

ISBN 978-0-230-03537-9

First published 2007

Original design by Georgia Liberopoulou
Page make-up by Anne Sherlock
Cover design by Macmillan Publishers Limited
Cover photograph Image 100

Authors' acknowledgements
The authors would like to thank Ruth Jimack and Lee Coveney for their valuable contributions to the planning, writing and editing of this book.

Printed and bound in Thailand

2016 2015 2014
10   9   8

Introduction

Overview

Destination B1: Grammar and Vocabulary has been designed for intermediate students at B1 (Threshold) level on the Council of Europe's Common European Framework scale. This book provides presentation and practice of all the key grammar, vocabulary and lexico-grammatical areas required for all main B1 exams. eg. Cambridge PET.
There are 42 units in the book: 28 grammar units and 14 vocabulary units.

Grammar

Each grammar unit begins with a clear one-page presentation of grammar rules and examples in table form. Important points are highlighted in Watch out! boxes.
The grammar practice exercises follow the order of the grammar presentation on a point-by-point basis, and are graded in difficulty through the unit. A wide variety of exercise types are used, including those found in major B1 level exams as well as exercise types from major B2 level exams which students are likely to encounter in the future.
In each set of two grammar units, the focus of the following related vocabulary unit is used as a context for presentation and text-based exercises.

Vocabulary

The vocabulary units are topic-based, covering topics appropriate to the level. Each vocabulary unit begins with a clear presentation table comprising five sections: topic vocabulary, phrasal verbs, prepositional phrases, word formation and word patterns.
The vocabulary exercises are organised according to these sections, and provide systematic practice of the vocabulary presented. Exercise types found in major B1 level exams are included, as are exercise types from major B2 level exams which students are likely to encounter in the future.
The grammar focus of the preceding unit is consolidated within these exercises.

Revision and consolidation

Strong emphasis is placed on revision and consolidation. The book includes:

- fourteen two-page reviews (after every three units)
- two four-page progress tests (after units 21 and 42)

Additional material

Additional reference and practice material is provided at the back of the book. This includes:

- a list of irregular present forms
- a list of irregular verbs
- a unit-by-unit glossary of all topic vocabulary with definitions and example sentences from the Macmillan Essential Dictionary
- a phrasal verb database, with definitions and example sentences
- a prepositional phrases database, with example sentences
- a word patterns database, with example sentences
- a word formation database, with example sentences

Contents

Units			Pages

Grammar

Present simple, present continuous, stative verbs

Present simple

Form

statement	negative	question
I/you/we/they **play** ...	I/you/we/they **do not (don't) play** ...	**Do** I/you/we/they **play** ...?
He/she/it **plays** ...	He/she/it **does not (doesn't) play** ...	**Does** he/she/it **play** ...?

Use	Example
Present habits	Marsha **goes** to dance lessons every Saturday.
Permanent situations	**Does** Dan **work** at the cinema?
States	I **like** the new James Bond film.
General truths	You **play** chess with 32 pieces.

 Watch out! The verbs *be* and *have* have irregular present forms. See page 182.

◉ Helpful hints

The present simple is often used with the following words and phrases:

adverbs
- always • usually • often
- sometimes • rarely • never

phrases
- every Monday/week/etc
- each Monday/week/etc
- once/twice a week/month/etc
- three times a week/month/etc

Remember that these adverbs usually go before the verb, but **after** the verb *be*.
- I **often** play football with my friends.
- I am **often** late for my piano lessons.

Present continuous

Form

statement	negative	question
I **am ('m) playing** ...	I **am not ('m not) playing** ...	**Am** I **playing** ...?
He/she/it **is ('s) playing** ...	He/she/it **is not (isn't / 's not) playing** ...	**Is** he/she/it **playing** ...?
You/we/they **are ('re) playing** ...	You/we/they **are not (aren't / 're not) playing** ...	**Are** you/we/they **playing** ...?

Use	Example
Actions happening now	Jan **is watching** a DVD upstairs.
Temporary situations	She **is working** at the museum until the end of the month.
Annoying habits (usually with *always*)	My brother **is always borrowing** my CDs without asking!

◉ Helpful hints

The present continuous is often used with the following words and phrases:
- now • right now • at the moment
- today • this week/month/etc

Stative verbs

Form

Stative verbs do not usually describe actions. They describe states (feelings, thoughts, etc). They are not normally used in continuous tenses.

✓ I **like** reading books in my free time.
✗ I ~~am liking reading books in my free time.~~

Some common stative verbs:

appear	include	see
be	know	seem
believe	like	taste
belong to	love	think
hate	need	understand
have	prefer	want

 Watch out! Some of these verbs (such as *be*, *have* and *think*) are used in continuous tenses when they describe actions.
✓ What **do** you **think** about his new song?
✓ I'm **thinking** about last night's match.

6

A Look at the pictures of Helen and use the prompts to write sentences. Use the correct form of the present simple.

every day / get up / at half past seven

once a week / watch a film at the cinema

often / eat fast food for lunch

rarely / go to the gym

in the evening / usually / meet her friends for coffee

have a driving lesson / twice a week

1 Every day, Helen gets up at half past seven.

2 ....

3 ....

4 ....

5 ....

6 ....

B Complete using the correct present continuous form of the verbs in brackets. You may have to use some negative forms.

1 Gordon? I think he .... (**write**) a letter at the moment.
2 Yes, the match is on TV now, but we .... (**lose**).
3 Right now, Margaret .... (**have**) a shower. Do you want to ring later?
4 Sally .... (**stay**) with her aunt for a few days.
5 I .... (**lie**)! It's true! I did see Madonna at the supermarket.
6 Josh .... (**always / use**) my bike! It's so annoying.
7 We .... (**have**) lunch, but I can come round and help you later.
8 .... (**you / play**) music up there? It's really noisy!

C Rewrite correctly. Change the words or phrases in bold.

1 **Are top musicians studying** for many years? ....
2 What's going on? I hope you **don't touch** my things! ....
3 It's a small business, so each person **is doing** lots of different jobs. ....
4 **Does Christine listen** to the radio, or is that the TV I can hear? ....
5 I **am usually buying** a special ticket each week for the bus because it's cheaper. ....
6 Our washing machine **is starting** when you press this button. ....
7 How's the match going? **Does our team win?** ....
8 Many people **are enjoying** spending time on the beach on holiday. ....

D Circle the correct word or phrase.

1 I **work / am working** at the local library for the summer.
2 We **don't go / aren't going** to the theatre very often.
3 Stacy **gets / is getting** ready for school, so she can't come to the phone.
4 **Does Gary ever talk / Is Gary ever talking** about his expedition to the Amazon jungle?
5 In squash, you **hit / are hitting** a ball against a wall.
6 I **read / am reading** a newspaper at least once a week.
7 **Do you practise / Are you practising** the piano for two hours every day?
8 Nadine and Claire **do / are doing** quite well at school at the moment.
9 A good friend **knows / is knowing** when you're upset about something.
10 How **do you spell / are you spelling** your name?

E Complete using the correct present simple or present continuous form of the verbs in the box. You may have to use some negative forms.

> belong • do • have • help • hold • move • use • watch

1 In Monopoly, you .... around the board, buying houses and hotels.
2 .... you .... this programme or can I turn the TV off?
3 Regular exercise .... you to stay healthy.
4 I .... my brother's guitar until I get a new one.
5 .... Simon always .... the washing-up after lunch?
6 .... you .... any sweaters in a larger size?
7 You .... the kite right. Let me show you.
8 Dad .... to the local astronomy club.

F Underline ten verbs in the wrong tense and rewrite them correctly.

> 'One game I am loving is backgammon. You are throwing the dice and then you move
> your pieces around the board. It is seeming quite easy, but in fact you are needing to be
> quite careful. When your piece lands on one of the other person's pieces, you are taking
> it off the board and you send it back to the beginning. You are winning by getting all your
> pieces to the end and off the board. Some people are preferring chess, but I am not
> understanding that game. Right now, I wait to have a game with my brother. He does his
> homework. I usually win, so I think he doesn't want to play a game with me!'

1 .... 4 .... 7 ....
2 .... 5 .... 8 ....
3 .... 6 .... 9 ....
                                                                         10 ....

Grammar

Past simple, past continuous, *used to*

Past simple

Form

statement	negative	question
I/you/he/she/it/we/they **played** …	I/you/he/she/it/we/they **did not (didn't) play** …	**Did** I/you/he/she/it/we/they **play** …?

Use	Example
Completed actions	I **saw** the new James Bond film yesterday.
Repeated actions in the past	I **went** to the theatre four times last month.
General truths about the past	Fifty years ago, people **didn't spend** as much on entertainment as they do today.
Main events in a story	Josh **pushed** the door open and **looked** inside the room.

Helpful hints

The past simple is often used with the following words and phrases:
- *yesterday*
- *last week/summer/year/etc*
- *in January/2001/etc*
- *an hour/a week/a year ago*

 Watch out! Some verbs have irregular past simple forms. See page 182.

Past continuous

Form

statement	negative	question
I/he/she/it **was playing** … You/we/they **were playing** …	I/he/she/it **was not (wasn't) playing** … You/we/they **were not (weren't) playing** …	**Was** I/he/she/it **playing**? **Were** you/we/they **playing**?

Use	Example
Actions happening at a moment in the past	At nine o'clock last night, I **was watching** TV.
Two actions in progress at the same time	I **was reading** a book while you **were doing** the washing-up.
Background information in a story	It **was raining** so Wendy decided to go to the cinema.

Helpful hints

The past continuous is often used with the following words and phrases:
- *at that moment*
- *at one/two/etc o'clock*
- *while*

 Watch out!
- When one action in the past happens in the middle of another, we use the past simple and the past continuous together.
  ✓ The phone **rang** while I **was watching** a DVD.
- We do not use the past continuous for regular or repeated actions in the past.
  ✗ ~~Last year, I **was going** to the cinema every weekend.~~

used to

Form

used to + bare infinitive

statement	negative	question
I/you/he/she/it/we/they **used to** …	I/you/he/she/it/we/they **never used to** … I/you/he/she/it/we/they **didn't use to** …	**Did** I/you/he/she/it/we/they **use to** …?

Use	Example
Distant past habits and states	When I was four, I **used to** eat ice cream every day.

A Complete using the correct past simple form of the verbs in the box. You may have to use some negative forms.

come • give • go • have • know • make • send • take

1 I got to the post office just before it closed and .... the letter.
2 We invited Stephanie to the party, but she ....
3 Jack lost his job because he .... too many mistakes.
4 Everyone .... that it was Bill's fault, but nobody said anything.
5 Karen .... the keys from the kitchen table and ran out the door.
6 I was bored, so Mum .... me some money to go shopping.
7 Do you remember the time we .... to India on holiday?
8 It started raining, but luckily I .... an umbrella in my bag.

B Look at the pictures and complete the sentences. Use the correct form of the past simple.

last week

yesterday

two years ago

last night

in June

a week ago

1 I don't want to go and see the film because <u>I saw it last week</u> ....
2 I don't need a football because ....
3 I know a lot about Paris because ....
4 I don't need to worry about my homework because ....
5 I haven't got a PlayStation any more because ....
6 Mum is angry with me because ....

C Complete using the correct past continuous form of the verbs in brackets.

1 Ted .... (**play**) his guitar at half past seven.
2 At midnight, I .... (**sleep**), but Jane .... (**listen**) to music.
3 Luke .... (**stand**) outside the bank when suddenly two robbers ran past him.
4 I know Doug .... (**work**) late at the office because I saw him when
   I .... (**leave**).
5 .... you .... (**have**) a shower when the earthquake happened?
6 Penny .... (**run**) to catch the bus when she slipped and fell.
7 When you saw Eugene .... he .... (**go**) home?
8 At midnight? Erm … we .... (**watch**) a DVD, I think.

D   Circle the correct word or phrase.

1 When we were in Canada, we **went / were going** skiing almost every day.
2 About four years ago, I **decided / was deciding** to become a chef.
3 Georgia **had / was having** a shower when someone knocked at the door.
4 Holly and I ran from the house to the taxi because it **rained / was raining** heavily.
5 Two men **argued / were arguing** outside, so I went to see what was happening.
6 Daniel **called / was calling** you at one o'clock yesterday, but you were here with me.
7 We **ate / were eating** breakfast when a letter came through the letter box.
8 As I walked past the window, I saw that Paula **made / was making** a cake.
9 I **dreamt / was dreaming** about my favourite band when the alarm clock went off.
10 While I **practised / was practising** the trumpet late last night, a neighbour came to complain.

E   Complete using the correct past simple or past continuous form of the verbs in the box.

> answer • be • continue • get • go • have • open • practise • put
> ring • say • shine • sing • wake

Amber's Big Match

One morning, Amber (**1**) .... up early. The sun (**2**) .... and the birds (**3**) .... Amber (**4**) .... very excited because it was the day of the big tennis match.

Amber (**5**) .... downstairs and into the kitchen, where her father (**6**) .... breakfast.

'Morning, Amber. Today's the day!' he (**7**) .... Amber smiled nervously. 'Don't worry!' he (**8**) .... 'You'll be fine.'

Amber (**9**) .... some toast into the toaster and (**10**) .... the fridge. Just as she (**11**) .... the butter out, the phone (**12**) .... Her father (**13**) .... it. After a few minutes, he put the phone down.

'Bad news, I'm afraid. The other player (**14**) .... yesterday when she had an accident. The match is off.'

Amber ate her toast slowly. She was surprised she didn't feel disappointed.

F   Complete using the correct form of *used to*. You may have to use some negative forms.

1 When I was younger, I .... eat pizza almost every day!
2 .... there .... be a supermarket on the corner?
3 Bradley is a teacher, but he .... want to be a train driver.
4 I .... like eating cabbage, but now I love it!
5 .... Rick .... have blond hair when he was a little boy?
6 I know Lily .... cook much, but now I think she makes dinner every day.

Vocabulary
Fun and games

● Topic vocabulary

see page 184 for definitions

beat (v)	concert (n)	organise (v)
board game (n phr)	defeat (v, n)	pleasure (n)
captain (n)	entertaining (adj)	referee (n)
challenge (v, n)	folk music (n phr)	rhythm (n)
champion (n)	group (n)	risk (v, n)
cheat (v)	gym (n)	score (v, n)
classical music (n phr)	have fun (v phr)	support (v, n)
club (n)	interest (v, n)	team (n)
coach (n)	member (n)	train (v)
competition (n)	opponent (n)	video game (n phr)

● Phrasal verbs

carry on	continue
eat out	eat at a restaurant
give up	stop doing sth you do regularly
join in	participate, take part
send off	make a player leave a game (eg, football)
take up	start (a hobby, sport, etc)
turn down	lower the volume of
turn up	increase the volume of

● Prepositional phrases

for a long time
for fun
in the middle (of)
in time (for)
on CD/DVD/video
on stage

● Word formation

act	action, (in)active, actor		**hero**	heroic, heroine
athlete	athletic, athletics		**music**	musical, musician
child	children, childhood		**play**	player, playful
collect	collection, collector		**sail**	sailing, sailor
entertain	entertainment		**sing**	sang, sung, song, singer, singing

● Word patterns

adjectives	bored with		*verbs*	feel like
	crazy about			listen to
	good at			take part in
	interested in		*nouns*	a book (by sb) about
	keen on			a fan of
	popular with			a game against

Topic vocabulary

A Complete the crossword.

Across

1 If he wins this match, he'll be the world .... ! (8)
4 I'm thinking of joining a .... to get more exercise. (3)
5 Our basketball .... said that I can play on Saturday! (5)
8 The .... blew his whistle and the game started. (7)
9 Which team do you .... ? (7)
11 Mark's band play traditional .... music – they often perform at country fairs and festivals. (4)

Down

2 I'm sorry, but you have to be a .... of the golf club to play here. (6)
3 My .... was a brilliant player and I didn't manage to win the match. (8)
6 Tom is really good at cards. He would never .... ! (5)
7 Lisa's .... has just reached number one with their new song! (5)
10 I took a big .... by doing the parachute jump, but I loved every second of it! (4)

B Complete using the correct form of the words and phrases in the box.

> beat • challenge • have fun • interest • organise • score • train

Start your *own* sports club!

Do you dream of (**1**) .... the winning goal in a football match, or (**2**) .... a top tennis player? Sport (**3**) .... most young people, and it's a great way to stay healthy and (**4**) .... at the same time. That's why the local council has decided to help young people who want to (**5**) .... their own sports club. We know it's a big (**6**) .... , and that's why we'll give you the money you need to get started. We'll help you find a place to (**7**) .... and give you money to find good players in your area. Contact the Town Hall for details.

C Circle the correct word.

1 I really like playing **board / video** games like Monopoly and Cluedo.
2 Roy was the best player, so he wasn't surprised when he became **captain / club** of the team.
3 Lots of people get **defeat / pleasure** from just watching sport from their armchairs.
4 I thought the music at the **concert / rhythm** we went to last night was great.
5 Everyone in my family supports the same **competition / team**.
6 I find **classical / entertaining** music really boring, and I prefer pop.

13

Phrasal verbs

D   Choose the correct answer.

1 You should take .... a sport and then you would get more exercise.
   A off   B up   C down

2 I'm trying to work! Could you please turn your music .... ?
   A down   B in   C out

3 Just ask and I'm sure the other children will let you join ....
   A out   B up   C in

4 The referee sent David .... for arguing with him.
   A off   B down   C up

5 This is my favourite song! Turn it .... !
   A off   B out   C up

6 A mobile phone rang, but the musician just carried .... playing.
   A on   B up   C in

7 We can't afford to eat .... very often.
   A off   B up   C out

8 I've decided to become a vegetarian and give .... meat.
   A up   B off   C out

Prepositional phrases

E   Write one word in each gap.

1 We were waiting outside the stadium .... a long time before they finally let us in.
2 I've got that concert .... DVD – it's fantastic!
3 I ran all the way home and I was just .... time for my favourite programme.
4 Everyone clapped when the singer came .... stage.
5 At the cinema, Mum sat on the right, Dad sat on the left and I sat .... the middle.
6 Ed doesn't want to become a professional footballer. He just does it .... fun.

Word formation

F   Complete by changing the form of the word in capitals when this is necessary.

1 What's the name of that .... you were singing earlier? **SING**
2 I started to learn the piano, but I don't think I've got much .... talent, to be honest. **MUSIC**
3 My dad used to be really fit and was on his college .... team. **ATHLETE**
4 When you were young, did you ever play in the street with other local .... ? **CHILD**
5 Alan is studying to be an .... , but I don't think he's enjoying it. **ACT**
6 They have a wonderful .... of old toys at the museum in town. **COLLECT**
7 My grandad loves to .... and we often go out on his boat. **SAIL**
8 You have to practise a lot if you want to work as a .... **MUSIC**

G   Use the word given in capitals at the end of each line to form a word that fits in the gap in the same line.

■ The need to play

Why are kittens such (**1**) .... animals? They love chasing a   **PLAY**

ball or a piece of wool, and they always play in a very (**2**) ....   **ATHLETE**

way. But why? All of a kitten's (**3**) .... when playing are, in   **ACT**

fact, important for the future. It might look like (**4**) .... , but   **ENTERTAIN**

the kitten is practising its hunting skills. That (**5**) .... jump   **HERO**

onto a toy teaches the kitten a lot. Think about your own (**6**) ....   **CHILD**

and you'll see that you learnt a lot through play.

Word patterns

H   Write one word in each gap.

Diana: Hello, is that Jenny? I'm bored (**1**) .... watching TV and I felt
(**2**) .... a chat. What are you doing?

Jenny: Hi, Diana. Well, I'm reading a book (**3**) .... a Russian writer. It's
(**4**) .... how to become a great actor.

Diana: Really? Oh, I'm really interested (**5**) .... acting. Tell me about it.

Jenny: He says it takes a long time to get good (**6**) .... acting. To become
popular (**7**) .... the public, you need to really understand people.

Diana: That sounds just like me! Tell me more. What else does he say?

I   Each of the words in bold is wrong. Write the correct word.

1 I'm completely crazy **with** skateboarding! I love it!   ....

2 In my free time I listen **on** music on CD or on the radio.   ....

3 Elsa isn't very keen **for** this group, but they're one of my favourites.   ....

4 Next week we've got a game **to** a team from Hungary.   ....

5 Is that Kylie? Oh, I'm a really big fan **from** hers.   ....

6 I was really scared when I took part **to** the singing competition last year.   ....

Review 1

A Use the word given in capitals at the end of each line to form a word that fits in the gap in the same line.

Collecting records

These days, most of us have a CD (**1**) .... Before the CD,   **COLLECT**
(**2**) .... made LPs, or 'long-playing' records. Although many   **SING**
(**3**) .... have never seen an LP, they were once very popular.   **CHILD**
To play these records, you needed a record (**4**) .... with a   **PLAY**
needle that ran along the record and produced the sound. Some
(**5**) .... say the sound of LPs was better than CDs – and   **MUSIC**
many (**6**) .... agree! LPs are no longer very popular as a   **COLLECT**
form of (**7**) .... , but many people buy and sell them. Some   **ENTERTAIN**
of them remember the LP from their (**8**) .... and listening to   **CHILD**
records reminds them of the past.

(1 mark per answer)

B Complete using the correct form of the verbs in the box. You have to use one word twice.

carry • eat • give • join • send • take • turn

9 Now, everyone knows this song, so I want you all to .... in with me!

10 It's so noisy in this restaurant. Could you ask them to .... the music down?

11 There was a fight during the match and the referee .... two players off.

12 We .... out about once a week and we cook at home the rest of the time.

13 I love this song! .... it up!

14 I used to play the trumpet, but I .... up last year because I didn't have time.

15 We stopped playing because of the rain, but when it stopped we .... on.

16 A good way of getting more exercise is to .... up a sport, like basketball.

(1 mark per answer)

C Complete each second sentence using the word given, so that it has a similar meaning to the first sentence. Write between two and five words.

17 Jack really likes football and never misses a match. **crazy**
   Jack .... football and never misses a match.

18 My uncle worked on a sailing boat until he was thirty. **was**
   My uncle .... until he was thirty.

19 Do you want to watch TV? **feel**
   Do you .... TV?

20 John participated in a swimming competition last week. **part**
   John .... in a swimming competition last week.

21 June and I had a game of tennis. **against**
   I had .... June.

22 I played chess almost every day when I was young. **used**
   I .... chess almost every day when I was young.

23 Volleyball doesn't really interest me. **in**
   I'm not .... volleyball.

24 I enjoyed myself at your birthday party. **fun**
   I .... at your birthday party.

25 Young children like Disneyland. **popular**
   Disneyland .... young children.

26 Karen doesn't like watching sport on TV. **keen**
   Karen .... watching sport on TV.

(2 marks per answer)

D Choose the correct answer.

27 When you rang, I .... my bike.
   A cleaned   C used to clean
   B was cleaning   D clean

28 At my last basketball club, we ....
   every Saturday for three hours.
   A were training   C train
   B training   D used to train

29 I really .... the meal we had at your
   house last Tuesday.
   A was liking   C like
   B liked   D am liking

30 We .... to the beach every day when
   we were on holiday.
   A went   C go
   B were going   D used to going

31 I broke my leg when Tony and I ....
   for the school sports day.
   A practised   C were practising
   B used to practise   D are practising

32 Leon never .... about it, but he was
   once a world champion skier.
   A talks   C was talking
   B is talking   D talk

33 I .... like golf, but now I really like it.
   A don't use to   C didn't used to
   B don't used to   D didn't use to

34 Denise .... at the stadium until she
   finds a better job.
   A works   C used to work
   B is working   D was working

(1 mark per answer)

E Match the two halves of the sentences.

35 I waited outside the tennis club for   ....   A fun, and I don't want to do it as a job.
36 When you rang, I was in   ....   B stage, with all the audience clapping.
37 We finally got to the stadium just in   ....   C time to see the match start.
38 I just play football for   ....   D a long time, but George didn't appear.
39 I loved that film and when it comes out   ....   E on DVD, I'll definitely get it.
40 It's great to appear on   ....   F the middle of cleaning my football boots.

(1 mark per answer)

Total mark: ..../50

Present perfect simple, present perfect continuous

Present perfect simple

Form

have/has + past participle

statement	negative	question
I/you/we/they **have ('ve) learnt** …	*I/you/we/they* **have not (haven't) learnt** …	**Have** *I/you/we/they* **learnt** …?

Use	Example
Situations that started in the past and are still true	*Mrs Jenkins* **has been** *the head teacher for three years.*
Completed actions at a time in the past which is not mentioned	*I***'ve** *already* **read** *that book.*
Completed actions where the important thing is the result now	*They***'ve** *all* **done** *their homework.*

Helpful hints

The present perfect simple is often used with the following words and phrases:

- *for* — *She's taught German here* **for** *over five years.*
- *since* — *Mr Gray has taught French here* **since** *2006.*
- *just* — *We've* **just** *done this exercise.*
- *already* — *We've* **already** *done this exercise.*
- *yet* — *We haven't checked the answers* **yet**.
- *ever* — *Have you* **ever** *had guitar lessons?*
- *never* — *I've* **never** *understood why they give us so much homework!*
- *it's the first time* — **It's the first time** *we've watched a video in class.*

 Watch out!

- We don't use the present perfect simple when we want to say **when** something happened in the past. We use the past simple.

  ✓ *I* **did** *my homework* **last night**.

- We don't use the past simple when we want to show that something happened **before now** or is **still important now**. We use the present perfect simple.

  ✓ *I***'ve finished**! *Can I go home now?*

- Some verbs have irregular past participle forms. See page 182.

Present perfect continuous

Form

have/has + *been* + *-ing*

statement	negative	question
I/you/we/they **have ('ve) been studying** …	*I/you/we/they* **have not (haven't) been studying** …	**Have** *I/you/we/they* **been studying** …?
He/she/it **has ('s) been studying** …	*He/she/it* **has not (hasn't) been studying** …	**Has** *he/she/it* **been studying** …?

Use	Example
Actions continuing up to now or just before now	*We***'ve been doing** *grammar exercises for over an hour. Can we have a break now?*
	*They're having a break now because they***'ve been working** *so hard.*

Helpful hints

The present perfect continuous is often used with the following words:

- *for* — *I've been learning English* **for** *over three years.*
- *since* — *He's been learning Chinese* **since** *2004.*
- *just* — *I've* **just** *been reading the school newspaper.*

 Watch out!

- The present perfect simple often emphasises the result of an action:

  ✓ *She***'s written** *an article for the school newspaper.* (= She's finished it.)

- The present perfect continuous often emphasises the action, and the time spent on the action, rather than the result:

  ✓ *She***'s been writing** *an article for the school newspaper.* (= She's started, but she hasn't finished it yet.)

A Complete using the correct present perfect simple form of the verbs in brackets.

1 I .... (**see**) this film already.
2 John and Julie .... (**had**) their car for about a year.
3 She .... (**not / take**) her driving test yet.
4 Sue .... (**be**) a tour guide since she left university.
5 .... (**you / ride**) into town on your new bike yet?
6 This new computer .... (**make**) my life a lot easier.
7 We .... (**not / decide**) what to get Mark for his birthday yet.
8 .... (**Paul / ever / meet**) a famous person?

B Choose the correct answer.

1 .... never played this game before.
   A I've   B I

2 Adam .... his room last night.
   A has tidied   B tidied

3 .... here since 2005?
   A Have you lived   B Did you live

4 Carol and I .... to the cinema three nights ago.
   A have been   B went

5 It's the first time .... our flat, isn't it?
   A you've visited   B you visited

6 They .... the baby a name yet.
   A haven't given   B didn't give

7 .... to New York when you went to the States last summer?
   A Have you been   B Did you go

8 .... an e-mail before?
   A Have you ever sent   B Did you ever send

C Look at the picture and use the prompts to write sentences. Use the correct form of the present perfect simple.

1 lesson / not / start / yet
   ....
   ....

2 teacher / already / write / on the board
   ....
   ....

3 Joe and Tim / just / come / into the classroom
   ....
   ....

4 Tony / not / finished / getting / books ready
   ....
   ....

5 Christine / already / open / book
   ....
   ....

6 Dave / drop / pen / on the floor
   ....
   ....

7 he / not / pick it up / yet
   ....
   ....

19

D Complete using the correct present perfect continuous form of the verbs in brackets. Use short forms where possible.

Mandy: Hi Matt. How are you? What (**1**) .... (**you / do**) recently?

Matt: Oh, hi Mandy! Well, (**2**) .... (**I / study**) for my exams.

Mandy: That sounds boring! (**3**) .... (**you / work**) hard?

Matt: Very! Basically, (**4**) .... (**I / just / sit**) at my desk in my bedroom for the past three weeks and (**5**) .... (**I / not / go**) out at all. (**6**) .... (**I / work**) with Michael, my best friend, some of the time, though, so at least I've had some company. How about you?

Mandy: Well, my mum and (**7**) .... (**I / paint**) my bedroom for the last few days. That has been fun! And (**8**) .... (**we / also / plan**) our summer holiday.

Matt: Great! Where are you going?

Mandy: Well, we haven't decided yet. (**9**) .... (**We / look**) at different places to see which we like best.

Matt: I'm sure you'll have a great time, wherever you go. Oh, by the way, (**10**) .... (**I / think**) of having a party when I finish my exams. Would you like to come?

Mandy: Sure! That would be great!

E Circle the correct word or phrase.

1 I think I've **heard / been hearing** that song before.
2 They haven't **arrived / been arriving** yet, but they should be here soon.
3 You've **written / been writing** that e-mail for over an hour. How long is it going to take you?
4 Have you **talked / been talking** on the phone since eight o'clock?
5 Jo has already **invited / been inviting** Shirley to dinner.
6 I've **read / been reading** an interview with Brad Pitt, but I haven't finished it yet.
7 Have the boys **played / been playing** computer games since this morning?

F Complete using the words in the box.

already • ever • for • just • never • since • yet

1 I haven't listened to their new CD .... Is it any good?
2 We've been waiting for you .... over an hour. Where have you been?
3 Have you .... been to the UK before?
4 I'm afraid we've .... made plans for this weekend, so we won't be free.
5 Pedro has been having English lessons .... he was five years old.
6 It's strange that you mention the film *Crash*. I've .... been reading about it in the paper.
7 I've .... heard of a 'sudoku'. What is it?

Grammar

Past perfect simple, past perfect continuous

Past perfect simple

had + past participle

statement	negative	question
I/you/he/she/it/we/they **had ('d) written** …	I/you/he/she/it/we/they **had not (hadn't) written** …	**Had** I/you/he/she/it/we/they **written** …?

Use	Example
Actions and states before a moment in the past	**I'd finished** my homework a few minutes before the lesson started. Mrs Cross **had been** a teacher for twenty years before she became a head teacher.
Finished actions and states where the important thing is the result at a moment in the past	We were happy because we'**d** all **done** our homework.

Helpful hints

The past perfect simple is often used with the following words and phrases:

- by — I'd finished my homework **by** eight o'clock.
- by the time — **By the time** I got to class, the lesson had started.
- before — The teacher had checked the answers **before** the lesson.
- after — I left **after** I'd finished the test.
- just — Simon had **just** finished the test when the bell rang.
- when — I left **when** I'd finished the test.

Watch out!
- Whether we use the past simple or the past perfect simple can change the meaning of a sentence.
  - ✓ The lesson **started** when I arrived. (= I arrived and then the lesson started.)
  - ✓ The lesson **had started** when I arrived. (= The lesson started and then I arrived.)
- Some verbs have irregular past participle forms. See page 182.

Past perfect continuous

had + *been* + *-ing*

statement	negative	question
I/you/he/she/it/we/they **had ('d) been writing** …	I/you/he/she/it/we/they **had not (hadn't) been writing** …	**Had** I/you/he/she/it/we/they **been writing** …?

Use	Example
Actions continuing up to, or stopping just before, a moment in the past	We'**d been doing** grammar exercises for over an hour, so we were really bored! They had a break because they'**d been working** so hard.

Helpful hints

The past perfect continuous is often used with the following words and phrases:

- for — Tony had been studying **for** hours, so he had a headache.
- since — She'd been hoping to win the competition **since** the summer.
- before — We'd been talking about the Internet **before** the lesson started.
- all day/night/etc — I'd been studying **all day**.

Watch out!
- The past perfect simple often emphasises the result of an action:
  - ✓ She'**d written** an article for the school newspaper. (= She'd finished it.)
- The past perfect continuous often emphasises the action, and the time spent on the action, rather than the result:
  - ✓ She'**d been writing** an article for the newspaper. (= She'd started, but she hadn't finished it.)

A Complete using the correct past perfect simple form of the verbs in brackets.

1 By the time I arrived, everyone .... (**leave**)!
2 Steve .... (**already / see**) the film, so he didn't come with us to the cinema.
3 Tina .... (**not / finish**) doing the housework by seven o'clock, so she called Andrea to tell her she would be late.
4 .... (**you / just / speak**) to Billy when I rang?
5 The car broke down just after .... (**we / set off**).
6 I didn't eat anything at the party because .... (**I / already / eat**) at home.
7 .... (**you / hear**) about the accident before you saw it on TV?

B Choose the sentence (A or B) which means the same as the first sentence.

1 We'd had dinner when Wendy arrived.
   A Wendy arrived and then we had dinner.
   B We had dinner and then Wendy arrived.

2 I read the book after I'd seen the film.
   A I saw the film and then I read the book.
   B I read the book and then I saw the film.

3 By the time Dad came home, I'd gone to bed.
   A I went to bed before Dad came home.
   B I went to bed after Dad came home.

4 She didn't go to bed until her mum had come home.
   A She went to bed and then her mum came home.
   B Her mum came home and then she went to bed.

5 Mr Banks hadn't arrived at the office by the time I got there.
   A I arrived before Mr Banks.
   B Mr Banks arrived before me.

6 They'd bought the plane tickets before they heard about the cheaper flight.
   A They bought the plane tickets and later they heard about the cheaper flight.
   B They heard about the cheaper flight and then they bought the plane tickets.

7 The girls had tidied the house when the visitors arrived.
   A The visitors arrived and later the girls tidied the house.
   B The girls tidied the house and then the visitors arrived.

C Write sentences using the prompts. One of the verbs must be in the past perfect simple.

1 we / just / hear / the news / when / you / ring
   ....

2 I / already / think of / that / before / you / suggest / it
   ....

3 when / I / turn on / the TV / the programme / already / start
   ....

4 she / be / hungry / because / she / not / eat / anything / all day
   ....

5 by the time / I leave / school / I / decide / to become / a musician
   ....

D Look at the pictures and complete the sentences. Use the correct form of the past perfect continuous.

1 She was tired because .... (**run**).

2 They were hot because .... (**dance**).

3 The garden was flooded because .... (**it / rain / all night**).

4 Did they crash because .... (**drive / too fast**)?

5 When I arrived, ... (**they / wait / for over half an hour**).

6 When I got there, ... (**they / not / wait / long**).

E Choose the correct answer.

1 I'd only .... the washing-up for a few minutes when Clare came home, so she offered to finish it.

A done   B been doing

2 Had you already .... James his birthday present when we gave him ours?

A given   B been giving

3 Gail hadn't .... me that she would help me, so I wasn't angry when she didn't.

A told   B been telling

4 Mum had .... her cup of tea for several minutes before she realised it had salt in it!

A drunk   B been drinking

5 We'd .... ready all day when they called to say the party had been cancelled.

A got   B been getting

6 It was a fantastic experience because I'd never .... in a plane before.

A flown   B been flying

F If a line is correct, put a tick (✓). If there is an extra word in a line, write the word.

Dear Diary,

1 ...... had	This morning my exam results finally ~~had~~ came. I'd been expecting
2	them for the last week. I knew I'd been done quite well, but I was
3	still nervous as I had opened the envelope. Before I'd had a chance to
4	look at them, my sister ran up and pulled them out of my hand! She
5	had read them out one by one. 'English A, maths A, biology A,
6	French A ... ' This was the news I'd been waiting for. I'd got As in
7	every subject – even geography, which I hadn't been making sure
8	about! When Mum and Dad heard the news, they immediately started
9	been shouting with joy. By the time I'd had breakfast, Mum had
10	already called Grandma and Grandpa and had yet told the neighbours!

Vocabulary
Learning and doing

Topic vocabulary

see page 185 for definitions

achieve (v)	guess (v, n)	report (n)
brain (n)	hesitate (v)	revise (v)
clever (adj)	instruction (n)	search (v, n)
concentrate (v)	make progress (v phr)	skill (n)
consider (v)	make sure (v phr)	smart (adj)
course (n)	mark (v, n)	subject (n)
degree (n)	mental (adj)	take an exam (v phr)
experience (v, n)	pass (v)	talented (adj)
expert (n, adj)	qualification (n)	term (n)
fail (v)	remind (v)	wonder (v)

Phrasal verbs

cross out	draw a line through sth written
look up	try to find information in a book, etc
point out	tell sb important information
read out	say sth out loud which you are reading
rip up	tear into pieces
rub out	remove with a rubber
turn over	turn sth so the other side is towards you
write down	write information on a piece of paper

Prepositional phrases

by heart
for instance
in conclusion
in fact
in favour (of)
in general

Word formation

begin	began, begun, beginner, beginning	**instruct**	instruction, instructor
brave	bravery	**memory**	memorise, memorial
correct	correction, incorrect	**refer**	reference
divide	division	**silent**	silence, silently
educate	education	**simple**	simplify, simplicity

Word patterns

adjectives	capable of		help (sb) with
	talented at		know about
verbs	cheat at/in		learn about
	confuse sth with		succeed in
	continue with	*nouns*	an opinion about/of
	cope with		a question about

Topic vocabulary

A Complete using the correct form of the words and phrases in the boxes.

achieve • fail • pass

1 We had our English exam this morning. I hope I've .... !
2 Pete couldn't answer any questions, so he thinks he has ....
3 Our teacher said that we've all .... a lot this year.

degree • experience • instruction

4 I've left you a list of .... on the kitchen table. Make sure you follow them!
5 Meeting Brad Pitt was an amazing .... !
6 My sister left Warwick University after she got her ....

course • qualification • skill

7 Being able to use a computer is a very useful ....
8 I'm thinking of going on a computer ....
9 You can only apply for this job if you've got a .... in website design.

make progress • make sure • take an exam

10 You've all .... a lot of .... this year. Well done!
11 I always get nervous before I ....
12 I .... that I'd answered all the questions and then I handed in my test paper.

B Circle the correct word.

1 I **search / wonder** how difficult the maths test tomorrow will be.
2 It's nearly the end of **term / mark**, so it will be the holidays soon!
3 Could you **revise / remind** me to take this book back to the library?
4 Carl is a computer **brain / expert**. Why don't you ask him to fix your computer?
5 Rosalind is a really **smart / talented** musician, but she doesn't practise enough.
6 Rebecca is really **clever / mental**. She always knows the answer!
7 I wasn't sure of the answer so I **guessed / hesitated** and I was right!
8 Have you ever **concentrated / considered** becoming a professional singer?
9 After every experiment in chemistry, we have to write a **subject / report** on what happened.

C Complete the crossword. All the answers are words in bold in exercise B.

Across

2 I want you to .... Unit 6 at the weekend because you've got a test on Monday. (6)

4 Another word for 'clever' is '........................'. (5)

6 What's your favourite .... at school? (7)

8 The other students were talking and laughing but Jamie .... on his work. (12)

Down

1 If you can do maths problems in your head, then you're good at .... arithmetic. (6)

3 I got a .... of nineteen out of twenty in the test. (4)

4 I'll have to .... for that book because I've no idea where it is. (6)

5 Kelly didn't know what to say so she .... before she answered. (9)

7 Everyone uses their .... when they think. (5)

Phrasal verbs

D Write one word in each gap.

24th June

We had our English exam today. It was a disaster! We all sat there nervously, waiting for Mrs Jennings to say we could start. Finally, she told us to turn our exam papers (1) .... Then she read (2) .... the instructions to make sure we all understood. We had to write three essays in two hours! We weren't allowed to look (3) .... any words in the dictionary, and we had to write in pen. That meant we couldn't rub anything (4) .... if we made a mistake. We had to cross it (5) .... neatly or just rip (6) .... the whole piece of paper and start again. So, I read through the three questions very carefully and thought about what I was going to write. I'd just written my name (7) .... at the top of the first piece of paper, and was about to start writing the first essay, when Mrs Jennings pointed (8) .... that there were only five minutes left. Oh dear!

Prepositional phrases

E Each of the words in bold is in the wrong sentence. Write the correct word.

1 We learnt that poem by **conclusion** but I've forgotten it now. ....

2 Are you in **general** of teenagers leaving school at the age of sixteen? ....

3 I thought the exam would be difficult but, in **instance**, it was really easy. ....

4 Many people, for **heart** my brother, prefer to do something active rather than do homework. ....

5 In **fact**, the teachers at this school are really nice, but some are nicer than others! ....

6 It's a good idea to start the final paragraph of your composition with the phrase 'In **favour**'. ....

Word formation

F Complete by changing the form of the word in capitals.

1 Do you think you get a good .... at your school? **EDUCATE**
2 I'm not an expert. I'm only a .... ! **BEGIN**
3 The police are going to give Tracy an award for .... **BRAVE**
4 I'm writing in .... to your advertisement for a guitar teacher. **REFER**
5 I want .... at all times during the exam. **SILENT**
6 Rupert is an .... at a local extreme sports centre. **INSTRUCT**
7 I'm afraid that answer is .... so you haven't won today's top prize.
   What a shame! **CORRECT**
8 You don't understand .... ? Look! Twelve divided by four is three.
   It's easy! **DIVIDE**
9 This is really difficult to understand. Why don't we .... it a little? **SIMPLE**
10 Actors have to .... a lot of words when they are in a play. **MEMORY**

Word patterns

G Write one word in each gap.

1 You didn't cheat .... the exam, did you?
2 We're learning .... dinosaurs at the moment at school.
3 What's your opinion .... children going to school at a very young age?
4 I think you've confused astronomy .... astrology – they're not the same!
5 I hope Mr Aziz doesn't ask me a question .... the book because I haven't read it!
6 I can't cope .... all this homework I've got to do!

H Complete each second sentence using the word given, so that it has a similar meaning to the first sentence. Write between two and five words.

1 Sasha is a really good tango dancer. **talented**
   Sasha is really .... tango dancing.

2 Our teacher wasn't feeling well but she didn't stop the lesson. **continued**
   Our teacher wasn't feeling well but she .... the lesson.

3 I've got no experience at designing clothes. **know**
   I .... designing clothes at all!

4 Dan couldn't do his homework on his own so I've been helping him. **helping**
   I've been .... his homework because he couldn't do it on his own.

5 No one can learn all that in one day! **capable**
   No one .... all that in one day!

6 I really hope you find a solution to the problem. **succeed**
   I really hope you .... a solution to the problem.

Review 2

A Complete using the words in the box.

> exam • fact • favour • heart • instance • mark • progress • skill

1 My German teacher says I've made a lot of .... this term!
2 What time are you taking the French .... tomorrow?
3 I'm not in .... of giving students lots of homework each night.
4 Being able to drive a car is a very useful ....
5 Have we got to learn all these irregular verbs by .... ?
6 Some languages, like Russian for .... , don't have words for 'a', 'an' and 'the'.
7 I got a very good .... in my geography test.
8 Many people hate learning phrasal verbs, but in .... they're not that difficult.

(1 mark per answer)

B Write a phrasal verb in the correct form to replace the words in bold. The first letter of the first word is given to help you.

9 Simon r........................... .... the wrong answer and wrote the right one. (**removed with a rubber**)
10 Why did you r........................... .... that piece of paper? (**tear into pieces**)
11 If you make a mistake, just c........................... it .... (**draw a line through**)
12 You should l........................... .... words you don't know in a dictionary. (**find information about**)
13 Carol, will you r........................... .... your poem to the class, please? (**say out loud**)
14 Our teacher p........................... .... that we only had five minutes left. (**said**)
15 Have you all w........................... .... what the homework is? (**made a note of**)

(2 marks per answer)

C Complete by changing the form of the word in capitals.

16 What's the name of Dave's driving .... ? **INSTRUCT**
17 Dictionaries and encyclopaedias are examples of .... books. **REFER**
18 I've only been learning Arabic for a few months, so I'm still a .... **BEGIN**
19 In maths, you have to learn to do addition, subtraction, multiplication and ....
    DIVIDE
20 Three of your answers were .... , so you got 17 out of 20. **CORRECT**
21 Are you really going to take part in the singing competition? I admire your .... !
    BRAVE

22 I think every child should get a good .... **EDUCATE**

23 There's a .... to Albert Einstein in the town square. **MEMORY**

24 I want complete .... , so no talking at all! **SILENT**

25 This maths problem is too difficult for you, so I'll .... it a little. **SIMPLE**

(1 mark per answer)

D Choose the correct answer.

26 It's the first time .... all the answers right in a test!
   A I've got   C I've been getting
   B I'd got   D I'd been getting

27 The exam .... when Jimmy finally found the right room.
   A has already started C had already started
   B already started   D already starts

28 .... that crossword for over an hour and you still haven't finished it!
   A You've done   C You've been doing
   B You'd done   D You'd been doing

29 When they let us go in, we .... outside the exam room for over half an hour.
   A have stood   C have been standing
   B had been standing D are standing

30 Clare hasn't finished her homework ....
   A already   C just
   B yet   D ever

31 Have you .... been on a school trip?
   A yet   C before
   B for   D ever

32 Lizzie has been having dance classes .... she was four years old.
   A for   C since
   B from   D when

33 Had you been learning French .... several years before you took your first exam?
   A for   C since
   B from   D when

(1 mark per answer)

E Write one word in each gap.

Cheating

You're doing a history test. Your friend, who's sitting next to you, really wants to succeed (**34**) .... the test. There's a question (**35**) .... the First World War, which you've been learning (**36**) .... recently. You know a lot (**37**) .... it, but your friend isn't really capable (**38**) .... answering the question properly. Your friend whispers 'Help me!' to you. What should you do? Should you help your friend (**39**) .... the question, or just continue (**40**) .... your own test? Every student has to cope (**41**) .... this difficult situation at some point. What's your opinion (**42**) .... cheating? Should you help your friend cheat (**43**) .... the test or not?

(1 mark per answer)

Total mark: ..../50

Grammar

Future time
(present continuous, *will*, *be going to*, present simple)

Present continuous

Form

For the form of the present continuous, see Unit 1.

Use	Example
Arrangements	We'**re driving** to Berlin this weekend.

Watch out!
- Things we want to do in the future but have not arranged are called 'intentions'. We do not use the present continuous for intentions. We use *be going to* instead.
  ✗ I'**m becoming** an explorer when I grow up.
- We do not use the present continuous for predictions. We use *will* or *be going to* instead.
  ✗ Do you think you'**re enjoying** your trip to Berlin next week?

will

Form

will + bare infinitive

statement	negative	question
I/you/he/she/it/we/they **will ('ll)** go …	I/you/he/she/it/we/they **will not (won't)** go …	**Will** I/you/he/she/it/we/they go …?

Use	Example
Facts about the future	The new airport **will** be the biggest in Europe.
Predictions	You'**ll** have a great time in the Bahamas.
Offers and requests	We'**ll** help you get ready for your holiday.
Decisions made now	I know! I'**ll** go to China this summer.

Watch out!
- With offers which are questions, we use *Shall* with *I* and *we*.
  ✓ **Shall** I drive you to the airport?
- We do not use *will* for arrangements.
  ✗ We'**ll visit** my grandma this weekend.

be going to

Form

be going to + bare infinitive

statement	negative	question
I **am ('m) going to** travel …	I **am ('m) not going to** travel …	**Am** I **going to** travel …?
He/she/it **is ('s) going to** travel …	He/she/it **is not (isn't / 's not) going to** travel …	**Is** he/she/it **going to** travel …?
You/we/they **are ('re) going to** travel …	You/we/they **are not (aren't / 're not) going to** travel …	**Are** you/we/they **going to** travel …?

Use	Example
Intentions	I'**m going to** become an explorer when I grow up.
Predictions (often with evidence we can see)	It'**s going to** rain, so take an umbrella.
Facts about the future	The new airport **is going to** be the biggest in Europe.

Present simple

Form

For the form of the present simple, see Unit 1.

Use	Example
Timetables	My plane **leaves** at six.

A   Look at Shelley's diary and use the prompts to write sentences. Use the correct form of the present continuous.

meet Alison - Friends Café

go shopping - Mum

catch train - Brighton

spend day - Charlie in Brighton

catch train - home - 10 am

work - Dad's shop - all morning

1 On Monday, she ....

....

2 On Tuesday, she ....

....

3 On Wednesday, she ....

....

4 On Thursday, she ....

....

5 On Friday, she ....

....

6 On Saturday, she ....

....

B   Complete using *will* or *shall* and the verbs in the box. You may have to use some negative forms.

be • come • find • have • lend • live • take • visit

1 This year, more than a million tourists .... our local area.
2 I'm sure we .... your bag soon. Where did you last see it?
3 .... you .... me some money until Saturday?
4 Everything on the menu looks delicious! Erm ... I .... Chicken Kiev, please.
5 I .... you to the bus station, if you like.
6 One day, people .... on Mars in special buildings.
7 No, there .... any problems with delivering your new furniture next week.
8 .... we .... at six to help you get things ready for dinner?

C   Complete using the correct form of *be going to* and the verbs in brackets. You may have to use some negative forms.

1 When I grow up, I .... (**play**) guitar in a rock group!
2 Rick and Mark .... (**start**) going to the gym twice a week.
3 .... Lauren .... (**tell**) her mum about what happened?
4 I .... (**look**) on the Internet for information about snowboarding.
5 No, Nadine .... (**invite**) everyone from class – just her close friends.
6 .... Harry .... (**be**) ready on time or not?
7 Careful! You .... (**break**) something with that ball! Go outside!
8 I .... (**lie down**) for half an hour. Call me at six o'clock.

D Complete using the correct present simple form of the verbs in the box.

arrive • come • leave • take

'I'm so excited about my holiday! My plane (**1**) .... the airport here at nine o'clock and we (**2**) .... in Paris two hours later. We then (**3**) .... the train from the airport to the city. We'll have a great week, and then we (**4**) .... back on the 17th. I can't wait!'

E Circle the correct word or phrase.

1 Oscar says he **is doing / will do** the washing-up after dinner.
2 I'm a bit scared because I **am seeing / will see** the dentist this afternoon.
3 What **are you going to do / do you do** this evening?
4 **Shall you tell / Will you tell** Rupert I'm sorry about yesterday?
5 My dad **will grow / is going to grow** a beard, but my mum doesn't like the idea.
6 I have to revise tonight because we **are having / will have** an exam tomorrow.
7 I **am remembering / will remember** this day for the rest of my life!
8 **Do you go / Are you going** to Australia next Christmas?
9 I'm sure you **are passing / will pass** your driving test. Don't worry.
10 If you want me to, I **will complain / am going to complain** to the manager about it.

F Choose the correct answer.

1 'Have you made plans for the summer?'
  'Yes. .... to Spain.'
  A We'll go   B We're going   C We go

2 'We're moving house tomorrow.'
  'Really? .... you with the furniture.'
  A I help   B I'm helping   C I'll help

3 'Do you need this paintbrush?'
  'Ah, yes. .... it to me, please?'
  A Do you pass   B Will you pass   C Are you passing

4 'What do you want to be when you grow up, Stevie?'
  '........................ a scientist. That's what I want to do, anyway.'
  A I be   B I'm going to be   C I'm being

5 'John is a better player than Martin, isn't he?'
  'Oh, yes. .... the match tomorrow, I expect.'
  A He'll win   B He wins   C He's winning

6 'The weather has been terrible, hasn't it?'
  'Yes, I think .... again later.'
  A it's going to rain   B it's raining   C it rains

Grammar

Prepositions of time and place

 in

Time		Place	
months	*Paris is wonderful **in** April.*	towns and cities	*There's a famous castle **in** Edinburgh.*
years	*I first went to Russia **in** 2005.*	countries and continents	*My brother is **in** Mexico.*
seasons	*We often go skiing **in** winter.*	areas and regions	*What's life like **in** the desert?*
parts of the day	*My train leaves **in** the afternoon.*	inside an object	*Your passport is **in** the drawer.*
		inside a room	*I've left the tickets **in** the living room!*
		inside a building	*Sharon has been **in** the travel agent's for an hour!*

> **Helpful hints**
>
> We also use *in* in the following phrases:
> • *in a minute/an hour* • *in front of*
> • *in the middle (of)* • *in the future*

Watch out! With verbs of motion (*come, go, move, run, walk*, etc), we usually use *to* instead of *in, on* or *at*.
✓ *Was it hot when you went **to** Japan?*

 on

Time		Place	
days	*I got a new car **on** Saturday.*	islands	*Last year, we stayed **on** Mykonos.*
dates	*My birthday is **on** 19th March.*	pages	*There are some useful Italian phrases **on** page 97.*
		on top of an object	*Did you put your car keys **on** the kitchen table?*
		on a surface	*There's a timetable **on** the wall.*

> **Helpful hints**
>
> We also use *on* in the following phrases:
>
> • *on the beach* • *on the left/right*
> • *on my birthday*

Watch out! • We say *in the morning/afternoon/evening*, but *on Monday morning/Wednesday evening/etc.*
✓ *We're flying to Washington **in the morning** / **on Tuesday morning**.*

• We don't use a preposition with *tomorrow, yesterday, tomorrow morning, yesterday evening*, etc.
✓ *We're flying to Washington **tomorrow afternoon**.*

 at

Time		Place	
clock times	*There's a bus **at** ten past three.*	exact places	*What's it like **at** the North Pole?*
holiday periods	*What are you doing **at** Christmas?*	addresses	*My cousin lives **at** 132 London Road.*
		buildings, when we are talking about the activities that happen there	*I think John is **at** the cinema, watching Titanic.*
		activities	*Rania isn't here. She's **at** a party.*

> **Helpful hints**
>
> We also use *at* in the following phrases:
> • *at the moment* • *at night* • *at the top/bottom*
> • *at the door/window*

Watch out! Compare how we use *in* and *at* for places. We use *in* for larger areas that are all around us when we are there. We use *at* for smaller places and points on a journey.
✓ *We're spending our next holiday **in** the countryside.* ✓ *Let's meet **at** the train station.*

A If the word in bold in each sentence is correct, put a tick (✓). If it is wrong, write the correct word.

1 We first visited China **on** 2006.   ....

2 My birthday is **at** the second of July.   ....

3 Let's meet **on** five o'clock, shall we?   ....

4 School starts again **in** September.   ....

5 There's a party at Emily's **at** Saturday.   ....

6 What do you want to do **on** the morning?   ....

7 Let's go and see Grandma **on** Easter.   ....

8 Where do you usually go **in** Christmas Day?   ....

B Complete using *on*, *in* or *at*.

1 There are lots of people .... the restaurant.

2 The people who live .... number 44 are away on holiday.

3 You should go to the Louvre when you're .... Paris.

4 Gorillas live .... forests in Africa and eat fruit.

5 What does that sign .... the wall say?

6 What did Ethan say .... his letter?

7 Have you heard of the strange statues .... Easter Island?

8 Do you really want to spend the whole day .... the beach?

C Look at the pictures and complete the sentences.

1 This photo was taken .... winter.

2 We're .... a concert.

3 She's .... the sea.

4 It's .... page 62.

5 It's .... the middle.

6 He's .... an island.

7 It's .... the mountain.

8 They're .... a wedding.

D Complete using the words in the box.

| at • in • on • to |

1 My aunt and uncle have decided to move .... New Zealand.
2 Do you want to go .... the theatre tomorrow?
3 We stayed .... a great hotel in Dubai.
4 Wait .... the end of the street and I'll come and meet you.
5 You can come .... my house for dinner, if you like.
6 Connor was walking .... the corner shop when he realised he'd lost his wallet.
7 We drove all night and finally arrived .... Lisbon at eight o'clock.
8 Did you leave your book .... the teacher's desk, so she can see it?
9 Look at those sheep .... that field over there.
10 It takes about six hours to fly .... Asia from here.

E Circle the correct word.

1 I'm meeting Andy **at / on** the cinema in an hour.
2 Have you seen the new building **at / in** front of the school?
3 My new job starts **in / on** the first day of August.
4 We're going to Martin's to see their new baby **in / on** Wednesday evening.
5 See if there are any tomatoes **at / in** the fridge, will you?
6 We'll all have computers connected to our brains **at / in** the future.
7 I don't feel like playing chess **at / on** the moment.
8 I think there's someone **at / in** the door. I'll go and check.

F Write one word in each gap.

Jetlag

When you travel (**1**) .... the other side of the world, jetlag is a real problem. You find yourself awake (**2**) .... the middle of the night and you feel like going to bed (**3**) .... the morning, just when everyone around you is getting up.
Jetlag happens when you go (**4**) .... a country where the time is very different. For example, you might leave London (**5**) .... midday and fly (**6**) .... Los Angeles. The flight takes about eleven hours, so when you arrive (**7**) .... Los Angeles airport, your body thinks you're there (**8**) .... 11 pm. But Los Angeles is eight hours behind London, so you actually get there (**9**) .... 3 pm local time. So, (**10**) .... midnight Los Angeles time, your body (which still thinks it's (**11**) .... London) says it's 8 am. It takes a few days for your body clock to change.

Unit 9 Vocabulary
Coming and going

see page 186 for definitions

Topic vocabulary

abroad (adv)	cruise (n)	pack (v)
accommodation (n)	delay (v, n)	passport (n)
book (v)	destination (n)	platform (n)
break (n)	ferry (n)	public transport (n phr)
cancel (v)	flight (n)	reach (v)
catch (v)	foreign (adj)	resort (n)
coach (n)	harbour (n)	souvenir (n)
convenient (adj)	journey (n)	traffic (n)
crash (v, n)	luggage (n)	trip (n)
crowded (adj)	nearby (adj, adv)	vehicle (n)

Phrasal verbs

get in(to)	enter a car
get off	leave a bus/train/etc
get on(to)	enter a bus/train/etc
get out (of)	leave a car/building/room/etc
go away	leave a place/sb
go back (to)	return (to)
set off	start a journey
take off	leave the ground

Prepositional phrases

by air/sea/bus/car/etc
on board
on foot
on holiday
on schedule
on the coast

Word formation

attract	attractive, attraction		**direct**	direction
back	backwards		**drive**	drove, driven, driver
choose	chose, chosen, choice		**fly**	flew, flown, flight
comfort	(un)comfortable		**travel**	traveller
depart	departure		**visit**	visitor

Word patterns

adjectives		*verbs*	
	close to		arrive at/in
	famous for		ask (sb) about
	far from		ask for
	late for		look at
	suitable for		prepare for
			provide sb with
			wait for

Topic vocabulary

A Complete using a word formed from the letters given.

1 The airline say my .... is too heavy and I have to pay extra. **E G U L G A G**
2 This model of Big Ben will be a lovely .... of our holiday. **E U N S V O R I**
3 Do you know which .... our train is on? **M L F R A P O T**
4 We've had a terrible .... and now I'm just happy to be home. **Y U N O R J E**
5 Let's walk around the .... and have a look at all the fishing boats. **B U R O H A R**
6 You have to choose your .... and the ticket machine gives you your ticket. **I N E T I D S O T A N**
7 This .... is suitable for city driving and for rough country roads. **H E I C E V L**
8 The .... to Australia takes 24 hours! **H I G L T F**
9 Look out! We're going to .... if you're not careful! **H A C S R**
10 The cost of the holiday includes .... at a five-star hotel. **C O N D I O M A C A O M T**
11 'Have you ever travelled .... ?' 'Yes, I went to Italy last year.' **D A R A O B**
12 Tina and Julie are going away on a weekend .... to Berlin. **K E R A B**

B Circle the correct word or phrase.

ferry / traffic

crowded / nearby

cruise / coach

convenient / foreign

passport / public transport

resort / trip

C Complete using the correct form of the verbs in the box.

> book • cancel • catch • delay • pack • reach

1 They've .... all today's trains. How are we going to get home?
2 What's the first thing you want to do when we .... New York?
3 It's cold in Moscow, so .... some warm clothes.
4 You .... the hotel room and I'll go and buy the train tickets.
5 Our plane has been .... by four hours.
6 If we're quick, then maybe we can still .... the bus.

Phrasal verbs

D Match to make sentences.

1 As the plane took ....
2 The door is open, so you can get ....
3 We were in a hurry and when we got ....
4 The man selling the tickets told us to go ....
5 It was raining when we set ....
6 We loved the hotel so we went ....
7 Ray fell as he was getting ....
8 The taxi driver asked us to get ....

A away and come back again later.
B back there the following year.
C off, I held my mum's hand tightly.
D off the bus and couldn't walk properly.
E off on our walk, but it soon stopped.
F in the car, if you like.
G out on the right because it was safer.
H on the bus, I realised I didn't have a ticket.

E Complete using the correct form of the phrasal verbs from exercise D.

1 Before Darren .... on his journey, he packed some boots and plenty of warm clothes.
2 Why don't you .... and think about what I've said to you?
3 We should .... the train at the next station and then find a taxi.
4 The helicopter .... and suddenly we were in the air!
5 There was a fire alarm and we all had to .... of the hotel.
6 Without saying anything, the man .... his car and drove up the road.
7 We ran to the train and .... just before it started to move.
8 My parents .... to the little Spanish town where they first met.

Prepositional phrases

F Complete using the words in the box. Add any other words you need.

> board • bus • coast • foot • holiday • schedule

1 When you go .... , it always takes a few days to completely relax.
2 I hope our plane arrives .... I'm bored just sitting here, waiting.
3 If you come .... , don't forget to get off at the stop outside the bank.
4 Living .... is great. I love walking on the beach every morning.
5 The cowboys got off their horses and went the rest of the way ....
6 Now we're .... the ship let's have a look around.

Word formation

G Use the word given in capitals at the end of each line to form a word that fits in the gap in the same line.

> ### Going abroad
>
> Up until the 1960s, not many British people had (**1**) .... abroad for   **FLY**
> their holidays. Although the idea was (**2**) .... , flying was still too   **ATTRACT**
> expensive for most people. The only (**3**) .... people had was to go   **CHOOSE**
> to British resorts. Instead of flying, families (**4**) .... to the British   **DRIVE**
> coast. Places like Blackpool and Brighton had millions of (**5**) ....   **VISIT**
> every year. During the 60s and 70s, prices dropped and (**6**) ....   **TRAVEL**
> began to visit places like Spain. At first, hotels were (**7**) .... , but   **COMFORT**
> they slowly got better. These days, the (**8**) .... lounges at airports   **DEPART**
> are full and people travel (**9**) .... and forwards across the world for   **BACK**
> work and on holiday. Every summer, tourists go in all (**10**) .... in   **DIRECT**
> search of the perfect beach and the perfect resort.

Word patterns

H Write one word in each gap.

1 Sydney is famous .... its harbour. You should also look .... the Opera House and the bridge while you're there.
2 We arrived .... the hotel and they provided us .... a map of the area.
3 When you're preparing .... a holiday, pack clothes that are suitable .... the place where you're going.
4 I prefer to be far .... other people when I'm on holiday. I don't like being close .... crowds of tourists.
5 While we were waiting .... our train, I asked someone .... the delay.
6 Will was late .... his appointment so he asked me .... some money for a taxi.

Units 7, 8 and 9 Review 3

A If a line is correct, put a tick (✓). If there is an extra word in a line, write the word.

Unseen London

1	....	Of course, London is famous for that its attractions like Big Ben
2	....	and the Tower of London. Millions of tourists look at these
3	....	buildings every year – but not far distance from these places,
4	....	there are other interesting sights. Next time you set off to visit
5	....	London, why not plan to go to some of the places close in to the
6	....	centre of the city that tourists rarely go to? Get into of a taxi and
7	....	ask the driver to take you to Billingsgate fish market, for
8	....	example. When you arrive there at the market, you'll be amazed
9	....	at the sights and sounds of real London. You can ask to the fish
10	....	sellers about their work – and you don't have to wait on for hours
		to get a ticket!

(1 mark per answer)

B Complete each second sentence using the word given, so that it has a similar meaning to the first sentence. Write between two and five words.

11 Did they give you a map of the area? **provide**
Did they .... a map of the area?

12 My intention is to travel to Malta by ferry. **going**
I .... travel to Malta by ferry.

13 I like staying by the sea when I'm on holiday. **coast**
I like staying .... when I'm on holiday.

14 Be careful when you leave the bus. **off**
Be careful when you .... the bus.

15 The beach is close to the hotel, so we can walk there. **foot**
We can .... from the hotel to the beach because it's close.

16 Why don't you drive to Brighton this weekend? **car**
Why don't you go to Brighton .... this weekend?

17 We're going to return to Bali again this summer. **back**
We're going to .... Bali again this summer.

18 I like to watch the planes leaving the ground when I'm at the airport. **off**
I like to watch the planes .... when I'm at the airport.

(2 marks per answer)

C Complete by changing the form of the word in capitals.

19 We thought of driving to Berlin, but in the end we .... **FLY**

20 Could you ask the .... to slow down a bit, please? **DRIVE**

21 Experienced .... will enjoy our hotel's comfortable double rooms. **TRAVEL**

22 Paris is really .... in the spring. Shall we go? **ATTRACT**

40

23 Let's fly in business class – it's much more .... than the cheap seats! **COMFORT**

24 Please check the .... time on your ticket carefully. **DEPART**

25 We looked at all the hotels and in the end we .... the Majestic. **CHOOSE**

26 I think we went in the wrong .... at the last turning and now we're lost. **DIRECT**

(1 mark per answer)

D Choose the correct answer.

27 I .... around the world one day.
A travel   C am travelling
B am going to travel   D travelled

28 Do you think Curtis .... the car race tomorrow?
A will win   C is winning
B wins   D won

29 What's the weather like .... Russia at the moment?
A on   C in
B at   D to

30 I can't come to your party because I .... my cousin that week.
A visit   C visited
B will visit D am visiting

31 I think there's a picture of the hotel .... the first page.
A on   C in
B at   D to

32 We usually go away somewhere on holiday .... New Year.
A on   C in
B at   D to

33 Watch out, or you .... off the boat!
A fall   C are falling
B are going to fall D fell

34 It's my birthday .... Friday, so we're spending the weekend in London.
A on   C in
B at   D to

(1 mark per answer)

E Choose the correct answer.

35 I got .... the car, turned the key and realised I didn't have any petrol!
A into   C onto
B off   D on

36 I hope our plane leaves on ....
A timetable   C schedule
B plan   D hour

37 My mum .... the bus to work every morning, but Dad drives.
A catches   C runs
B does   D goes

38 We had a long way to go so we .... off very early.
A made   C put
B set   D had

39 I prepared .... my trip very carefully,

and I still forgot my toothbrush!
A with   C about
B on   D for

40 Public .... in this city is quite good, and it's not expensive.
A travel   C vehicle
B journey   D transport

41 Mum .... away on business quite often.
A sets   C does
B takes   D goes

42 It's easier to travel abroad when you can speak .... language like English.
A a strange   C an unknown
B a foreign   D an outside

(1 mark per answer)

Total mark: ..../50

Grammar
The passive 1

The passive (present simple, past simple, *will*)

Form

be in the right form + past participle

statement	negative		question
Everyone **is invited**!	Some people **aren't (are not) invited**.		**Is** everyone **invited**?

	Active	Passive
present simple	They always invite Grandma.	Grandma **is** always **invited**.
past simple	They invited Uncle Adrian.	Uncle Adrian **was invited**.
will	They **will / won't** invite the neighbours.	The neighbours **will / won't be invited**.

Use	Example
When we don't know who does something	My sister's bike **was stolen** yesterday.
When we don't want or need to say who does something	**Was** Simon **invited**?

●Helpful hints

If you are not sure how to form a passive sentence, think of the **active** sentence first.

Active sentence: **Someone <u>stole</u> <u>my sister's bike</u> yesterday.**

Passive sentence: **<u>My sister's bike</u> <u>was stolen</u> yesterday.**

- Look at the active sentence. The verb is *stole* and the object is *my sister's bike*.

- The object of the active sentence (*my sister's bike*) becomes the subject of the passive sentence.
  My sister's bike …

- Then we need the verb *be* in the same tense as the verb in the active sentence. Here, *stole* is past simple, so we need *was*.
  My sister's bike was …

- Then we need the past participle of the verb in the active sentence. The past participle of *steal* is *stolen*.
  My sister's bike was stolen …

- Finally, we finish the sentence in the right way.
  My sister's bike was stolen yesterday.

- When the verb in a passive sentence is a phrasal verb, don't forget to include the particle.
  They **picked up** the broken glass. ⟶ The broken glass was **picked up**.

- Some verbs have irregular past participle forms. See page 182.

A The words and phrases in bold in each sentence are wrong. Write the correct word or phrase.

1 Every year, several prizes are **giving** to the best students. ....
2 When the pizza was **delivering**, it was cold. ....
3 You will be **telling** when you can come in. ....
4 That song **doesn't** played on the radio very often, is it? ....
5 **Your money was stealing** out of your bag? ....
6 We **haven't** allowed to use a dictionary in the exam yesterday. ....
7 That film won't **have** shown in our local cinema for a long time. ....
8 **I will be** picked up from the station on Saturday? ....

B Complete using the correct passive form of the verbs in brackets.

1 When people .... (**arrest**), they .... (**take**) to the police station.
2 Milk .... (**usually / keep**) in the fridge.
3 .... (**we / tell**) what's in next week's test?
4 How did people communicate over long distances before the phone .... (**invent**)?
5 .... (**you / allow**) to come to the party next Saturday?
6 You .... (**give**) your exam results next Monday.
7 .... (**Aidan's bike / find**) yesterday?

C Look at the pictures and complete the sentences. Use the correct passive form of the verbs in the box. Add any other words you need.

call • catch • find • investigate • rob • send

1 At ten o'clock yesterday morning, the local bank in the high street ....
2 At one minute past ten, the police ....
3 A few minutes later, the police arrived at the bank. The crime scene ....
4 At twenty past ten, the robbers' fingerprints ....
5 At half past eleven, the robbers ....
6 Next week, they ....

D Answer the questions using your own ideas.

1 Where are cars usually fixed?
They ....

2 Where will the next Olympic Games be held?
They ....

3 Who are Oscars usually awarded to?
They ....

4 What are you not allowed to do at school?
I ....

5 What were you given for your birthday last year?
I ....

6 What will you be given for your next birthday?
I'll probably ....

E Complete each second sentence using the word given, so that it has a similar meaning to the first sentence. Write between two and five words.

1 Will they send the letters first class? **sent**
Will .... first class?

2 I'm not sure if they eat pizza in China. **is**
I'm not sure if .... in China.

3 Someone told me that they don't make cars in the UK anymore. **made**
Someone told me that .... in the UK anymore.

4 Do they usually feed the animals three times a day? **fed**
Are .... three times a day?

5 Mr Jones is ill, so he won't give us a geography test today! **be**
Mr Jones is ill, so .... a geography test today!

6 Did they take her to hospital in an ambulance? **she**
Was .... to hospital in an ambulance?

F Write one word in each gap.

───────── *The National Trust* ─────────

There are lots of beautiful, large houses in Britain. Many of them (**1**) .... built hundreds of years ago. In the past, they (**2**) .... owned by very rich families. Today, many of them (**3**) .... owned by an organisation called The National Trust, which (**4**) .... created to look after them. The houses (**5**) .... kept in perfect condition, and visitors (**6**) .... allowed to look round them. It's interesting to learn how different life was in an old house. Milk was (**7**) .... kept in the fridge, because they didn't have fridges! Washing machines (**8**) .... only invented very recently, so washing (**9**) .... done by hand. In some cases, the house (**10**) .... still lived in today. When this happens, visitors (**11**) .... only shown part of the house. The private rooms (**12**) .... kept closed to the public. These houses often have beautiful gardens, too. The gardens (**13**) .... looked after by professional gardeners.

You usually have to pay to look round National Trust houses. Members of the National Trust (**14**) .... given a discount. This year, millions of people (**15**) .... be given the chance to see what life in an old country house was like.

Grammar
The passive 2

The passive (present continuous, present perfect simple, past continuous, past perfect simple, *be going to*, modals)

Form

be in the right form + past participle

statement	negative	question
The pizzas **are being**	The pizzas **aren't (are not) being**	**Are** the pizzas **being**

	Active	Passive
present continuous	*My aunt is doing the washing-up.*	*The washing-up **is being done** by my aunt.*
present perfect simple	*My cousin has sent the invitations.*	*The invitations **have been sent** by my cousin.*
past continuous	*My uncle was cleaning the car.*	*The car **was being cleaned** by my uncle.*
past perfect simple	*Our neighbours had taken the twins to the zoo.*	*The twins **had been taken** to the zoo by our neighbours.*
be going to	*They're going to invite Phil to the party.*	*Phil **is going to be invited** to the party.*
modals	*They might invite Kyle to the party.*	*Kyle **might be invited** to the party.*
	We should tell Jenny about the party.	*Jenny **should be told** about the party.*
	We must tell Dominic about the concert.	*Dominic **must be told** about the concert.*
	We can hold the party at Jack's house.	*The party **can be held** at Jack's house.*

For the passive form of the present simple, past simple and *will*, see Unit 10.
For the uses of the passive, see Unit 10.

Watch out!

- We can use *by* to emphasise who does something.
  - ✓ *My sister's bedroom was painted **by** my parents.* (= My parents painted my sister's bedroom.)
- We can use *with* to emphasise what someone uses.
  - ✓ *Soup is usually eaten **with** a spoon.* (= You usually use a spoon to eat soup.)
- We don't use *by* or *with* when we don't need to say, or don't know, who does something.
  - ✓ *Mrs Fisher was taken to hospital yesterday.*

A Look at the picture and match to make sentences.

1 The carnival lorry is ....
2 The lorry has ....
3 The gorilla has ....
4 Everyone watching is ....
5 The best song might ....
6 Have the costumes ....

A been given a banana by the pirate.
B going to be given a balloon by the astronaut.
C be sung by the cowboy.
D being driven by a clown.
E been bought from a fancy-dress shop?
F been decorated with lots of flowers.

B Look at the picture again and circle the correct word.

1 The balloons had all been **blowing / blown** up before the carnival started.
2 The bananas **haven't / aren't** all been eaten yet.
3 The lorry isn't **been / being** driven by the gorilla.
4 A young boy **was / has** just taken a balloon from the astronaut.
5 A prize is going to **have / be** given to the person in the best fancy dress.
6 The prize might not be **awarding / awarded** to the clown.
7 **Has / Is** the lorry been decorated well?
8 Can songs be sung **by / with** people in the crowd, too?

C Complete using *by* or *with*.

1 That book was written .... my uncle!
2 Are the best photos usually taken .... digital cameras?
3 That song has been sung .... lots of famous singers.
4 Is your hair cut .... a professional hairdresser?
5 Should the paper be cut .... a pair of scissors?
6 All the candles had been lit .... the same match.
7 The film isn't going to be directed .... Steven Spielberg after all.

D Complete each second sentence so that it has a similar meaning to the first sentence. Write no more than four words.

1 I think John has taken my jacket.
   I think my jacket .... John.

2 You should cook the chicken for at least an hour.
   The chicken .... for at least an hour.

3 They're showing that film at the cinema in town.
   That film .... at the cinema in town.

4 They hadn't invented digital cameras when we took that photo.
   Digital cameras .... when that photo was taken.

5 When I got there, Carly was doing the ironing, so I didn't have to do it!
   When I got there, the ironing .... Carly, so I didn't have to do it!

6 They were using hot soapy water to wash all the cars.
   All the cars .... hot soapy water.

E Read the text and answer the questions. Use the correct form of the passive.

Doing the housework

by Lisa Porter, Class 4b

At home, we all share the housework. My dad loves cooking, so he cooks all the food. Sometimes we help him, though. Next weekend, for example, we're having a party so I'm going to help him. In the past, my mum did all the shopping. She started a new job last year though, so I've done most of the shopping since then. It's easy, because I shop online. That means I order everything on the Internet (my dad lets me use his credit card!) and someone from the supermarket delivers it to our house.

My brother, Andy, cleans the bathroom nearly every day. He didn't do it yesterday, so he might do it later today. My sister Angelina sweeps the floors. She uses a really old brush. I think she should use a vacuum cleaner! You can save time if you use electrical equipment.

1 Does only one person do the housework in Lisa's house?
   No, the housework ....

2 Who cooks the food?
   The food ....

3 Who is going to help Lisa's dad next weekend?
   Lisa's dad ....

4 Who did all the shopping until about a year ago?
   Until about a year ago, the shopping ....
   ....

5 Who has done most of the shopping since then?
   Since then, most of the shopping ....
   ....

6 Does Lisa take the shopping home from the supermarket?
   No, it ....

7 How often does someone clean the bathroom?
   It ....

8 When might someone next clean the bathroom?
   It ....

9 How does Angelina sweep the floors?
   The floors ....

10 What does Lisa think Angelina should use?
   Lisa thinks a vacuum cleaner ....
   ....

Vocabulary
Friends and relations

Topic vocabulary

see page 187 for definitions

apologise (v)	generous (adj)	ordinary (adj)
boyfriend (n)	girlfriend (n)	patient (adj)
close (adj)	grateful (adj)	private (adj)
confident (adj)	guest (n)	recognise (v)
cool (adj)	independent (adj)	relation (n)
couple (n)	introduce (v)	rent (v, n)
decorate (v)	loving (adj)	respect (v, n)
defend (v)	loyal (adj)	single (adj)
divorced (adj)	mood (n)	stranger (n)
flat (n)	neighbourhood (n)	trust (v, n)

Phrasal verbs

bring up	take care of a child until he or she becomes an adult
fall out (with)	have an argument with sb and stop being friends
get on (with)	have a good relationship (with)
go out with	be the boyfriend/girlfriend of
grow up	become older (for children)
let down	disappoint
look after	take care of
split up	end a relationship

Prepositional phrases

by yourself
in common (with)
in contact (with)
in love (with)
on purpose
on your own

Word formation

able	ability, disabled, unable		**honest**	dishonest, honesty
admire	admiration		**introduce**	introduction
care	careful, careless		**lie**	liar, lying
confident	confidence		**person**	personality, personal
forgive	forgave, forgiven, forgiveness		**relate**	relative, relation, relationship

Word patterns

adjectives	fond of		apologise (to sb) for
	jealous of		argue (with sb) about
	kind to		care about
	married to		chat (to sb) about
	proud of	*nouns*	an argument (with sb) about
verbs	admire sb for		a relationship with

Topic vocabulary

A Complete using the words in the box.

close • confident • cool • divorced • generous • grateful
independent • loving • loyal • ordinary • patient • private • single

1 Thanks for looking after my dog for the weekend. I'm really ....
2 Judy is one of the most .... people I know. She's always giving me presents!
3 I don't want a girlfriend. I like being ....
4 It will take a while for Simon to forgive you. You'll just have to be ....
5 Adam's parents are .... , so he only sees his dad at the weekend.
6 Cats are more .... than dogs. They live their own lives and don't need human company.
7 I'm very .... to my best friend. I'd never talk about her behind her back.
8 Sandy's such a .... dog. He's always so happy to see us when we come home!
9 I'm not a very .... person. I get nervous when I have to speak in public.
10 My diary is .... No one is allowed to read it apart from me.
11 I tell my sister all my problems and secrets. We have a very .... relationship.
12 My uncle's really .... ! He's in a rock band!
13 I'm just a/an .... person with a normal life – but I'm quite happy!

B Complete using a word formed from the letters given.

1 Don't you think Ben and Angie make a lovely .... ? **L E O P U C**
2 How many .... are staying at the hotel at the moment? **S E G U T S**
3 All our .... are coming to the wedding. **S N O R E A L I T**
4 A .... is just a friend you haven't met yet! **G R A N T E R S**
5 How long have you been going out with your .... ? **D R I N F E Y O B**
6 Why are you in such a bad .... ? **O D O M**
7 My grandparents live in a really quiet .... **O H I D R O U G H B O N E**
8 My cousin has just moved into a .... in the city centre. **A T L F**
9 I'm going to the cinema with my .... tonight. **R E D G I N F L I R**

C Each of the words in bold is in the wrong sentence. Write the correct word.

1 I was first **respected** to Jake at a party. ....
2 I shouldn't have **rented** you. Now I know you can't keep a secret! ....
3 Our house is being **recognised** so we're staying with my grandparents at the moment. ....
4 Everyone **apologised** Mr Turner because he was strict but fair. ....
5 Have you **introduced** to Kelly for losing her CD? ....
6 Sarah said I was a liar but Carol **trusted** me and said I wasn't. ....
7 We **decorated** a small house in the countryside for the summer. ....
8 No one **defended** Phil when he came to the party dressed as an old man. ....

Phrasal verbs

D   Circle the correct word.

1   I thought I could trust you! You've really let me **off / down**.
2   Do you get **on / in** well with your older sister?
3   As children grow **off / up**, they want more independence from their parents.
4   Dave has fallen **off / out** with Jason and they're not talking to each other at the moment.
5   Ed was brought **in / up** by his aunt because his parents lived abroad.
6   I used to go **out / by** with Tony but we split **off / up** about a year ago.
7   I hate looking **after / over** my baby brother!

E   Write one word in each gap.

Advice for parents of teenagers

You've always (**1**) .... up your children to come to you when they're in trouble. You feel it's your job to (**2**) .... after them when they're having problems. But now, as your children are (**3**) .... up, they often don't want to share their problems with you. That's perfectly normal, so don't worry! Of course, you want to (**4**) .... on well with your children, but that means you have to give them some freedom.

Maybe they've (**5**) .... out with their best friend and feel upset and angry. Maybe they've just (**6**) .... up with the boyfriend or girlfriend they've been (**7**) .... out with. Maybe they've been (**8**) .... down by a friend who they trusted. Teenagers go through all these problems. If they want to talk to you about it, then that's fine. But if they don't, don't force them. They'll come to you when they're ready.

Prepositional phrases

F   Each of the words in bold is wrong. Write the correct word.

1   Are you still **on** contact with any friends from university?   ....
2   I'm going to split up with Dan because we've got nothing **from** common.   ....
3   I don't think I'd like to live **on** myself.   ....
4   Would you like to live **by** your own?   ....
5   Fiona didn't break your MP3 player **with** purpose. It was an accident!   ....
6   Guess what! Mike and Julie are **at** love with each other.   ....

Word formation

G   Complete by changing the form of the word in capitals.

1   I'm asking for your .... ! **FORGIVE**
2   Doug is such a .... I never believe a word he says! **LIE**
3   Be .... ! I've just painted the walls and they're wet. **CARE**
4   Lying to your dad like that was really .... **HONEST**
5   My brother is .... but that doesn't stop him from doing lots of sport. **ABLE**
6   I haven't got the .... to go up to a stranger at a party and introduce myself. **CONFIDENT**
7   My best friend gives me lots of help with my .... problems. **PERSON**
8   My .... with Chris lasted for over three years. **RELATION**

H   Complete the words.

1   Liz has got a really lively person............................ .
2   Roger is always losing things. He's so care............................ !
3   I really admire you for your honest............................ .
4   I have a lot of admir............................ for Linda. She's achieved such a lot.
5   Uncle Alan has an amazing mental ab............................ – he can guess the number you're thinking of.
6   In the introduc............................ to this book, it says that moving house is extremely stressful.
7   Most of my relat............................ live in Canada so I don't see them very often.

Word patterns

I   Write one word in each gap.

I'm very fond (**1**) .... my husband, William. I've been married (**2**) .... him for over sixty years. I know he cares (**3**) .... me now just as much as when we first met all those years ago. I'd got lost, and I asked him for directions. He was so kind (**4**) .... me. He offered to drive me wherever I wanted to go. It was love at first sight and since then my relationship (**5**) .... him has always been wonderful.

William is proud (**6**) .... my success as an artist, and he's never been jealous (**7**) .... my fame. I really admire him (**8**) .... supporting me so much over the years. Every evening, we chat (**9**) .... each other (**10**) .... the day's events. Of course, we do sometimes argue (**11**) .... things. All couples do. But whenever I have an argument (**12**) .... him, we soon start laughing and both apologise (**13**) .... each other (**14**) .... getting angry. I can't imagine life without him!

Review 4

A Complete using the verbs in the box.

| apologise • defend • introduce • recognise • rent • respect • trust |

1 'Who's that over there?'
'That's Graham Western, the actor. Let me .... you.'

2 'Hi, Harry!'
'Oh! Hi, Rita! I didn't .... you with your new hair style!'

3 'I'm really sorry!'
'There's no need to ....'

4 'I'm thinking of moving house soon.'
'Do you want to buy or .... a place?'

5 'I wish I hadn't told Rebecca some of my secrets.'
'Don't worry. You can .... Rebecca. She won't tell anyone.'

6 'Mr Parker is going to run a marathon for charity.'
'Yes, I really .... Mr Parker. He does such a lot of charity work.'

7 'I'm sure Billy didn't say that!'
'Why do you always .... Billy? He's not perfect, you know!'

(1 mark per answer)

B Write one word in each gap.

8 Could you look .... our rabbit while we're on holiday?

9 Tim was Sandy's boyfriend, but they split .... last month.

10 Kim and Katy have fallen .... with each other, so Kim isn't going to invite Katy to her party.

11 Phil was brought .... by his uncle and aunt.

12 Is Gareth really going .... with Liz?

(1 mark per answer)

C Complete by changing the form of the word in capitals.

13 I've got so much .... for Darren. **ADMIRE**

14 Susie is so .... She's always breaking things! **CARE**

15 Tony said his dad is a millionaire, but he's such a .... **LIE**

16 Lots of .... people live full and happy lives. **ABLE**

17 Karen apologised, so I .... her immediately. **FORGIVE**

18 Andrea has got a great .... You'll really like her! **PERSON**

19 I'm not sure I've got the .... to sing in public! **CONFIDENT**

20 I hate people who are .... **HONEST**

(1 mark per answer)

D Complete each second sentence using the word given, so that it has a similar meaning to the first sentence. Write between two and five words.

21 We gave my dad a surprise party on his fortieth birthday. **was**
My dad .... a surprise party on his fortieth birthday.

22 After the play, they introduced us to all the actors. **we**
After the play, ...
.... to all the actors.

23 They've caught the person who stole your bike! **has**
The person who stole your bike ....
.... caught!

24 No one had told me that Jill was coming! **been**
I .... that Jill was coming!

25 Our English teacher and our German teacher are husband and wife. **married**
Our English teacher ....
.... our German teacher.

26 A neighbour is feeding our dog while we're away. **being**
Our dog .... a neighbour while we're away.

27 Use a sharp knife to cut the cake. **should**
The cake .... a sharp knife.

28 I'm not interested in what you think! **care**
I .... what you think!

29 My parents don't let me watch much TV at home. **allowed**
I .... to watch much TV at home.

30 They're going to invite over a hundred people to the wedding reception. **going**
Over a hundred people ....
.... to the wedding reception.

(2 marks per answer)

E Choose the correct answer.

Parents and friends

We can choose our friends, but we can't choose our (**31**) .... That doesn't mean, though, that members of our family can't also be our friends. Many children have such a good relationship (**32**) .... their parents that they see them as friends. Of course, when you're a teenager, you'll have (**33**) .... with your parents. There will be times when you don't (**34**) .... on very well with them. That's only natural. There will be times when you want to be (**35**) .... and solve your problems (**36**) .... yourself. You'll also (**37**) .... your parents down sometimes. After all, nobody's perfect and we all make mistakes. But your parents understand that. And as you grow (**38**) .... and become an adult, you'll probably realise you have lots of things in (**39**) .... with your mum and dad and become even (**40**) .... to them.

31	A couples	B guests	C strangers	D relations
32	A by	B for	C with	D from
33	A moods	B arguments	C lies	D dishonesty
34	A get	B take	C put	D set
35	A divorced	B single	C grateful	D independent
36	A on	B by	C for	D with
37	A let	B make	C take	D fall
38	A on	B over	C out	D up
39	A private	B common	C contact	D love
40	A fonder	B more proud	C closer	D more ordinary

(1 mark per answer)

Total mark: ..../50

Grammar
Countable and uncountable nouns

Countable nouns

Form

Countable nouns have a singular and a plural form and take a singular or plural verb.

Countable nouns	Example
shop / shop**s**	There are over 100 **shops** in the new shopping centre.
baby / bab**ies**	They've got some great toys for **babies** in there.
dish / dish**es**	We need to get some new **dishes** for this evening.

⦿Helpful hints

We use these words with countable nouns:
- *a, an*
- *many*
- *a few*
- *one, two, etc*

Watch out! A few countable nouns have irregular plurals. They include:

- *one child, two children*
- *one foot, two feet*
- *one man, two men*
- *one person, two people*
- *one tooth, two teeth*
- *one woman, two women*

Uncountable nouns

Form

We cannot count some nouns (*uncountable nouns*). They do not have a plural form and take a singular verb, even if they end in -s.

Some uncountable nouns	Example
advice, bread, fruit, furniture, hair, homework, information, money, news, paper, rice, work	My **money is** in my wallet. Your **hair is** really long! The **news was** a complete shock.

⦿Helpful hints

We use these words with uncountable nouns:
- *a little*
- *much*
- *a bit of*
- *a piece of*

We use these words with both countable and uncountable nouns:
- *a lot of*
- *some*
- *lots of*
- *the*

We can use *any* in questions and negative statements with both uncountable nouns and plural countable nouns:
- Have we got **any** homework today?
- There aren't **any** eggs left.

Watch out!
- There are a few uncountable nouns that are plural and are followed by a plural verb. Be careful with the following words.

  - *clothes*
  - ✓ Your clean **clothes are** on the bed.

  - *jeans*
  - ✓ Your new **jeans look** great!

- Some nouns are uncountable with one meaning and countable with another meaning.
  - ✓ Get me some **paper** when you go to the shops. (= a packet of paper to write on)
  - ✓ Get me **a paper** when you go to the shops. (= a newspaper)

A Complete using the plural form of the words in the box.

> child • foot • man • person • puppy • tooth • watch • woman

1 Did you know that Jason's dog has had three beautiful .... ?
2 The *Spice Girls* was an all-girl band, so there weren't any ....
3 It's a bit strange that Victor wears two .... – one on each arm.
4 If .... do the same jobs as their husbands, they should be paid the same.
5 The dentist says I have to have two .... taken out!
6 How many .... were there at the show?
7 We've walked miles! My .... are hurting!
8 Mrs Jenkins has just had a baby, so she's got three .... now.

B Circle the correct word or phrase.

1 Your money **is / are** on the table in the dining room.
2 The advice you gave me **was / were** really useful. Thanks!
3 The cakes in that shop **looks / look** absolutely delicious.
4 There **has / have** been a lot of bad news recently.
5 Your homework **was / were** late. Please do it sooner next time.
6 **Does / Do** the information about the museum include the opening times?
7 We need new furniture in the dining room. **It's / They're** very old and scratched.
8 The fish in this tank all **seems / seem** to be ill.
9 I love your hair. **It's / They're** really soft.
10 Oh, no! The rice **has / have** gone all over the floor!

C Complete using the phrases in the box. You have to use some phrases more than once. Where there is more than one answer, write all the answers.

> a few • a little • a piece of • some

....
sugar

....
bread

....
bottles

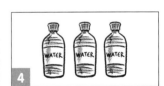
....
water

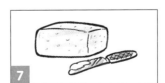
....
fruit

....
toys

....
butter

....
music

D Complete each second sentence using the word given, so that it has a similar meaning to the first sentence. Write no more than three words.

1 We don't know anything about the problem. **information**
  We don't .... about the problem.

2 Is it okay if I have some cheese? **bit**
  Is it okay if I have .... cheese?

3 There's only a little coffee left in the jar. **much**
  There .... coffee left in the jar.

4 I try not to drink too much Coca-Cola in a week. **cans**
  I try not to drink too .... of Coca-Cola in a week.

5 Would you like some more chocolate? **piece**
  Would you like .... chocolate?

6 I don't want a lot of cream on my strawberries. **cream**
  I only want .... on my strawberries.

E Choose the correct answer.

1 Be careful with that vase because it's made of .... !
  A glass   B a glass

2 I started coughing because I had .... at the back of my throat.
  A hair   B a hair

3 Don't put your hot cup on my new table! It's .... and I don't want you to burn it.
  A wood   B a wood

4 We should all recycle .... so that it can be used again.
  A paper   B a paper

5 My dad gets .... every day on his way to work.
  A paper   B a paper

6 Of course you can have some milk. Get .... out of the cupboard.
  A glass   B a glass

F Write one word in each gap.

◖ ◗ **Open-air markets**

Even if you only have a (**1**) .... money, you can still have a great time at your local open-air market. The clothes (**2**) .... cheap, and the fruit (**3**) .... cheap, too! Often, the food in your local supermarket (**4**) .... travelled a long way, but at the market you know that you'e buying food which has been produced locally. The vegetables (**5**) .... fresh, even if you go late in the day when there are only a (**6**) .... left. Support your local market and help local farmers. Contact your Town Hall to find out if there are (**7**) .... open-air markets in your area.

Grammar

Articles

a (indefinite article)

Use	Example
singular countable nouns (not specific)	I need to get **a** new coat.

Form

an (indefinite article)

Use	Example
instead of *a* when the next word begins with a vowel sound	I don't have enough money for **an** expensive dress.

Form

> **Watch out!** Whether we use *a* or *an* with a word depends on the sound, not the spelling. Be careful with the following words and phrases.
> - *an honest person* • *an hour* • *a euro* • *a uniform*

the (definite article)

Use	Example
singular countable nouns (specific)	Let's go to **the** new shopping centre.
plural countable nouns (specific)	Where are **the** books I ordered?
uncountable nouns (specific)	I gave the shop assistant **the** money and then left.

Form

No article (zero article)

Use	Example
plural countable nouns (general)	Prices have gone up a lot recently.
uncountable nouns (general)	Fresh fruit is really good for you.

Form

Special rules

Use	Example
places	**the**: seas (**the** Atlantic), rivers (**the** Amazon), areas (**the** Antarctic), some countries (**the** USA, **the** UK), public buildings (**the** theatre), **the** Earth, **the** world, **the** sky, **the** moon, **the** sun, **the** sea, **the** environment **no article**: towns and cities (Moscow), most countries (France), continents (Europe), streets (Baker Street), planets (Mars)
activities	**a/an**: have **a** job, work as **a** … **the**: on **the** radio, **the** media, play **the** piano **no article**: go to work, on TV, go shopping, play tennis, listen to music, go to work, go to school, be at school, be at university, school subjects (maths)
time	**the**: in **the** morning/afternoon/evening, on **the** 20th March, in **the** 1950s **no article**: days (Thursday), months (May), years (2009), at night
people	**the**: **the** King, **the** Prime Minister, **the** army, **the** navy, **the** police, **the** Germans, **the** English **no article**: become king, he's English, speak English

Form

A Complete using *a*, *an* or *the*.

1 We had .... really good science lesson at school today.
2 I found .... unusual insect on the wall outside our house.
3 It's your birthday next week. Are you going to have .... party?
4 We waited for hours, but we finally saw .... Queen.
5 Why don't we listen to .... radio?
6 Have you got .... euro I could borrow?
7 Mum has gone to .... bank, but she'll be back soon.
8 Where have you been? I've been waiting for over .... hour!

B Write an article in each gap where necessary. If an article is not necessary, put a dash (–).

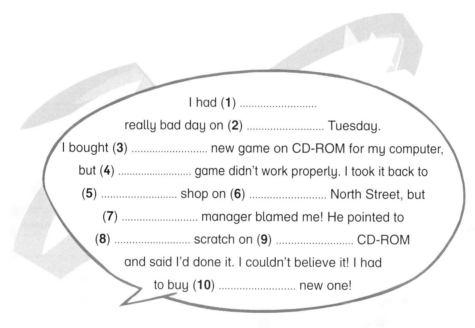

I had (**1**) ....
really bad day on (**2**) .... Tuesday.
I bought (**3**) .... new game on CD-ROM for my computer,
but (**4**) .... game didn't work properly. I took it back to
(**5**) .... shop on (**6**) .... North Street, but
(**7**) .... manager blamed me! He pointed to
(**8**) .... scratch on (**9**) .... CD-ROM
and said I'd done it. I couldn't believe it! I had
to buy (**10**) .... new one!

C Circle the extra word in each sentence.

1 Do you think we will ever send a person to the Mars?
2 When you go to the London, don't forget to see the London Eye.
3 When we use the cars, we damage the environment.
4 I'm not telling a lies! It's the truth.
5 I'm looking for a teacher who can teach me the German.
6 Ray needs a warm hat and a new coat for his visit to the Russia.
7 Dad has gone to a work and forgotten the car keys.
8 Some people have an unusual pets, such as lions or tigers.

D In each sentence there is a word missing. Put an arrow (↑) to show where the missing word should go and write the word.

1 English music was popular in America in 1960s. ....
2 Would you prefer to read book or watch television? ....
3 We had maths at school yesterday and our teacher gave us surprise test! ....
4 Peter joined police and caught ten thieves in his first month! ....
5 Gordon wanted to be writer, so he studied English at university. ....
6 Suddenly, two UFOs appeared in sky over Washington. ....

E Rewrite the sentences correctly, adding articles where necessary.

1 We had great time in USA.
....

2 Let's go to Belgium for week this summer.
....

3 Where's money I gave you on fifteenth of last month?
....

4 I'd like to join army and become soldier.
....

5 For Christmas, I got book, DVD and latest CD by my favourite band.
....

6 They say that English drink lot of tea.
....

7 I heard song on radio that I really liked.
....

8 Do Japanese and other people in Asia eat cheese?
....

F Underline ten mistakes in the dialogue and correct them.

Gary: It's the lovely day, isn't it? Let's walk down to a shops and look around.

Helen: That's an good idea. I'll just have a look in a kitchen and see what we need.

Gary: I got a milk yesterday, so we don't need any more. We might need a bread, though.

Helen: Okay. Bread … oh, and the packet of sugar. After shopping, we could go to a new market in a town centre and see what they have.

Gary: Right. You get your coat and I'll get a car keys.

Vocabulary
Buying and selling

Topic vocabulary

see page 189 for definitions

advertisement (n)	demand (v)	property (n)
afford (v)	export (v)	purchase (v, n)
bargain (n)	fee (n)	receipt (n)
brand (n)	fortune (n)	require (v)
catalogue (n)	import (v)	sale (n)
change (n)	invest (v)	save (v)
coin (n)	obtain (v)	select (v)
cost (v, n)	owe (v)	supply (v, n)
customer (n)	own (v)	variety (n)
debt (n)	profit (n)	waste (v, n)

Phrasal verbs

add up	find the total of
come back (from)	return (from)
give away	give sth free of charge
hurry up	do sth more quickly
pay back	return money (to sb)
save up (for)	save money (for a specific purpose)
take back	return sth to the place it came from
take down	remove (from a high place)

Prepositional phrases

by credit card/cheque
for rent
for sale
in cash
in debt
in good/bad condition

Word formation

add	addition		**judge**	judgement
afford	affordable		**serve**	service, servant
compare	comparison		**true**	truth, untrue, truthful
decide	decision		**use**	useful, useless
expense	(in)expensive		**value**	valuable

Word patterns

adjectives	wrong about/with			decide on
verbs	belong to			lend sth to
	borrow sth from			pay for
	buy sth from			spend sth on
	choose between		*nouns*	an advert(isement) for
	compare sth to/with			

Topic vocabulary

A   Circle the correct word.

'Getting to the Top' business seminar

So, you've seen **(1) an advertisement / a bargain** for someone to work in business? But do you really know what you're doing? Do you know how to keep the **(2) customers / debts** happy? Can you make a **(3) cost / profit** again and again? At *'Getting to the Top Business Education'* we'll help you to help yourself. Why don't you attend our specialist business seminar and … learn how to make a **(4) catalogue / fortune** in business! Our course leader, Richard Sugar, says, 'Being big in business **(5) exports / requires** a certain way of thinking. You need to know what your customers will **(6) afford / demand** and then find a way to **(7) owe / supply** them with it at the right price.' Come and join our seminar and we'll … 'get you to the top'!

B   Complete using the correct form of the verbs in the box.

import • invest • obtain • own • purchase • save • select • waste

1 We've decided to .... money in Jake's new business. Hope it's successful!
2 Let's stay in tonight and .... our money for the trip next week.
3 Don't .... all your pocket money on sweets and chocolate.
4 The company has .... permission to start selling in China.
5 You usually have to pay tax when you .... things from other countries.
6 Colin is so rich that he .... four Rolls-Royces!
7 Joan .... a few pairs of jeans and went to try them on.
8 It says here that they give you a free glass with every pint of milk you ....!

C   Each of the words in bold is in the wrong sentence. Write the correct word.

1 We don't usually get that **property** of washing powder.   ....
2 We can only take the item back if you've still got the **change**.   ....
3 The best thing about the new shopping centre is that there's a lot of **fee**.   ....
4 What's the design on a French one euro **sale**?   ....
5 Carter and Sons have got some really good things in the **receipt**.   ....
6 My mum didn't like me selling my bike, but she said it was my **coin**, so   ....
   it was my decision.
7 When we bought the house, we had to pay a huge **brand** to a lawyer. ....
8 The taxi driver wasn't very happy when I told him I didn't have any **variety**.   ....

Phrasal verbs

D Write one word in each gap.

He's taking it ....

She's .... up.

He's trying to ....
up.

They're ....
them away.

He's .... it up.

She's paying him ....

He's just .... back.

She's .... it back.

Prepositional phrases

E Complete using the words in the box. You have to use some words more than once.

by • for • in

1 It can be very worrying when you're .... a lot of debt.
2 Can I pay for this .... cheque?
3 Did you see that the house next door is .... sale?
4 They took ten per cent off because I paid .... cash.
5 We need to find an office .... rent in the centre of town.
6 I got quite a lot of money for the car because it was .... such good condition.

62

Word formation

F   One of the words in each sentence is in the wrong form. Write the correct word.

1 The serve in this place is absolutely terrible and I want to see the manager.   ....
2 Could you help me make a decide? I don't know which phone to get.   ....
3 Even very good quality clothes are quite afford in this shop.   ....
4 Companies should always tell the true in advertisements.   ....
5 Credit cards are really use, but you have to be careful with them.   ....
6 I read a compare of all the supermarkets and Safeshop was the most expensive.   ....
7 My grandma had no idea that her old vase was so value.   ....
8 Pete never shops at Mayfield's because he says it's too expense.   ....
9 Before you borrow from the bank, you have to make a judge about whether   ....
   you can pay it back or not.
10 Is the bill right? Could you just check your add, please?   ....

Word patterns

G   Circle the correct word.

1 Don't lend any money **on / to** George because you'll never get it back.
2 Where did you buy your new shoes **at / from**? They're great!
3 Let me just pay **about / for** these things and then we can go home.
4 There's something wrong **in / with** the CD player I've just bought.
5 Carol seems to spend all her pocket money **for / on** going out.
6 Look inside the wallet and maybe we can find out who it belongs **in / to**.
7 Have you decided **in / on** a name for your new business?

H   Complete using the words in the box. Add any other words you need.

> advertisement • borrowed • choose • compare • wrong

1 I need to get a new bag for school but I can't .... these two. What do you think?
2 This CD player seems expensive, but if you .... it ....
   the one in the other shop, it's actually not bad.
3 Madeleine .... a really nice top .... me and she still hasn't given it back!
4 The .... the website said you could sell your old things to people all over the country.
5 The shop assistant was .... the price so I had to show her the label.

Review 5

A Write one word in each gap.

eBay

One of (**1**) .... websites that has been very successful in recent years is eBay. On eBay, people take things that belong (**2**) .... them and offer them for sale. Other people offer (**3**) .... amount of money, and (**4**) .... person who offers the most money wins the item. They then pay (**5**) .... the item (**6**) .... cheque or credit card. It's (**7**) .... simple idea, but it's become a very popular way of buying and selling. Even if you only have a (**8**) .... of money, you can often find something you want on eBay. Most of the items are (**9**) .... good condition, and eBay has a (**10**) .... of happy users.

(1 mark per answer)

B Complete by changing the form of the word in capitals when this is necessary.

11 I've made my .... (**DECIDE**). I'm going to buy the blue one.

12 This dress is wonderful – but it's a little too .... (**EXPENSE**) for me.

13 I've broken my new CD player and now it's .... (**USE**)!

14 In the past, rich people often had .... (**SERVE**) to do everything for them.

15 We offer top quality products at .... (**AFFORD**) prices!

16 The advert was .... (**TRUE**), so I complained to the manager.

17 Please be careful with that painting – it's extremely .... (**VALUE**).

18 When you .... (**COMPARE**) our prices with other shops, we're the cheapest!

(1 mark per answer)

C Complete each second sentence using the word given, so that it has a similar meaning to the first sentence. Write between two and five words.

19 Could you lend some money to me until the weekend? **from**
Could I .... you until the weekend?

20 I can't decide which shoes I like most, the blue ones or the green ones. **choose**
I can't .... the blue shoes and the green shoes.

21 Why don't you return the sweater to the shop you got it from? **back**
Why don't you .... to the shop you got it from?

22 It can be very worrying when you owe money to the bank. **debt**
It can be very worrying when you .... to the bank.

23 We need to go quickly or the shops will be closed. **up**
We need to .... or the shops will be closed.

24 I paid for the CD using notes and coins and then left the shop. **cash**
I paid for the CD .... and then left the shop.

25 I don't agree with your opinion of the new shopping centre. **wrong**
   I think you .... the new shopping centre.

26 Do they rent cars here? **rent**
   Do they have .... here?

(2 marks per answer)

D Choose the correct answer.

27 I heard there's .... new sports shop in town. Let's see what they have.
   A a   C an
   B the   D one

28 I don't have .... money, so I'll have to wait to get a new coat.
   A a piece of   C much
   B a few   D many

29 It's going to be very expensive to send a person to ....
   A a Mars   C the Mars
   B one Mars   D Mars

30 I don't know much about computers, so I asked the assistant for .... advice.
   A a lot   C a few
   B many   D a little

31 In my experience, ... are very friendly.
   A Chinese   C the Chinese
   B a Chinese   D this Chinese

32 Dad has to go to .... early tomorrow to meet an important customer.
   A work   C a work
   B the work   D that work

33 Which is more important – money or .... ?
   A environment   C an environment
   B the environment   D one environment

34 Apparently, it's the largest computer store in ....
   A an Europe   C the Europe
   B a Europe   D Europe

(1 mark per answer)

E Choose the correct answer.

35 Let me just add .... what I'm buying to see if I've got enough money.
   A on   C over
   B up   D in

36 Bob .... a lot of money in his brother's business and made a profit.
   A spent   C saved
   B invested   D owed

37 I'm saving all my pocket money .... to buy a new PlayStation.
   A out   C up
   B down   D away

38 The old man took the book .... from the shelf and looked at the price.
   A up   C out

B down   D back

39 I couldn't sell my old magazines, so I gave them ....
   A over   C up
   B off   D away

40 I gave the waiter a €50 note and waited for my ....
   A change   C cash
   B supply   D cost

41 *Home Lovers* have got lots of .... in their sale this year.
   A debts   C bargains
   B fortunes   D fees

42 I usually spend any money I have .... sweets and video games.

(1 mark per answer)

Total mark: ..../50

Grammar

Pronouns and possessive determiners

Subject pronouns

Form

I / you / he / she / it / we / they

Use	Example
The subject of a verb	**They** built the first aeroplane.
	Alexander Fleming discovered penicillin, but **he** did it by mistake!

Object pronouns

Form

me / you / him / her / it / us / them

Use	Example
The object of a verb	Could you give **me** that equipment?
	Could you give that equipment to **me**?

Possessive determiners

Form

my / your / his / her / its / our / their

Use	Example
To show who owns or has something	That's **their** car.

Helpful hints

- Possessive determiners are always followed by a noun.
  ✓ Is this **my coffee**?

 Watch out! *Its* and *it's* do not mean the same thing.
✓ Here's the dog's water and here's **its** food. (= the dog's food)
✓ **It's** the best camera I've ever had. (= It is …)

Possessive pronouns

Form

mine / yours / his / hers / ours / theirs

Use	Example
To show who owns or has something	That car is **ours**.

Helpful hints

- Possessive pronouns are not followed by a noun.
  ✗ This is hers car.

 Watch out! There is no possessive pronoun for *it*.

Reflexive pronouns

Form

myself / yourself / himself / herself / itself / ourselves / yourselves / themselves

Use	Example
To describe actions where the subject and object are the same	My computer turns **itself** off after half an hour.
To emphasise who does something	Nobody helped me. I did it **myself**!

A Complete using the words in the box. You have to use some words more than once.

| I • you • he • she • it • we • they |

1 .... asked Mr Simons, my science teacher, what glass was and .... said that .... is a liquid!
2 Hi Diana! Are .... still coming shopping with us tomorrow?
3 My mum studied history at university. .... says .... was a really interesting course.
4 Scientists are working hard to find cures for lots of diseases, but .... haven't found a cure for the common cold yet.
5 Adam, do .... think .... should all bring some food with us to your party?
6 Dad, do .... know if .... sell computer games in the market?

B Replace each word or phrase in bold with a word from the box. You have to use some words more than once.

| him • her • it • us • them |

1 Did you give **that book** back to Alicia?   ....
2 I told **Bill** that you don't eat meat.   ....
3 Why does she always give **our class** more tests than the other class?   ....
4 They paid **Kate Winslet** a lot of money to be in this film.   ....
5 I haven't seen **Rich and Andy** for ages.   ....
6 Did you give an invitation to **Mr and Mrs Clark**?   ....
7 A TV channel has invited **my family** to take part in a game show!   ....

C Rewrite the sentences using the word given.

1 This is where we live. **house**
   This is ....

2 That wallet belongs to me! **That**
   .... wallet!

3 Do those shoes belong to you? **your**
   Are .... ?

4 That car doesn't belong to them. **car**
   That's ....

5 This is where she sleeps. **bed**
   This ....

6 That isn't what he does. **job**
   That ....

7 Have you seen the dog's blanket? **its**
   Where's .... ?

D If a sentence is correct, put a tick (✓). If there is an extra word in a sentence, write the word.

1 Is that my milkshake or yours milkshake? ....

2 Look where the dog has put its bone! ....

3 I haven't got a camera with me because I've lent mine to my brother. ....

4 Your DVD player is just the same as theirs is. ....

5 Was it your decision or hers decision? ....

6 You can borrow my laptop, but why aren't you using yours laptop? ....

7 I think those are your CDs and these are ours. ....

8 This is her book, these are your books and these two are mine books. ....

9 That video belongs to Carol and Doug – at least, I think it's theirs video. ....

E Each of the words in bold is in the wrong sentence. Write the correct word.

1 That's great, Cathy. Did you make that **herself**? ....

2 Doug hit **myself** in the eye by mistake with his toothbrush! ....

3 Cats can look after **yourself**, can't they? ....

4 I hope you all enjoy **himself** on holiday! ....

5 Dad didn't help me. I did it all **themselves**! ....

6 We painted the room **yourselves**; we didn't pay anyone to do it. ....

7 This kitchen isn't going to clean **ourselves**, you know! ....

8 Wendy decided that she would buy **itself** a new dress in the sales. ....

F Complete using the correct pronouns or determiners.

Inventions

If you invented something important, (**1**) .... would want to make money out of
(**2**) .... , right? Most of us would want to make some money from (**3**) .... invention.
It seems only fair – we did the work, so the money should be (**4**) .... too. Many inventors who
have had (**5**) .... inventions produced, have become rich and famous and we shouldn't blame
(**6**) .... for that.

But have (**7**) .... heard of Tim Berners-Lee? (**8**) .... invented the World Wide Web
on the Internet, one of the most important inventions of the last fifty years. Millions of lives have been
changed by (**9**) .... introduction.

When Tim Berners-Lee invented the Web, he made a promise to (**10**) .... – that he wouldn't
make any money out of it, and that he would give (**11**) .... invention to the world. He did,
and now the Web belongs to all of (**12**) ....

Ask (**13**) .... what life would be like if the World Wide Web wasn't free. We should be grateful
to Tim Berners-Lee, and thank (**14**) .... for (**15**) .... amazing gift to the world.

Grammar
Relative clauses

Relative pronouns

We use relative pronouns in relative clauses.
We use relative clauses to give more information about something, without having to start a new sentence.
That man over there is called Bill Gates. He started Microsoft. ⟶
That man over there, who's called Bill Gates, started Microsoft.

Use	Example
who for people	*What's the name of the man who created the Internet?*
which for things and animals	*The experiment which worked was the last one.*
where for places	*This is the town where Albert Einstein was born.*
whose to show possession	*That's the man whose sister discovered a new planet.*

● We can use *who* for animals when we give them a personality.
  ✓ *Our dog, who's called Benji, is eight years old.*

● When there is a relative pronoun, remember not to repeat the subject/object.
  ✗ *What's the name of the man who he created the World Wide Web?*
  ✗ *This is the experiment which I'm doing it at the moment.*

Non-defining relative clauses

Non-defining relative clauses give extra information. The sentence makes sense without the relative clause.
That man over there, who is called Bill Gates, started Microsoft.
If we remove the relative clause, the sentence still makes sense:
That man over there started Microsoft.

Use	Example
To give extra information	*This program, which is totally free, protects your computer against viruses.*

Helpful hints

We use commas with non-defining relative clauses.
✓ *Carl, whose sister is famous, is a friend of mine.*

Defining relative clauses

Defining relative clauses give very important information. If we remove a defining relative clause, the sentence doesn't make sense.
Imagine that there are lots of people in a room. Only one of them is wearing a blue shirt.
The person who is wearing the blue shirt started Microsoft.
If we remove the relative clause, we won't know which person it is.
✗ *The person started Microsoft.*

Use	Example
To define who or what we are talking about	*This is the TV which works. This is the TV which doesn't work.*

Helpful hints

● We don't use commas with defining relative clauses.
● We can use *that* instead of *who* and *which*.
  ✓ *Did you see the programme about the woman who invented Tippex?*
  ✓ *Did you see the programme about the woman that invented Tippex?*

A Complete using the words in the box. You have to use some words more than once.

> where • which • who • whose

1 There's a film on tonight .... I really want to see.
2 Do you know any restaurants .... they serve vegetarian dishes?
3 Can you remember .... told you about the new nightclub?
4 The film, ... stars Tom Hanks, is based on a book by Dan Brown.
5 I've never met anyone before .... mother was famous!
6 Lorenzo, ... is from Spain originally, has lived here for about ten years.
7 Carla, ... parents are from Mexico, was born in the UK.
8 Here's a photo of the hotel .... we stayed.

B Circle the extra word in each sentence.

1 The boy who he sits next to me in class is called Vladimir.
2 This book, which I started reading it last week, is really funny.
3 Jean, whose her mother is a nurse, wants to be a doctor.
4 My mum and dad, who they got married fifteen years ago, met over thirty years ago.
5 The jeans which I was telling you about them are over there.

C Rewrite as one sentence using a relative clause.

1 My grandfather was an airline pilot. He is sixty-five years old now.
   My grandfather, who is sixty-five years old now, was an airline pilot.

2 *Friendly People* is a comedy. It's my favourite programme.
   ....

3 My friend Michael often comes to play with me. He hasn't got any brothers and sisters.
   ....

4 My sister loves wearing hats. Her hair is brown.
   ....

5 New York is an enormous city. It's where I was born.
   ....

6 This CD is scratched. I only bought it yesterday.
   ....

7 My brother George has got some great shirts! He hates me borrowing his clothes.
   ....

8 Our neighbours have never invited us to dinner. Their house is directly opposite ours.
   ....

D Look at the pictures and use the prompts to write sentences.

1 A tree / tall / have / leaves
   The tree which is tall doesn't have any leaves.
   ....

   B trees / have / leaves / be / short
   ....

2 A bottle / big / full
   ....

   B bottles / small / empty
   ....

3 A girl / has / short hair / be called / Melissa
   ....

   B girls / hair / be / long / be called / Lucy, Tina and Debbie
   ....

4 A boy / hold / black basketball / wear / school uniform
   ....
   ....

   B boys / basketballs / be / white / wear / tracksuits
   ....
   ....

E Tick (✓) the sentences in exercise D where the relative pronoun can be replaced by the word *that*. Put a cross (✗) where *that* cannot replace the relative pronoun.

1 A ....   B ....   4 A ....
   B ....   3 A ....   B ....
2 A ....   B ....

F Write one word in each gap.

Actuaries

Did you know that there are people (**1**) .... are paid to predict the future? They're called 'actuaries'. I'd never heard of actuaries until my friend Greg, (**2**) .... mother is an actuary, told me about them. It's a job (**3**) .... sounds quite interesting.

Actuaries usually work for companies, like insurance companies, (**4**) .... deal with the chances of things happening in the future. Actuaries have to decide how probable it is that something will happen. For example, it's more probable that buildings will be flooded in places (**5**) .... it rains a lot. Greg's mum, (**6**) .... has been an actuary for about five years, is involved with car insurance. She works in an office (**7**) .... they decide how much car insurance people should pay. It's more probable that a car (**8**) .... is new is safer and more reliable than a very old car, so people (**9**) .... cars are new pay less insurance. If there are drivers (**10**) .... she thinks will probably have more accidents, she makes them pay more insurance!

Vocabulary
Inventions and discoveries

Topic vocabulary

see page 190 for definitions

artificial (adj)	experiment (v, n)	operate (v)
automatic (adj)	gadget (n)	plastic (n, adj)
complicated (adj)	hardware (n)	program (v, n)
decrease (v, n)	invent (v)	research (n)
digital (adj)	involve (v)	run (v)
discover (v)	laboratory (n)	screen (n)
effect (n)	lack (v, n)	software (n)
equipment (n)	laptop (n)	sudden (adj)
estimate (v)	maximum (adj)	technology (n)
exact (adj)	minimum (adj)	unique (adj)

Phrasal verbs

break down	stop working (for a machine, etc)
come across	find sth by chance
find out	discover information, etc
make up	invent an explanation, excuse, etc
pull off	break by pulling
throw away	put sth in a rubbish bin
turn off	stop a machine working
turn on	start a machine working

Prepositional phrases

at last
by chance
in my opinion
in the end
in the future
out of order

Word formation

boil	boiler, boiling	**history**	historic, historian
chemist	chemical, chemistry	**identical**	identically
conclude	conclusion	**long**	length
examine	exam(ination), examiner	**measure**	measurement
fascinate	fascination, fascinating	**science**	scientist

Word patterns

adjectives	different from/to		result in
	full of	*nouns*	a difference between
verbs	begin sth with		an idea about
	connect sth to/with		a number of
	disconnect sth from		a reason for
	fill sth with		a type of

Topic vocabulary

A Match the pictures with the words in the box.

> equipment • experiment • gadgets • hardware • laboratory • laptop • screen • software

....

....

B Complete using the words in the box.

> artificial • automatic • complicated • digital • exact • maximum
> minimum • plastic • sudden • unique

1 It's not a/an .... watch. It's got hands.
2 If you play this stereo on .... volume, you'll go deaf!
3 It's not a/an .... experiment. In fact, it's really simple.
4 Are leather chairs more comfortable than .... ones?
5 There aren't any windows in the lab, so all the light is ....
6 Was it a/an .... decision, or had you thought about it for a long time?
7 The lights are .... – they come on when you enter the room, and go off when you leave.
8 Each person's fingerprints are .... No two people have the same fingerprints.
9 The .... number of patients necessary to test the new drug is 50. Any less than that and the scientists won't know if it works properly or not.
10 I can't remember the .... year it was discovered, but it was around 1976.

C Circle the correct word.

1 Do you know who **invented / discovered** the planet Mars?
2 The number of people dying of malaria has **run / decreased** enormously over the last 100 years.
3 You need at least three people to **operate / estimate** this machine safely.

4 Modern **technology / equipment** makes all our lives easier.
5 We've done a lot of **research / experiment** into why people are scared of spiders.
6 I'm using a computer **research / program** that translates from English into Greek.
7 This drug seems to have no **effect / lack** on humans at all.
8 The experiment just **involves / operates** answering a few questions.
9 Could you **program / estimate** how many times a week you eat cheese?
10 Do you think anyone will ever **invent / discover** a time machine?
11 Professor Reinhart **decreases / runs** the computer lab with her three assistants.
12 There's **a lack / an effect** of phones in this office. We need some more!

Phrasal verbs

D Choose the correct answer.

1 I .... across this book about the moon in the library. It's really interesting!
A went   C came
B found   D looked

2 Jenny pulled .... the handle so we can't open the cupboard now.
A off   C in
B away   D over

3 I'd like to find .... more about being a computer programmer.
A across   C off
B up   D out

4 Our car has broken .... again.
A off   C out
B down   D in

5 Dean was late for physics so he ....

up a story about being attacked by a cat!
A took   C created
B wrote   D made

6 .... the TV off. This show is boring.
A Put   C Turn
B Set   D Make

7 I'm going to throw these old shoes .... I never wear them anymore.
A off   C down
B away   D back

8 I turned .... the tap but no water came out.
A over   C round
B up   D on

Prepositional phrases

E Complete using the words in the box.

| chance • end • future • last • opinion • order |

1 These toilets have been out of .... for a week now. When are they going to fix them?
2 In my .... , humans will never live on other planets.
3 Alexander Fleming discovered penicillin by .... He didn't expect to find it at all.
4 I wonder what new technology will be invented in the ....
5 Helen couldn't get the experiment to work for ages, but in the .... it was fine.
6 It's so nice to have my own computer at ....

Word formation

F Use the word given in capitals at the end of each line to form a word that fits in the gap in the same line.

Mr Thomas

Mr Thomas was a teacher at our school. He'd trained as a (**1**) .... **HISTORY**
and usually taught history. He definitely wasn't a (**2**) .... , but for **SCIENCE**
some strange reason he taught us (**3**) .... for a term. His lessons **CHEMIST**
were always (**4**) .... , but that was mainly because his experiments **FASCINATE**
always went wrong! If he was supposed to use (**5**) .... water for **BOIL**
an experiment, Mr Thomas would use cold water by mistake. Once, he was measuring
the (**6**) .... of some pieces of sodium. I can't remember exactly **LONG**
why he needed this (**7**) .... , but I think he wanted all the pieces **MEASURE**
to react (**8**) .... As he picked up the ruler, his arm knocked over **IDENTICAL**
a jug of water and the sodium caught fire. He almost burnt the lab down and they had
to call the fire brigade. I think after that Mr Thomas came to the
(**9**) .... that he should stick to history! I learnt a lot from him, **CONCLUDE**
though. Whenever there was a question in a science (**10**) .... **EXAMINE**
about what happens when sodium reacts with water, I always got the answer right!

Word patterns

G Match to make sentences.

1 What's the difference   ....   A in us having to call the fire brigade.
2 This box is full   ....   B to that piece of equipment over there.
3 This resulted   ....   C about how to do this experiment.
4 Connect this cable   ....   D between H_2O and H_2SO_4?
5 I've had an idea   ....   E with water?
6 Could you fill this bottle   ....   F of old camping equipment.

H Write one word in each gap.

1 This program is very different .... the one you're using at the moment.
2 Let's begin the lesson .... a short test on the names of the different parts of an insect.
3 Disconnect your PC .... the power supply before you take the case off.
4 There are a number .... different ways of doing this experiment.
5 How many types .... building can you think of?
6 What were your reasons .... choosing to do biology at university?

Review 6

A Complete each second sentence using the word given, so that it has a similar meaning to the first sentence. Write between two and five words.

1 I found the photo by chance when I was tidying my room. **across**
   I .... the photo when I was tidying my room.

2 Fridges and freezers are not the same thing. **difference**
   There .... fridges and freezers.

3 Scientists should never invent their results. **made**
   Results should never .... scientists.

4 Don't put those plastic bags in the bin – use them again! **away**
   Don't .... – use them again!

5 Our car stopped working on the motorway, so we had to call a mechanic. **down**
   We had to call a mechanic when our car .... on the motorway.

6 A new medicine was developed because of the work Dr Wang did. **resulted**
   Dr Wang's .... a new medicine being developed.

7 There are quite a few things that I'd like to invent! **number**
   There are .... things that I'd like to invent!

8 Make sure you fill the bottle with water before you start the experiment. **full**
   Make sure the bottle .... water before you start the experiment.

(2 marks per answer)

B Write one word in each gap.

9 Turn all the lights .... when you leave the room. We don't want to waste electricity!

10 .... my opinion, modern technology has improved all our lives.

11 Could you disconnect your laptop .... the Internet when you've finished checking your e-mail?

12 We thought the experiment would work, but .... the end it didn't.

13 .... last, someone has built a battery-powered skateboard!

14 How many different types .... building can you think of?

15 That programme is about to start, so I'll turn .... the TV.

16 Ice floats in water. Can you think of a reason .... that?

(1 mark per answer)

C Complete by changing the form of the word in capitals.

17 The .... (**LONG**) of the train is exactly 100 metres.

18 I think astronomy is absolutely .... (**FASCINATE**)!

19 Lee and Greg are twins, but they don't dress .... (**IDENTICAL**).

20 I've come to the .... (**CONCLUDE**) that no one should have a car.

21 Why do all .... (**SCIENCE**) have untidy hair?

22 Pour the .... (**BOIL**) water over the tea bag and leave for a few minutes.

23 Make sure your .... (**MEASURE**) are accurate.

24 My brother is studying .... (**CHEMIST**) at university.

(1 mark per answer)

D Choose the correct answer.

25 Did someone help Alison or did she do all the calculations .... ?
   A her   B hers   C herself

26 That's not your calculator. It's ....
   A me   B mine   C my

27 Einstein is the person .... showed that time can speed up and slow down.
   A which   B who   C whose

28 Do you know .... idea it was? Was it Greg's or Fiona's?
   A who   B which   C whose

29 This is the laboratory .... we do all the experiments.
   A that   B which   C where

30 Novosibirsk, ... is a big city in Siberia, is famous for its university.
   A who   B which   C where

31 That's the girl .... father says he's invented a time machine!
   A who   B whose   C that

32 Is this our DVD or is it .... ?
   A them   B their   C theirs

(1 mark per answer)

E Choose the correct answer.

Technology and the young

Modern technology is changing and improving all the time. Every month, scientists (**33**) .... new gadgets and (**34**) .... to help us with our daily lives, and (**35**) .... ways to make existing technology faster and better. Our homes are full of hardware (such as DVD players and computers) and (**36**) .... (such as computer games and MP3s).
(**37**) .... suggests, however, that it's young people who are best able to deal with this change. Whereas teenagers have no problem (**38**) .... a DVD player, their mums and dads and grandparents often find using new technology (**39**) .... and difficult.
But if you're a teenager who criticises your parents for their (**40**) .... of technological awareness, don't be too hard on them! Some time (**41**) .... the future, when you've got children of your own, your ability to deal with new technology will probably (**42**) .... and your children will feel more comfortable with new technology than you do. You won't want them to criticise you, will you?

33	A estimate	B invent	C involve	D experiment
34	A experiments	B effects	C laboratories	D equipment
35	A involve	B discover	C decrease	D connect
36	A screens	B gadgets	C software	D laptops
37	A Research	B Experiment	C Program	D Technology
38	A involving	B operating	C discovering	D inventing
39	A automatic	B unique	C sudden	D complicated
40	A research	B experiment	C effect	D lack
41	A to	B in	C on	D at
42	A decrease	B involve	C lack	D estimate

(1 mark per answer)

Total mark: ..../50

Grammar
Modals 1: ability, permission, advice

Introduction to modals

Form

The modal verbs are:

statement	negative	statement	negative
can	can't / cannot	could	couldn't / could not
may	may not	might	mightn't / might not
will	won't / will not	would	wouldn't / would not
shall	shan't / shall not	should	shouldn't / should not
must	mustn't / must not		

All modal verbs:

- have only one form
  I/you/he/she/it/we/they **may** write an e-mail.
- are followed by the bare infinitive
  You should **call** Stella.
- do not have an infinitive

Semi-modals

There are also some phrases that we use like modals:

- ought to (ought not to)
- have to (don't have to)
- need to (don't need to / needn't)

Like modals, *ought to* doesn't change.
Have to and *need to* change for person and tense like normal verbs and have infinitives.

- We form questions with modal verbs like this:
  ✓ **Can you** understand what he's saying?
- We use modals with the passive voice like this:
  ✓ The address **should be written** clearly on the front of the envelope.

Ability

Use	Modal	Example
Ability now or generally	can	**Can** you use a fax machine?
Ability in the past	could	Tom **could** read when he was two years old.

We use *be able to* to form other tenses.
✓ It's useful **to be able to** order things by e-mail. (infinitive)
✓ Soon, I'**ll be able to** speak Italian quite well. (future)
✓ **Have** you **been able to** speak English for a long time? (present perfect)

Permission

Use	Modal	Example
Asking for permission	can / could / may	**Can / Could / May** I use the phone?
Giving permission	can / may	You **can / may** send the fax when you like.

May is more polite than *could* and *could* is more polite than *can*.

Advice

Use	Modal	Example
Asking for and giving advice	should	Liam **ought to / should** watch less TV.
	ought to	

A Underline the mistake in each sentence and write the correct words.

1 My older brother can to ride a motorbike, but I can't. ....
2 He'll has his dinner early today because he's going out. ....
3 Do you can come to my party? ....
4 You should to see a doctor about your foot. ....
5 I couldn't bought any bread because the baker's was closed. ....
6 You needn't to do the washing-up. I've already done it. ....
7 The school ought listen to pupils' opinions. ....
8 People shouldn't to drop their rubbish in the street. ....

B Look at the pictures and complete the sentences using *can, could* or the correct form of *be able to*. You may have to use some negative forms.

Amy really loves playing chess and she (**1**) .... play very well. When she was a baby she (**2**) .... play chess. She thinks that when she's older, she'll (**3**) .... win the national championships!

Amy has (**4**) .... ride a bicycle since she was three. She wants to learn to drive when she grows up, though. When she's eighteen, she hopes she'll (**5**) .... do her driving test. She (**6**) .... drive a car now though. It's against the law!

C Write what they say using the word given.

1 Tony wants to borrow his friend's pencil. **could**
'Could I borrow your pencil .... ?'

2 Alex wants to allow her friend to use her dictionary. **can**
'........................ .'

3 Julie wants permission from her teacher to leave the classroom. **may**
'........................ ?'

4 Lou wants to wear his brother's new trainers. **can**
'........................ ?'

5 Terry wants to ask her boss for permission to take the day off work. **could**
'........................ ?'

6 Diane wants to use her dad's car this weekend. **can**
'........................ ?'

7 A teacher wants to give her students five extra minutes to finish the test. **may**
'........................ .'

D Rewrite the sentences using *should* or *ought to* and the words in brackets.
You may have to use some negative forms.

1 'I need to earn more money.' (**a**, **get**, **job**, **new**, **you**)
'You should/ought to get a new job .... '

2 'Brenda is angry about what I said.' (**are**, **say**, **sorry**, **you**, **you**)
' .... '

3 'Tom doesn't understand his homework.' (**about**, **ask**, **it**, **he**, **his**, **teacher**)
' .... '

4 'I'd like to learn to play the piano.' (**having**, **lessons**, **start**, **you**)
' .... '

5 'Tina is often tired at work.' (**at**, **late**, **night**, **she**, **TV**, **watch**)
' .... '

6 'I don't seem to have much energy at the moment.' (**exercise**, **get**, **some**, **you**)
' .... '

E Circle the correct word or phrase.

1 I've been having swimming lessons and now I **can / could** swim really well.
2 Please **could / should** I use your mobile phone? Mine doesn't have any power.
3 Sam **could / ought** to get a job instead of complaining about having no money.
4 Okay, yes – you **can / should** leave five minutes early today.
5 Do you think I **must / should** tell Michael the truth about what happened?
6 I **can't / couldn't** read until I was five years old.
7 I'm sorry, but you **can't / couldn't** leave your car there.
8 If you want to pass the exam, you **can / ought to** do some revision.
9 I know John lived in Tokyo, but I don't think he **can / may** speak Japanese.
10 Tracy **can / could** sing really well now that she's had a few lessons.

F Match to make sentences.

1 There's a lot of washing-up; I think we should .... A wait for their flight in the VIP area.
2 It's getting quite late and we ought .... B borrow some if you need it.
3 I don't have much money, but you can .... C to think about getting a taxi.
4 It's amazing that Andrew could .... D offer to do it.
5 Passengers travelling in first class may .... E walk when he was just six months ol

Grammar

Modals 2: obligation, probability, possibility

For general information about modals, see Unit 19.

 Obligation

Use	Modal	Example
Present or future obligation	must / mustn't have to need to	All visitors **must** turn off their mobile phones. You **have to/need to** press 'send'.
No present or future obligation	don't have to don't need to needn't	You **don't have to/don't need to/needn't** pay to send an e-mail.
Past obligation	had to	Yesterday, Sam **had to** buy more stamps.
No past obligation	didn't have to didn't need to	I learnt a little Italian, but everyone spoke English, so I **didn't have to/didn't need to** use it.

> **Helpful hints**
>
> In spoken English, *have to* is more common than *must*. *Must* is often used in written notices and instructions.
> ✓ 'We **have to** pay the phone bill today,' Rita said.
> ✓ Passengers **must** turn off all mobile phones.

> **Watch out!** *Mustn't* and *don't have to* do not mean the same.
> ✓ You **mustn't** do that! (= Don't do that!)
> ✓ You **don't have to** do that. (= You can do that if you want to, but it's not necessary.)

 Probability and possibility

Use	Modal	Example
Present strong probability	must can't couldn't	The phone is ringing – it **must** be Simon. This letter **can't/couldn't** be from Japan because it's got a French stamp.
Present and future probability	should ought to	We **ought to/should** hear from Cheryl this weekend.
Present and future possibility	could may might	I'm not sure what language it is – it **could/may/might** be Polish.

> **Helpful hints**
>
> We often use *must*, *can't* and *couldn't* for probability when we have some evidence for our opinion.
> ✓ I just rang Paul, but there's no answer. He **must** be out.

> **Watch out!** To talk about possibility and probability about the past, we use a modal and the perfect infinive.
> See Unit 22.

A Choose the sentence (A, B or C) which means the same as the first sentence.

1 We have to pay the electricity bill before Friday.
   A We can pay it if we want to.
   B We must pay it.
   C We've already paid it.

2 You don't need to buy me a birthday present.
   A You must buy me a birthday present.
   B It's not necessary to buy me a birthday present.
   C You mustn't buy me a birthday present.

3 I have to do some work on my project this evening.
   A I haven't got time to do the work.
   B I've already done the work.
   C I need to do the work.

4 Lenny didn't have to see the head teacher after all.
   A It wasn't necessary for Lenny to see the head teacher.
   B Lenny went to see the head teacher.
   C Lenny is waiting to see the head teacher.

5 Students mustn't run in school buildings.
   A They can run if they want to.
   B Students don't like running.
   C Running isn't allowed.

6 All passengers must fasten their seatbelts.
   A They have to fasten their seatbelts now.
   B They don't have to fasten their seatbelts.
   C They can fasten their seatbelts.

7 Mr Reed had to go to the police station to answer some questions.
   A Mr Reed was able to go to the police station.
   B Mr Reed forgot to go to the police station.
   C Mr Reed was obliged to go to the police station.

8 It's kind of you to offer to help, but you really don't need to.
   A I don't want you to help me.
   B Your help isn't necessary.
   C You won't be able to help me.

B Circle the correct word or phrase.

1 'Smoking isn't allowed in the airport.'
   You **mustn't / don't have to** smoke in the airport.

2 'It's not necessary to come to the train station to meet me.'
   You **have to / don't have to** meet her at the train station.

3 'We were forced to wait for over two hours in the rain.'
   They **had to / didn't need to** wait for over two hours in the rain.

4 'The instructions tell you to write in pencil.'
   You **must / needn't** write in pencil.

5 'You can contact us by either phone or e-mail.'
   You **mustn't / don't have to** phone them.

6 'In my country, you can carry your passport with you if you want, but it's not necessary.'
   In her country, you **don't need to / mustn't** carry your passport with you.

7 'My grandfather was made to start work when he was just fourteen years old.'
   He **had to / must** start work when he was just fourteen years old.

8 'It's not necessary to book a hotel; you can stay in our spare room.'
   You **mustn't / don't have to** stay in a hotel.

C Complete using the correct form of *have to*. You may have to use some negative forms.

1 Jade can't come out tonight. She .... look after her little brother.
2 I didn't have enough money, so I .... borrow some from Yuri.
3 It's raining really hard, but luckily we .... go out this evening.
4 To start the laptop you .... press the power button.
5 Robbie worked last weekend, but I ....
6 ....you .... go to piano lessons when you were younger?

D Match the sentences with the explanations. You have to use some of the explanations more than once.

1 'Someone is at the door. It must be Mrs Johnson from next door.' ....

2 'Lena might not know where the cinema is.' ....

3 'Dad should know what the capital of New Zealand is.' ....

4 'Greg can't be in the final! He's a terrible player!' ....

5 'The dog is wet. It must be raining outside.' ....

6 'We may go to the Canary Islands for Easter.' ....

7 'Ken must like that film. He's seen it six times!' ....

8 'Barry ought to be able to cook Chinese food. He lived there for two years.' ....

A I'm almost certain.

B It's probable.

C Maybe / Perhaps.

E Rewrite the sentences using the words given.

1 You're expecting David to ring. The phone rings. **must**

'... ,

2 Anna is a better runner than Rula. You think Anna will probably win the race tomorrow. **should**

'... ,

3 A letter arrives. It's possible that it's from your cousin, Janice. **could**

'... ,

4 There's a knock at the door. Your mum says it might be Colin, but you know Colin is on holiday. **can't**

'... ,

5 You see someone wearing a costume. You think there's a strong probability that she's going to a fancy-dress party. **must**

'... ,

6 Your sister is looking for her hairbrush. You think it's possible that it's in the living room. **might**

'... ,

7 You're waiting for Harriet to arrive. You think she'll probably be there in half an hour. **should**

'... ,

8 You're talking about why James seems to be sad. You think it's possible he's in trouble at school. **could**

'... ,

83

Vocabulary
Sending and receiving

Topic vocabulary

see page 191 for definitions

accent (n)	informal (adj)	publish (v)
announcement (n)	Internet (n)	report (v, n)
broadcast (v, n)	interrupt (v)	request (v, n)
channel (n)	link (v, n)	ring (v)
clear (adj)	media (n)	signal (n)
click (v)	mobile phone (n phr)	swear (v)
contact (v, n)	online (adj, adv)	type (v)
file (n)	pause (v, n)	viewer (n)
formal (adj)	persuade (v)	website (n)
image (n)	pronounce (v)	whisper (v, n)

Phrasal verbs

call back	ring again on the phone
come out	be published
cut off	disconnect (phone, electricity, etc)
fill in	add information in the spaces on a form, etc
hang up	put the receiver down to end a phone call
log off	disconnect from the Internet/a website
log on(to)	connect to the Internet/a website
print out	make a paper copy of sth on a computer

Prepositional phrases

by e-mail/phone/letter
on the Internet
on the news
on the phone
on the radio
on TV

Word formation

certain	certainly, certainty	**inform**	informative, information
communicate	communication	**predict**	prediction, (un)predictable
connect	connection, disconnect	**secret**	secretly, secrecy
deliver	delivery	**speak**	spoke, spoken, speaker, speech
express	expression, expressive	**translate**	translation, translator

Word patterns

verbs	comment on		talk (to sb) about
	communicate with		tell sb about
	glance at		translate (from sth) into
	receive sth from		write (to sb) about
	reply to	*nouns*	information about
	send sth to sb		a letter (from sb) about

Topic vocabulary

A Complete using a word formed from the letters given.

1 You can tell Martin is from Denmark by his .... **N C E C T A**

2 Did the .... say that our plane was delayed or cancelled? **E U N T N E C M A N O N**

3 We've got relatives in Canada, but we don't have much .... with them. **T T A C N C O**

4 You need to save what you've written as a .... and then send it to me by e-mail. **E I L F**

5 The first .... that was sent by radio from New York to London was a picture of the American president. **A I E G M**

6 The .... started in the 1980s and now it connects millions of computers around the world. **T N R T N E I E**

7 You need to .... the computers together and then you can send things directly from one to the other. **N I K L**

8 You shouldn't believe everything you read or hear in the .... **D E A I M**

9 According to the .... on the TV news, the Prime Minister is coming to our town soon. **T O E P R R**

10 You can't listen to the radio when you're on the underground because the .... isn't strong enough. **A N G S I L**

11 If you're a regular .... of our programme, then you'll know that we often interview ordinary people. **I E V R E W**

12 I got the information from a .... Hang on and I'll give you the address. **I B E S W T E**

B Complete using the correct form of the verbs in the box.

broadcast • click • interrupt • pause • publish • ring • swear • type

1 You have to .... on the picture by pressing the left button on your mouse.

2 Writing and sending e-mails is a lot faster if you learn how to .... properly.

3 I couldn't believe it when Greg .... in front of the head teacher!

4 The man on the telephone .... for a moment and then said, 'Tell no one!'

5 This programme was first .... in 1967 and hasn't been shown on TV since then.

6 Please don't .... me. Let me finish what I wanted to say.

7 Our school might .... a weekly magazine to keep parents and students informed about what's happening.

8 You should .... Michael and let him know about the plan for this evening.

C Circle the correct word or phrase.

1 What John said on the phone wasn't very **clear / online** so I asked him to repeat it.

2 Sandy waited until the teacher was looking the other way. 'Meet me after school,' he **whispered / requested** quietly in my ear.

3 How do you **persuade / pronounce** your name?

4 You should use **formal / informal** language when you're writing to someone you don't know personally.

5 Why do you keep on switching **channels / mobile phones**? I'm trying to watch this film!

Phrasal verbs

D Complete using the correct form of the phrasal verbs in the box.

> call back • come out • cut off • fill in • hang up • log off • log on(to) • print out

1 I've got an e-mail from Mick! Wait a second and I'll .... it .... so you don't have to read it on the screen.
2 I was talking to Matt on the phone when the train went into a tunnel and we were ....
3 You just have to .... this form and we'll send the money for you.
4 My favourite magazine, *Teen Scene*, ... every Friday.
5 Len was talking on the phone, but when I entered the room he ....
6 I can't .... because I can't remember my password.
7 I'm afraid Mr Brown isn't here. Could you .... in an hour?
8 Tom surfed the Internet for hours and .... at three in the morning!

Prepositional phrases

E Write one word in each gap.

> ### News travels fast
>
> These days, there's no excuse for not knowing what's happening in the world. (**1**) .... TV and on (**2**) .... radio, news programmes keep us up to date with all the important events. We read about problems on the other side of the world (**3**) .... the Internet as soon as they happen, and we see live pictures (**4**) .... the news 24 hours a day. Even personal news travels fast today. Whether we keep in touch (**5**) .... phone or e-mail, we're never more than a few seconds away from friends and family. The days when the only means of communication was (**6**) .... letter are gone forever. So, the next time you're (**7**) .... the phone, just remember how things have changed.

Word formation

F Complete by changing the form of the word in capitals.

1 My .... is that one day all phone calls will be free. **PREDICT**
2 Politicians often have a .... with them when they go to other countries. **TRANSLATE**
3 I would hate to give a .... in front of hundreds of people! **SPEAK**
4 Who knows what means of .... will be invented in the future? **COMMUNICATE**
5 There's something wrong with my .... to the Internet, so I can't send and receive e-mails. **CONNECT**
6 The mobile phone has .... made life a lot easier. **CERTAIN**

G | Use the word given in capitals at the end of each line to form a word that fits in the gap in the same line.

The Secret Message

I was walking down the street when a woman appeared in front of me. 'Please! You must help me!' she cried. I could tell from her (**1**) .... that she was frightened. She   **EXPRESS**

(**2**) .... English with a Russian accent. She put a piece of paper into my hand.   **SPEAK**

'This contains important (**3**) .... I can't say any more, but there will be a   **INFORM**

(**4**) .... tonight.' She started to leave. 'Contact the person in the message.   **DELIVER**

But do it (**5**) .... ! No one must know!' I looked at the message but didn't   **SECRET**

understand. When I looked up, she was gone. That was how my adventures began …

Word patterns

H | Write one word in each gap.

1 I didn't read the newspaper properly. I just glanced .... it, really.
2 I've got an e-mail in Spanish. Could you translate it .... English for me?
3 My grandma says people don't talk .... each other like they used to.
4 You should receive a letter .... our company in the next few days.
5 Press this button to reply .... the e-mail.
6 I got a letter from Alex .... her new job. It sounds interesting.

I | Complete each second sentence using the word given, so that it has a similar meaning to the first sentence. Write between two and five words.

1 Did Olivia say anything about your website? **comment**
   Did Olivia .... your website?
2 Carl described his new mobile phone to me. **told**
   Carl .... his new mobile phone.
3 This website describes the history of communication. **information**
   This website has .... the history of communication.
4 Remind me to send Nigel a letter about our plans. **write**
   Remind me to .... our plans.
5 Some chimpanzees use sign language to talk to people. **communicate**
   Some chimpanzees .... people through sign language.
6 Could you tell Gail about the party by e-mail? **send**
   Could you .... Gail about the party?

Use the word given in capitals at the end of each line to form a word that fits in the gap in the same line.

From one language to another

Finding an accurate (**1**) .... from one language to another is	**TRANSLATE**
not always easy and the job of an interpreter can be (**2**)	**PREDICT**
Many (**3**) .... in one language don't work in another language	**EXPRESS**
and trying to give a good idea of what a (**4**) .... wants to say	**SPEAK**
can be difficult. The most important thing is that no (**5**)	**INFORM**
should be lost. The interpreter has to have complete (**6**)	**CERTAIN**
that they understand the message and their (**7**) .... language	**SPEAK**
has to be very good. Interpreters can provide a real (**8**)	**CONNECT**
for people who speak different languages. They are (**9**)	**CERTAIN**
an important part of international (**10**)	**COMMUNICATE**

(1 mark per answer)

Write one word in each gap.

11 When does Stephen King's new book come .... ?
12 We didn't pay the bill, so they cut our phone ....
13 Could you ask Mr Jones to call me .... later today?
14 The woman on the phone started shouting at me, so I hung ....
15 I'd like to print this e-mail .... Is that possible?
16 I logged .... my favourite website and started reading the latest news.
17 You have to fill .... a form to enter the competition.
18 I finished reading the web page, logged .... and then went to watch TV.

(1 mark per answer)

Complete each second sentence using the word given, so that it has a similar meaning to the first sentence. Write between two and five words.

19 Katy sent me a text message. **received**
    I .... Katy.
20 It's not necessary to pay to use the office phone. **have**
    You .... pay to use the office phone.
21 Mike is able to read and write Japanese. **can**
    Mike .... Japanese.
22 It wasn't necessary for me to buy a stamp for my letter. **need**
    I .... to buy a stamp for my letter.
23 It's possible that the e-mail is from Alex. **might**
    The e-mail .... from Alex.

24 Jill described her holiday to me. **told**
Jill .... her holiday.

25 Companies shouldn't ring people at home to sell them things. **ought**
Companies .... ring people at home to sell them things.

26 I'm almost certain this phone is broken because I can't hear anything. **must**
This phone .... because I can't hear anything.

(2 marks per answer)

D Choose the correct answer.

27 I couldn't .... the programme so I turned the TV up.
A hear   C hearing
B heard   D to hear

28 My brother .... write when he was just three years old.
A can   C might
B could   D should

29 .... I use your computer to check my e-mail?
A Will   C May
B Ought   D Would

30 My teacher thinks I .... to pay more attention in class.
A might   C ought
B may   D would

31 All compositions .... be handed in to me by Friday at the latest.
A must   C have
B need   D ought

32 That .... be my mobile – mine is silver and that one is black.
A mustn't   C wouldn't
B shouldn't   D can't

33 I sent the letter yesterday, so it .... get there tomorrow.
A can   C should
B need   D ought

34 Did you .... to pay to send the package back?
A must   C ought
B should   D have

(1 mark per answer)

E Choose the correct answer.

35 Did you write to Irina .... her visit this summer?
A for   C on
B of   D about

36 You have to .... on the word 'Next' to see the next web page.
A press   C push
B click   D hit

37 I read about the accident .... the Internet.
A on   C to
B in   D at

38 Please don't .... me when I'm speaking.
A break   C pause
B prevent   D interrupt

39 When you have written your letter, save the .... in 'My Documents'.
A paper   C file
B notebook   D line

40 I finally managed to .... Simon to lend me his laptop.
A persuade   C say
B make   D allow

41 Even when he's very angry, my dad never .... or uses bad language.
A swears   C whispers
B tells   D broadcasts

42 I didn't read the message carefully. I just glanced .... it.
A with   C on
B to   D at

(1 mark per answer)

Total mark: ..../50

Progress Test 1

A Choose the correct answer.

1 When you get to your .... , you have to show your ticket to leave the station.
  A destination   B harbour   C souvenir   D passport

2 Brazil .... coffee all over the world.
  A invests   B demands   C exports   D affords

3 How do you .... 'csar'?
  A interrupt   B swear   C guess   D pronounce

4 Dogs make very .... pets. They'll always stay by your side.
  A mental   B private   C loyal   D digital

5 Let's go for a swim as soon as we .... the hotel!
  A arrive   B get   C reach   D meet

6 You have to .... or you won't understand the explanation.
  A concentrate   B contact   C consider   D involve

7 There's a train coming. Don't stand at the edge of the ....
  A property   B link   C platform   D resort

8 I .... a lot of money on my credit cards and I don't know if I can pay it back.
  A own   B obtain   C cost   D owe

(1 mark per answer)

B Write one word in each gap.

Lucky accidents

Sometimes, scientists know what they (**9**) .... looking for and they find it. At other times, things (**10**) .... discovered by accident. Two famous examples of this are gravity and penicillin.

Isaac Newton, (**11**) .... first used maths to describe gravity, was sitting (**12**) .... his garden when he saw (**13**) .... apple fall – some say it fell on his head! This made him think about why, and he realised he (**14**) .... explain it using maths.

Alexander Fleming discovered penicillin, (**15**) .... was the first antibiotic. It completely changed medicine. He was working (**16**) .... his laboratory when he saw that something (**17**) .... started growing on one of his experiments. He analysed it and realised that it (**18**) .... be very useful in fighting disease. Sometimes luck can be a big help!

(1 mark per answer)

C Complete each second sentence using the word given, so that it has a similar meaning to the first sentence. Write between two and five words.

19 My computer doesn't work, so I can't e-mail you. **wrong**
   There's .... my computer, so I can't e-mail you.

20 When we started our journey towards the mountains, the sun was shining. **off**
   When we .... towards the mountains, the sun was shining.

21 Did you mention the plans for this weekend to Matt? **talk**
Did you .... the plans for this weekend?

22 I think we should build a new theatre in town. **favour**
I'm .... building a new theatre in town.

23 You lost Jill's camera and I think you should say sorry. **apologise**
I think you should .... losing her camera.

24 Have you ever participated in a swimming race? **part**
Have you ever .... in a swimming race?

25 Remove any mistakes you make using a rubber. **rub**
If you make any mistakes, ... with a rubber.

26 Please play your electric guitar more quietly! **down**
Please .... your electric guitar!

27 How long has Alice been Tony's girlfriend? **out**
How long has Alice been .... Tony?

28 When was the last time you heard from Nigel? **contact**
When was the last time you were .... Nigel?

(2 marks per answer)

D Use the word given in capitals at the end of each line to form a word that fits
in the gap in the same line.

Top tips for writers

None of us find writing easy. When you can't see the person who you're talking
to, (**29**) .... is much more difficult. You have to be   COMMUNICATE
(**30**) .... to communicate your message clearly, but how   CARE
do you do that? The first thing you must think about is who you're writing to.
Then you can make a (**31**) .... about how formal it   DECIDE
should be. A letter to a friend is more like (**32**) ....   SPEAK
English, so your (**33**) .... should be in your writing, while a   PERSON
letter to a hotel manager is formal. You also need to think about what kind of
thing you're writing. The language in a story, for example, should be
(**34**) .... , but the language in a report or an article   EXPRESS
should be much more (**35**) .... When you're writing a   INFORM
formal essay giving your opinion, make sure the (**36**) ....   INTRODUCE
gives a general idea of the subject. Later, in the (**37**) .... ,   CONCLUDE
you should summarise your opinion. Each time you write, you have to make
(**38**) .... about what you're going to do. If you do that right,   CHOOSE
then there's nothing to stop you becoming a good writer!

(1 mark per answer)

91

E Write one word in each gap.

39 Why don't you borrow a pencil .... someone else?

40 I don't think I can cope .... studying and having a job at the same time.

41 I finally succeeded .... jumping over the box on my skateboard.

42 My uncle asked me to help him translate a menu .... English.

43 Ed glanced .... the message on his mobile phone and then carried on talking.

44 Did you know that our head teacher is married .... an actress? I had no idea.

45 This area is famous .... its cheese and its bread.

46 I don't know very much .... cooking, but I can make an omelette!

47 I've always been interested .... insects and spiders. I don't know why!

48 Jessie seemed to be getting a bit bored .... the game, so I suggested watching TV.

(1 mark per answer)

F Match to make sentences.

49 I think I'm going to take   .... A off, I held my dad's hand tightly.

50 As our plane took   .... B after my younger sister when she was small.

51 Mr and Mrs Davies have split .... C out where the concert is going to happen.

52 I hope we manage to find   .... D off the TV and find something else to do.

53 I often had to look   .... E up me and my brother because my parents worked.

54 You should turn   .... F up a musical instrument, maybe the violin.

55 I've fallen   .... G out with Kelly because she hurt my feelings.

56 My grandmother brought   .... H up after more than twenty years together.

(1 mark per answer)

G One word in each sentence is in the wrong form. Write the correct form.

57 It's true! Don't call me a lie.   ....

58 I need a new chair for my bedroom – this one is so comfort!   ....

59 After not speaking to her for a week, I finally forgive Gemma for not inviting me.   ....

60 It's important to get a good educate if you want a good job.   ....

61 The book is €10 and you have to pay €2 for deliver.   ....

62 Losing your keys while playing football was really care!   ....

63 I would love to be a music, but I don't play any instruments.   ....

64 Mum can speak four languages and she works as a translate.   ....

65 I spent my child on a farm, so I know a lot about animals.   ....

66 Do we have to memory all these words?   ....

(1 mark per answer)

H Complete using the words in the box.

> chance • common • foot • fun • heart • instance • purpose • schedule

67 Did you break the window on .... or was it an accident?
68 The weather was really bad, but our boat still left on ....
69 Our car broke down, so we had to go the rest of the way on ....
70 I loved the poem so much that I learnt it by ....
71 I knew I had a lot in .... with Yiota the first time I met her.
72 We use lasers in all kinds of things these days – DVD players, for ....
73 I sing for .... – I don't want to do it as a job.
74 I hadn't planned to meet Wendy in London. It happened completely by ....

(1 mark per answer)

I Write one word in each gap.

75 Why won't this dog just go .... and leave me alone?
76 When does the new *Movie Magazine* come .... ?
77 If you're not sure how to spell a word, look it .... in a dictionary.
78 I was trying to open the door when I pulled the handle .... Oops!
79 Could you please read .... what you've written so that everyone can hear?
80 I was looking for something when I came .... a very old picture of my dad.
81 What do you want to be when you grow .... ?
82 Did you really see an alien, or are you making it .... ?

(1 mark per answer)

J Choose the correct answer.

83 'What .... when you saw the man?' the police officer asked.
  A have you done   B were you doing   C are you doing   D do you do

84 Thomas Edison, ... was American, invented many things, including the light bulb.
  A which   B who   C that   D what

85 I hope we're staying .... a good hotel this time!
  A at   B to   C with   D on

86 I know London quite well because I .... there.
  A used live   B used to living   C was used to live   D used to live

87 My bike .... ! Call the police!
  A was being stolen   B has been stolen   C stole   D was stealing

88 I'm tired because I .... since eight this morning.
  A have been working   B work   C am working   D had worked

89 Do you think I could have .... water, please?
  A a few   B much   C few   D a little

90 Is that Paul? He must .... from Australia.
  A return   B had returned   C have returned   D returning

(1 mark per answer)

Total mark: ..../100

Unit 22 — Grammar

Modals 3: the modal perfect

Form

Modals + the perfect infinitive

modal + *have* + past participle

statement	negative	question
*You **should have told** me you were going shopping.*	*You **shouldn't (should not) have told** Liz what Bill said.*	***Should** I **have invited** Carol to the party?*

Watch out! Some verbs have irregular past participle forms. See page 182.

Ability

Use	Modal	Example
To say that someone had the opportunity or ability to do something, but didn't do it	*could*	*We **could have gone** to the party, but we decided not to in the end.*

Watch out! We use *this* for things that someone didn't actually do. For general ability in the past, we use *could* + bare infinitive (see Unit 19).
✓ *I **could play** the guitar when I was seven.* (= I knew how to play the guitar.)
✓ *I **could have played** the guitar.* (= I had the opportunity to play the guitar, but I didn't actually play it.)

Criticism

Use	Modal	Example
To say that someone's past behaviour was bad or wrong	*ought to / should*	*You **should have invited** Carol to your party.* (= You didn't invite Carol and that was wrong.)

Probability and possibility

Use	Modal	Example
Strong probability	*must / can't*	*They **must have had** a lovely holiday!* (= It's almost certain that they had a lovely holiday.) *They **can't have had** any sleep!* (= It's almost certain that they didn't have any sleep.)
Possibility	*could / may / might*	*Helen **might have found** a new house.* (= It's possible, but I'm not certain.)

Expectation

Use	Modal	Example
To show you expected the past to be different from what actually happened	*ought to / should*	*Jim **should have arrived** half an hour ago. I wonder where he is.*

A Complete using the correct form of the verbs in brackets.

1 We could .... (**take**) the bus, but in the end we decided to walk.
2 Although I could .... (**buy**) the DVD, I actually got the video.
3 Alan could .... (**go**) to the concert with Sindy, but he stayed at home instead.
4 They could .... (**catch**) an earlier plane, but they decided to get the later one.
5 Could you .... (**stay**) longer or did you have to leave then?

B Look at the pictures and complete the sentences. Use *should* or *shouldn't* and the correct form of the verbs in the box.

eat • get • kick • take • tidy • wear

1 Mr Appleby .... an umbrella with him.
2 Jenny .... her room.
3 Alex .... the ball so hard.
4 Tim .... a fancy-dress costume.
5 They .... there earlier.
6 They .... so much!

C Complete each second sentence using the word given, so that it has a similar meaning to the first sentence. Write between two and five words.

1 I expect Adrian did a lot of revision. **must**
   Adrian ....
   a lot of revision.

2 I don't believe that Jim stole the money. **can't**
   Jim .... the
   money.

3 It's possible that I have made a mistake.
   could
   I .... a mistake.

4 There's a chance that someone saw us. **may**
   Someone .... us.

5 It's possible that Tim hasn't arrived yet. **might**
   Tim .... yet.

6 I'm sure that Irene wasn't at the party because she was ill. **have**
   Irene .... at the
   party because she was ill.

D Complete each second sentence so that it has a similar meaning to the first sentence.

1 We were expecting Dave to call, but he hasn't.
Dal should have called ....

2 They said they were going to deliver the computer at lunchtime, but they didn't.
They should ....

3 I was expecting the film to come out at the cinema last week.
The film ought ....

4 The shop wasn't supposed to close so early.
The shop shouldn't ....

5 Was the programme supposed to start at eight o'clock?
Should .... ?

E Choose the correct answer.

1 Ronny .... have gone to Switzerland, but I'm not totally sure.
A must   C can't
B could   D should

2 You .... have lied to me! Why didn't you tell me the truth?
A mustn't   C shouldn't
B might not   D couldn't

3 Helen .... to have seen a doctor weeks ago. Why didn't she?
A ought   C must
B should   D can't

4 They .... have seen the play last night as they went to a football match instead.
A could   C might
B must   D can't

5 Carl .... have been here by now. Maybe he got stuck in traffic.
A might   C should
B must   D can't

6 You .... have been really excited when you heard you'd won the competition!
A must   C might
B should   D could

F Write one word in each gap.

My cousin Tina

My cousin Tina is a professional dancer. Her mum – my aunt – says that Tina (**1**) ....
dance really well even before she was able to walk!

When Tina was ten, she could (**2**) .... gone to a special school for dancers in New
York, but she decided not to because she didn't want to leave her friends. Even today, Tina's mum thinks
that Tina (**3**) .... have gone to the school. I'm sure it (**4**) ....
have been a very difficult decision for Tina to make, but she says that she doesn't regret not going. She
carried on dancing in her spare time, often getting up at five o'clock in the morning for a dance lesson
before school. That can't have (**5**) .... much fun!

Today, she's really successful. She's been in lots of shows and she's even appeared on TV a few times.
In fact, she (**6**) .... have got the main part in a new show in London. She's not sure
yet. They (**7**) .... to have contacted her yesterday about it, but they didn't. Hopefully
she'll hear in the next few days. Whether she gets the part or not, I'm really proud of my cousin!

Grammar

Questions, question tags, indirect questions

Questions

Form

Normal main verbs	Simple tenses	• **Do** you **feel** cold? • **Did** they **go** shopping?
	Continuous tenses	• **Am** I **annoying** you? • **Were** they **waiting** for you?
	Perfect tenses	• **Have** you **seen** this film? • **Had** it **started**?
Be as a main verb		• **Am** I late? • **Were** you all right? • **Have** you **been** ill?
Have as a main verb		• **Does** she **have** a bath every day? • **Did** they **have** lunch at one o'clock?
Modals		• **Should** I **call** the police? • **Could** you **call** me later?
Question words		• **Who** was in prison? • **What**'s your name? • **Where** do they live? • **Why** did you do that?

Watch out!
• To form questions in the passive, we put the auxiliary verb before the subject. If there is more than one auxiliary verb, only the first one goes before the subject.
  ✓ **Was** Mr Jenkins arrested yesterday?
  ✓ **Has** Mr Jenkins **been** arrested?

• With the question words *who* and *what*, we use *do* as an auxiliary verb if the question word refers to the **object** of the verb.
  ✓ Who **told** you? (= Someone told you. Who?)
  ✓ Who **did** you **tell**? (= You told someone. Who?)

Questions tags

Form

Use	Example
To ask someone to agree with us	It's confusing, **isn't it**?
To check whether something is true	You haven't been to prison, **have you**?

Normal main verbs	Simple tenses	• Phil **works** here, **doesn't** he? • They **didn't leave**, **did** they?
Continuous tenses		• You **are** coming, **aren't** you? • They **weren't looking**, **were** they?
	Perfect tenses	• They**'ve gone**, **haven't** they? • You **hadn't** seen it, **had** you?
Be as a main verb		• He**'s** new here, **isn't** he? • You **weren't** old enough, **were** you?
Have as a main verb		• They **have** a car, **haven't / don't** they? • You **didn't have** a shower every day, **did** you?
Modals		• Jan **should** be here by now, **shouldn't** she? • You **won't** make a mess, **will** you?

⊙Helpful hints

In sentences with *I am*, we use *aren't I?* In sentences with *I'm not*, we use *am I?*
✓ **I'm** right, **aren't I**?   ✓ **I'm not** stupid, **am I**?

Watch out!
With *Let's*, we use *shall* in the question tag.
  ✓ **Let's** do the washing-up later, **shall we**?

Indirect questions

Form

Phrase + clause with normal word order

Use	Example
To ask questions politely	**Can/Could you tell me** where the bank is?
	Can/Could you let me know what time the film starts?
	Do you know if Alison lives there?
	I wonder if you could tell me where the toilets are.
	I wonder if you know how much this costs.

Watch out! We don't use question word order in the second half of the sentence.

A The words and phrases in bold in each sentence are wrong. Write the correct word or phrase.

1 Does Debbie **likes** Greek food? ....

2 Did Anne and Carlo **went** to Spain last year? ....

3 **Was** Dawn and Jennifer with you? ....

4 **Has Claudia** a haircut every Thursday? ....

5 Have you **buy** the new *Arctic Monkeys'* CD yet? ....

6 **Does** Tim going to be in the school play? ....

7 **It would be** the best thing to do? ....

8 Were you **play** basketball when it started snowing? ....

B Write one word in each gap.

Rachel: Hi, Ben! (**1**) .... are you?

Ben: I'm fine. (**2**) .... you hear about Mr Watkins, the maths teacher?

Rachel: No. (**3**) .... happened to him?

Ben: He fell out of the window of his classroom!

Rachel: (**4**) .... pushed him?

Ben: No one!

Rachel: So how (**5**) .... it happen?

Ben: He was sitting on the windowsill and he just fell backwards!

Rachel: Oh dear! Poor Mr Watkins. (**6**) .... he hurt?

Ben: No. Luckily his classroom is on the ground floor.

Rachel: That's lucky! (**7**) .... you there at the time?

Ben: Yes! We were having a maths lesson.

Rachel: So (**8**) .... did you all do?

Ben: We ran outside to help him. We were all laughing, though!

Rachel: (**9**) .... he think it was funny, too?

Ben: Not at first, but he laughed about it afterwards.

C Match to make sentences.

1 You live in a village, ... A weren't they?

2 You're not fifteen years old, ... B have you?

3 Carol has a maths test tomorrow, ... C don't you?

4 They were having lunch at the time, ... D didn't they?

5 You've been to France, ... E are you?

6 I'm not the only one, ... F haven't you?

7 They all passed the test, ... G will she?

8 You haven't seen Linda anywhere, ... H doesn't she?

9 She won't tell anyone else, ... I isn't it?

10 This is the right DVD, ... J am I?

D Complete the question tags.

1 Mark doesn't eat meat, ... he?
2 We should phone Grandma, ... we?
3 I didn't get you into trouble, ... I?
4 You weren't waiting for me, ... you?
5 Jill has finished her homework, ... she?
6 You'll call me later, ... you?
7 Let's go out tonight, ... we?
8 I'm going to pass the exam, ... I?

E Choose the correct answer.

1 Excuse me. Could you tell me how much .... , please?
  A are these jeans   B these jeans are

2 Can you let me know what time .... ?
  A does the train arrive   B the train arrives

3 Do you know if .... at seven o'clock?
  A the show starts   B does the show start

4 I wonder if you could tell me what ....
  A is the difference   B the difference is

5 I wonder if you know who .... ask.
  A I should   B should I

F Complete each second sentence so that it has a similar meaning to the first sentence.

1 Where's the post office?
  I wonder if you could tell me ....

2 Why did you do that?
  Could you tell us .... ?

3 How much will the holiday cost?
  Can you let me know .... ?

4 Are there any cafés near here?
  Could you tell me if .... ?

5 Does Jim like jazz music?
  Do you know .... ?

99

Unit 24 — Vocabulary

People and daily life

Topic vocabulary

see page 192 for definitions

admit (v)	habit (n)	routine (n, adj)
arrest (v)	identity card (n phr)	schedule (n)
charity (n)	illegal (adj)	situation (n)
commit (v)	politics (n)	social (adj)
community (n)	population (n)	society (n)
court (n)	prison (n)	steal (v)
criminal (n, adj)	protest (v, n)	tradition (n)
culture (n)	resident (n)	typical (adj)
familiar (adj)	responsible (adj)	vote (v, n)
government (n)	rob (v)	youth club (n phr)

Phrasal verbs

break in(to)	enter illegally
catch up (with)	reach the same point/level as
get away with	escape punishment for
get up	leave your bed
move in	start living in a new house, etc
put away	return sth to where it belongs
wake up	stop being asleep
wash up	wash plates, cups, cutlery, etc

Prepositional phrases

against the law
at the age of
in public
in response to
in touch (with)
in your teens/twenties/etc

Word formation

agree	agreement, disagree	**life**	live, alive
belief	believe, (un)believable	**nation**	nationality, (inter)national
courage	courageous	**peace**	peaceful(ly)
elect	election	**prison**	prisoner
equal	equality, unequal	**shoot**	shot, shooting

Word patterns

adjectives	angry (with sb) about		forget about
	guilty of		forgive sb for
verbs	accuse sb of		invite sb to
	blame sb for		punish sb for
	blame sth on		share sth with
	criticise sb for		smile at

Topic vocabulary

A Circle the correct word.

1 Is it **illegal / familiar** to drive without wearing a seatbelt?
2 Rob is very **typical / responsible**. You can trust him completely.
3 The area where I live has a lot of **illegal / social** problems.
4 Her face looked **responsible / familiar** but I wasn't sure who she was.
5 It was just another **typical / social** day at the office.

B Complete the crossword.

Across

2 If you've broken the law, you're a .... (8)
7 A new .... is elected every four years. (10)
9 Are you a .... or are you just visiting? (8)
10 How much money do you give to .... ? (7)
12 I really feel part of the local .... (9)
14 The .... of our village is decreasing. Soon there will be no one living here at all. (10)
16 It's a .... in my family to go for a walk on New Year's Day. (9)

Down

1 Biting your fingernails is a horrible .... ! (5)
3 The police officer asked to see my .... card. (8)
4 I've had to change my .... now I start work earlier. (7)
5 She's got a very busy .... today. (8)
6 Let's go to the .... club after school! (5)
8 He was sent to .... for six years. (6)
10 The judge entered the .... and everyone stood up. (5)
11 I'm in a very difficult .... I should tell my parents that I lost the money, but I'm afraid they'll be angry! (9)
13 In a democratic .... , people have the right to vote. (7)
15 My brother is very interested in .... He'd like to be a member of parliament one day. (8)

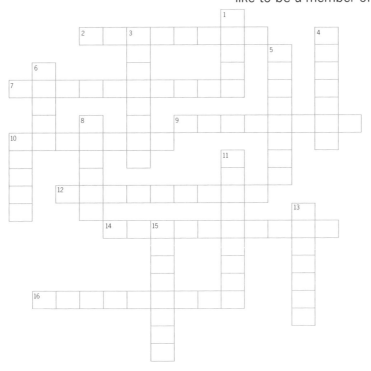

C Complete using the correct form of the verbs in the box.

admit • arrest • commit • protest • rob • steal • vote

1 You've never .... a crime, have you?
2 Most people who .... banks get caught eventually.
3 I think we should .... about the council's plans to close the playground.
4 John finally .... that he had broken the window after all.
5 If you didn't have enough money for food, would you .... from a supermarket?
6 A man has been .... in connection with the bank robbery last Tuesday.
7 Are you going to .... in the local elections next week?

Phrasal verbs

D Match to make sentences.

1 Someone has broken   ....   A up with the rest of the class quite quickly.
2 I missed a few lessons but I'm catching ....   B those plates up, aren't you?
3 You'll never get   ....   C up when the alarm clock rang this morning
4 I didn't want to get   ....   D up, I realised I was late for school.
5 Our new neighbours moved   ....   E into my car and stolen the CD player.
6 Do you want me to help you put ....   F all these clothes away?
7 When I woke   ....   G away with this!
8 You're going to wash   ....   H in next door today.

Prepositional phrases

E Write one word in each gap.

Dear Sir,

I am writing (**1**) .... response (**2**) .... the letter from Mrs A Taylor, which was published in the last issue of The Village Times.

Mrs Taylor spoke quite rudely about the young people who hang around in the park after school and at weekends. She seems to suggest that a group of teenagers meeting and having fun (**3**) .... public is (**4**) .... the law. Well, it isn't! She should try to remember what she was like (**5**) .... the age (**6**) .... fifteen. I know several people (**7**) .... their teens who like to spend time in the park. They are polite, honest and helpful, and I am proud to have them in the village. Perhaps I could put Mrs Taylor (**8**) .... touch (**9**) .... them. They might teach her not to be so rude and unpleasant in future.

Yours,

Wendy Partridge

Word formation

F Complete by changing the form of the word in capitals.

1 Running after that thief was very .... of you! **COURAGE**
2 You looked so .... when you fell asleep on the sofa. **PEACE**
3 All four of my grandparents are still .... **LIVE**
4 Did you vote in the last .... ? **ELECT**
5 It can be very difficult for .... when they leave prison and go back into the community. **PRISON**
6 At the end of the film, you hear a single .... and then Al Pacino falls to the ground. **SHOOT**
7 It's .... ! I've lost my glasses again! **BELIEVE**
8 I think we're all in .... that something must be done about the problem. **AGREE**
9 Should I write 'British' or 'English' as my .... ? **NATION**
10 We'll only have real .... when women earn as much money as men. **EQUAL**

Word patterns

G Circle the correct word.

1 Don't blame the theft **on / for** Tim. He didn't steal anything!
2 I'll share these sandwiches **to / with** you, if you like.
3 They accused Tonya **of / for** telling lies, but she was telling the truth.
4 Are you still angry **with / about** me?
5 I'd completely forgotten **for / about** the party. I'm not ready!
6 Trudy is such a lovely baby. She always smiles **at / to** you when you sing to her.

H Write one word in each gap.

1 You can't blame me .... the bad weather!
2 You shouldn't criticise people .... the way that they look.
3 I'm thinking of inviting Eliot .... the barbecue.
4 You're not angry .... what I said, are you?
5 The head teacher is going to punish us .... being late for class.
6 Ronald Jennings, you have been found guilty .... murder.
7 I'll never forgive you .... what you've done!

Review 8

A Choose the correct answer.

1 You should .... me you were going to be late!
  A tell   C to tell
  B have told   D to have told

2 The football match .... have finished by now. It started over four hours ago!
  A must   C can't
  B ought   D wouldn't

3 I wonder if you know where ....
  A is the post office?   C the post office is?
  B is the post office.   D the post office is.

4 You don't eat meat, ... you?
  A are   C have
  B eat   D do

5 Let's see what's on at the cinema, ... ?
  A do we   C shall we
  B shall us   D let us

6 She .... have bought the tickets today, but I can't be sure.
  A must   C can't
  B might   D shouldn't

7 Could you tell us ....
  A when you were born?   C when were you born?
  B when you were born.   D when were you born.

8 I'm sleeping in Jim's room tonight, ... I?
  A am not   C aren't
  B don't   D isn't

(1 mark per answer)

B Match to make sentences.

9 Someone broke .... A up at half past seven.
10 I'll just put .... B into our neighbour's house yesterday.
11 Mum always wakes me .... C in whenever you like.
12 If you wash these plates .... D up soon, you'll be late for school.
13 The flat is empty, so you can move .... E these things away and then I'll be ready.
14 If you don't get .... F up, I'll start cooking dinner.

(1 mark per answer)

C Complete each second sentence using the word given, so that it has a similar meaning to the first sentence. Write between two and five words.

15 I'm almost certain I didn't leave my wallet in the café. **can't**
   I .... my wallet in the café.

16 They'll find out that you've lied to them about your age. **away**
   You won't .... lying to them about your age.

17 Todd lost my favourite CD, but I've forgiven him. **for**
   I've forgiven .... my favourite CD.

18 The woman said that my uncle was a thief! **accused**
   The woman .... a thief!

19 Why didn't you check the time of the film? **should**
You .... the time of the film!

20 It'll be difficult to reach the others as they're a long way ahead. **up**
It'll be difficult to .... the others as they're a long way ahead.

21 Everyone said that I'd stolen the money! **blamed**
Everyone .... stealing the money.

22 It's possible that Jean saw Don in the town centre. **may**
Jean .... Don in the town centre.

23 Our teacher thought that Trudy was responsible for the damage, but she wasn't. **blamed**
Our teacher .... Trudy, but she didn't do it.

24 It was wrong of you to take that money. **have**
You .... that money.

(2 marks per answer)

D Complete using the words in the box.

age • card • club • law • public • response • teens • touch

25 I've got a passport, but I haven't got an identity ....
26 That kind of behaviour is okay in private, but not in .... !
27 I learnt to ride a bike at the .... of three.
28 It's against the .... to drive a car without a driving licence.
29 Could you put me in .... with someone who knows about starting a website?
30 Shall we go to the youth .... tonight?
31 When I was in my .... , I wanted to break all the rules!
32 I am writing in .... to your letter of 15th November.

(1 mark per answer)

E Use the word given in capitals at the end of each line to form a word that fits in the gap in the same line.

A politician speaks …

It's my (**33**) .... that we all have some very important questions | **BELIEVE**
to ask in this (**34**) .... What kind of a country do we want to | **ELECT**
live in? How can we achieve (**35**) .... for everyone? How can | **EQUAL**
we all live (**36**) .... with each other? I think that everyone here | **PEACE**
who was (**37**) .... 20 or 30 years ago will be in complete | **LIVE**
(**38**) .... that life is better now than it was then. But there are | **AGREE**
still many local and (**39**) .... problems to solve. Who's going | **NATION**
to solve them? My political party, or the other parties? I want you, the voter, to be
(**40**) .... and vote for the only person who can really make a | **COURAGE**
difference. Me!

(1 mark per answer)

Total mark: ..../50

105

Grammar

So and *such*, *too* and *enough*

so and such

Use

Both *so … that* and *such … that* are used to show the results of a situation or action. They take the following structures:

Form	Example
with an adjective: *so* + adjective + *that*	Al is **so good that** he was made manager.
with a noun: *so* + *many/much* + noun + *that* *such* + *a/an* + adjective + noun + *that* *such* + adjective + plural noun + *that* *such* + *a lot of* + noun + *that*	Al sells **so many cars that** he was made manager. Al is **such a good worker that** he was made manager. Al gets **such good results that** he was made manager. Al makes **such a lot of money for the company that** he was made manager.
with an adverb: *so* + adverb + *that*	Al **works so well that** he was made manager.

too and enough

Use

Both *too* and *enough* are used to talk about how much or how little of something there is. We use *too* to describe the negative effect of having more than necessary. We use *enough* to describe the effects of having/not having the right amount of something.

Form	Example
with an adjective: *too* + adjective (+ full infinitive) adjective + *enough* (+ full infinitive)	It's **too cold** to work in the garden. Carol isn't **patient enough** to work as a teacher.
with a noun: *too* + *many/much* + noun (+ full infinitive) *enough* + noun (+ full infinitive)	Jonty works **too many hours** to have any hobbies. We don't have **enough money** to pay our bills.
with an adverb: *too* + adverb (+ full infinitive) adverb + *enough* (+ full infinitive)	I got there **too late** to see the manager. Jack did the work **quickly enough** to finish half an hour early.

Watch out!

- *Too* does not mean the same as *very*. We only use *too* when we are describing something negative.
  ✓ I've got **too** much work. I can't come out tonight.
  ✗ ~~This job is great because you get paid **too** much money.~~

- *Enough* always comes after the adjective.
  ✓ You're not old **enough** to work here.
  ✗ ~~You're not **enough** old to work here.~~

- Both *too* and *enough* can be followed by *for*.
  ✓ It's too hot **for** me in this office.
  ✓ You're not old enough **for** the army.

A Complete using *so* or *such*.

1 The pan was .... hot that I nearly dropped it!
2 Mr Jones was .... a kind man that I was sad when he moved to another town.
3 We have .... many pets that sometimes it's really noisy!
4 Alicia is .... good at basketball that I think she could be a professional.
5 There was .... a lot of smoke that I couldn't see.
6 Tyrone ran .... fast that no one had a chance in the race.
7 Cherie is .... popular that everyone wants to be friends with her.
8 Would you like to have .... long hair that you can sit on it?

B If the phrase in bold is correct, put a tick (✓). If it is wrong, write the correct phrase.

1 Paris Hilton is **such famous that** she gets recognised wherever she goes.
   ....

2 There were **so many customers in the shop that** I couldn't move!
   ....

3 The man spoke **such quickly that** I couldn't understand a word he said.
   ....

4 I had **so good marks that** my dad bought me a new computer!
   ....

5 Victoria is **so old that** she can remember seeing a car for the first time.
   ....

6 There was **so a long queue that** we decided to go home.
   ....

7 I've got **so a lot of friends that** I don't have time to see them all.
   ....

8 Big Brother was **such successful that** they're making another series.
   ....

C Complete each second sentence using the word given, so that it has a similar meaning to the first sentence. Write between two and five words.

1 I have a lot of money and I don't know what to do with it. **such**
   I have .... that I don't know what to do with it.
2 Adrian fell asleep during the film because he was very tired. **so**
   Adrian .... he fell asleep during the film.
3 Today was so hot that I didn't want to do anything. **such**
   Today was .... that I didn't want to do anything.
4 I didn't have time to open all my Christmas presents because I got so many! **such**
   I got .... Christmas presents that I didn't have time to open them all!
5 They closed the funfair because it was very dangerous. **that**
   The funfair .... they closed it.
6 The food was so spicy that I couldn't eat it. **such**
   We had .... that I couldn't eat it.

107

D Circle the correct word or phrase.

1 This soup is **very salty / too salty** to eat.
2 If you run **too fast / fast enough**, you might win the race.
3 Don't drive **too fast / fast enough** or you might have an accident.
4 Have we got **too much / enough** time or do we need more?
5 Do you think you're **too strong / strong enough** to lift this heavy chair?
6 There are **too many / enough** questions here! I can't do all of them in five minutes!
7 Are you **enough warm / warm enough**? Shall I put the heating on?
8 This tea is **too / enough** hot to drink. I'll wait for it to cool down.

E Complete using a word from box A and a word or phrase from box B. You have to use the words in box A more than once.

A   enough • so • such • too

B   a long time • a lot of fun • beautiful • early • hard • hot • many things • sweets

1 We were having .... at the party that I didn't want to come home.
2 I put .... in the plastic bag and it broke.
3 We didn't have .... for everyone to have one.
4 Nancy is .... that I think I'm falling in love with her.
5 It's raining .... to go out. Let's stay in and watch TV.
6 When the milk is .... , pour it into the cup and stir with a spoon.
7 We waited for .... that I thought the bus was never going to come!
8 Stacy got to the theatre .... that there was no one there.

F Write *so, such, too* or *enough* in each gap.

My first – and last! – day at work

I'll never forget my first day at work. It was (**1**) .... a disaster that I lost my job! The boss explained what I had to do, but she did it (**2**) .... quickly that I didn't understand. I wasn't brave (**3**) .... to ask her to repeat it, so I pretended I knew what to do. It wasn't difficult at first – just putting numbers into a computer. Soon, though, I was (**4**) .... busy that I started making more and more mistakes. I made (**5**) .... a lot of mistakes that the other workers noticed. They tried to help me, but it was (**6**) .... late. In the end, I just had (**7**) .... much to do that I gave up. I sat there and stared at my computer for two hours! The boss came back and she was (**8**) .... shocked that she fired me immediately! My first day was also my last!

Grammar
Comparatives and superlatives

Comparatives

Use	Example		
To compare things/people/actions that are different	My new job is **more enjoyable** than my old one. I'd like you to get to the office **earlier** tomorrow.		
	adjective	⟹	comparative
one syllable	hard	+ -er	harder
one syllable ending in -e	late	+ -r	later
one syllable ending in vowel + consonant	big	double last letter + -er	bigger
two syllables ending in -y	pretty	-y ➡ -ier	prettier
two or more syllables	interesting	more/less + adjective	more/less interesting
irregular adjectives / quantifiers	good ➡ better / bad ➡ worse	little ➡ less / far ➡ farther/further	many ➡ more / much ➡ more
	adverb	⟹	comparative
regular adverbs	carefully	more/less + adverb	more/less carefully
irregular adverbs	well ➡ better / badly ➡ worse / early ➡ earlier	near ➡ nearer / late ➡ later	fast ➡ faster / far ➡ farther/further

⊙ Helpful hints

The comparative form is often followed by *than*. ✓ My working day is **longer than** it used to be.

Superlatives

Use	Example		
To compare one member of a group of things/people/actions with the whole group	Out of all the jobs in the company, John's is the **hardest**. The person who does **best** will get a pay rise.		
	adjective	⟹	superlative
one syllable	hard	+ -est	hardest
one syllable ending in -e	late	+ -st	latest
one syllable ending in vowel + consonant	big	double last letter + -est	biggest
two syllables ending in -y	pretty	-y ➡ -iest	prettiest
two or more syllables	interesting	most/least + adjective	most/least interesting
irregular adjectives / quantifiers	good ➡ best / bad ➡ worst	little ➡ least / far ➡ farthest/furthest	many ➡ most / much ➡ most
	adverb	⟹	superlative
regular adverbs	carefully	most/least + adverb	most/least carefully
irregular adverbs	well ➡ best / badly ➡ worst / early ➡ earliest	near ➡ nearest / late ➡ latest	fast ➡ fastest / far ➡ farthest/furthest

⊙ Helpful hints

We usually use *the* before the superlative form. ✓ Today was **the worst** day since I started working there.

A Complete using the comparative form of the words in brackets.

1 Wait! Your bicycle is .... (**fast**) than mine!
2 Phew! It's much .... (**hot**) than it was yesterday, isn't it?
3 I think you look .... (**pretty**) when you wear your hair up.
4 The price of batteries has gone up. They're a lot .... (**expensive**) than last time.
5 Angus hasn't been practising the piano and he's got a lot .... (**bad**).
6 His new film is much .... (**entertaining**) than his last one. I loved that one!
7 Tell us another joke – but a .... (**short**) one this time! That one took forever!
8 I didn't win the lottery. Maybe I'll be .... (**lucky**) next time.
9 The Russian athlete threw the discus .... (**far**) than all the others and won gold.
10 I think these biscuits are even .... (**nice**) than the last ones you made!

B The words in bold in each sentence are wrong. Write the correct word.

1 We lost the match because we played **badly** than the other team did. ....
2 It rains a lot in England, so the countryside is a lot **green** than in Greece. ....
3 You gave Sarah a really small piece of cake – and you've given me even **little**! ....
4 I must have lost weight. These jeans seem **large** than they were before. ....
5 I got to the party **early** than everyone else, so I had to wait. ....
6 I hear her new CD is **good** than her last one. What do you think? ....
7 Our cat seems to be getting **fat** every day – maybe she should go on a diet! ....
8 I'm disappointed. I think you could have done a lot **well** on this test. ....

C Rewrite the sentences using the correct comparative form of the words in the box.

bad • beautiful • confident • fat • happy • near (to) • short • young

1 Joshua is much taller than Alex.
   Alex is ....
2 Theresa is more confident than Amy.
   Amy is a lot ....
3 Your house is further from the school than mine.
   My house is ....
4 Jude is less happy than Andy about the decision.
   Andy is ....
5 Bill is thinner than Simon.
   Simon is ....
6 Terry is older than Sarah-Jane.
   Sarah-Jane is ....
7 Patricia is better than her sister on the clarinet.
   Patricia's sister is ....
   ....
8 The houses here are uglier than in my grandparents' village.
   The houses in my grandparents' village
   ....

D Complete using the correct form of the words in the box.

> bad • big • far • funny • hard • kind • scary • tasty

1 This really is the .... song I've ever heard! It's terrible!
2 Ivy is the .... woman I know. She'll do anything for anybody.
3 Listen! I promise you, this is the .... joke ever! Well, a man goes into a shop …
4 Mmm! This is the .... soup you've made so far.
5 What's the .... thing about English grammar for you?
6 Ben appeared and he was carrying the .... present I'd ever seen. It was huge!
7 We had a competition to see who could swim the ....
8 Sandra told us the .... ghost story she could, and it was really frightening!

E Complete using the correct form of the words in brackets.

> I think this is the (**1**) .... (**bad**) job I've ever had. My last job was much
> (**2**) .... (**good**) than this one. I had a lot (**3**) .... (**little**) work
> there and my boss was really nice. My boss here is the (**4**) .... (**strict**) in the whole
> firm, and the working day is (**5**) .... (**long**) than in my last job, too. The
> (**6**) .... (**good**) thing about it is that the office is (**7**) ....
> (**close**) to my house than the old one. At least now I get home (**8**) .... (**early**) than
> I used to.

F Complete using the correct form of the words in the box.

> clean • dirty • fast • old • slowly • young

'I walk (**1**) ....
than him.'
'I walk the (**2**) ....
.... of all.'

'I ran (**6**) ....
of all.'
'I ran (**7**) ....
than everyone except him.'
'They both ran (**8**) ....
than me.'

'I'm the (**3**) ....
pigeon.'
'I'm (**4**) ....
than they are.'
'I'm the (**5**) ....
pigeon.'

'I'm the (**9**) ....
in the family.'
'And I'm the (**10**) ....'

Vocabulary
Working and earning

Topic vocabulary

see page 194 for definitions

ambition (n)	earn (v)	poverty (n)
application (n)	fame (n)	pressure (n)
bank account (n phr)	goal (n)	previous (adj)
boss (n)	impress (v)	profession (n)
career (n)	income (n)	retire (v)
colleague (n)	industry (n)	salary (n)
company (n)	interview (v, n)	staff (n)
contract (n)	leader (n)	strike (n)
department (n)	manager (n)	tax (v, n)
deserve (v)	pension (n)	wealthy (adj)

Phrasal verbs

call off	cancel
give back	return sth you have taken/borrowed
go on	happen
put off	delay to a later time
set up	start (a business, organisation, etc)
stay up	go to bed late
take away	remove
take over	take control of (a business, etc)

Prepositional phrases

at the moment
in charge (of)
on business
on strike
on time
on/off duty

Word formation

assist	assistant, assistance		**occupy**	occupation
beg	beggar		**office**	officer, (un)official
boss	bossy		**retire**	retired, retirement
employ	(un)employment, employer, employee, unemployed		**safe**	save, unsafe, safety
fame	famous		**succeed**	success, (un)successful

Word patterns

adjectives	careful with			depend on
	difficult for			inform sb about
	fed up with			refer to
	ready for			work as
	responsible for			work for
verbs	apply for		*nouns*	a kind of

Topic vocabulary

A Choose the correct answer.

1 Bob joined the .... about six years ago.
   A ambition   B fame   C pension   D company

2 We lost £10 million last year because of the workers' .... over money.
   A strike   B department   C colleague   D tax

3 I'm sure it's good to be well known, but .... isn't everything.
   A boss   B interview   C fame   D poverty

4 Don't sign the .... until you've read every word of it!
   A industry   B contract   C staff   D profession

5 My grandfather stopped working two years ago and now he gets a ....
   A pressure   B leader   C pension   D department

6 Charles worked in the same job for almost the whole of his ....
   A colleague   B manager   C industry   D career

7 You should be able to save a little money with a/an .... of €30,000 per year.
   A application   B income   C leader   D goal

8 Can I introduce you to Isaac, a .... of mine from work?
   A profession   B department   C colleague   D salary

B Complete using a word formed from the letters given.

1 I had a lot more responsibility in my .... job. **I O R V U E P S**
2 Why not open one of our new Supersaver bank .... ? **C S N O A U C T**
3 It's always been my .... to work in advertising. **B T M O I I A N**
4 Frank left university and got a job in the computer .... **D Y T U R S I N**
5 The family lived in .... after Mr Bucket lost his job. **T O Y V E P R**
6 His parents left him a lot of money and now Neil is extremely .... **A E H Y L T W**
7 You usually need a degree and some training to join the teaching ....
   O R I O F S P N S E
8 All members of .... here get three weeks holiday a year. **A T F S F**

C Complete using the correct form of the verbs in the box.

deserve • earn • impress • interview • retire • tax

1 Isabelle really .... her manager and soon she was given a better job.
2 My dad said that he wants to .... when he's sixty.
3 We .... everyone who applies for a job before making our decision.
4 The government .... everyone who works and then spends the money on roads, hospitals and things like that.
5 Wendy works hard for the company and I think she .... a more challenging job.
6 I read recently that women still .... less than men for the same job and I don't think it's fair.

113

Phrasal verbs

D Write one word in each gap.

1 A Japanese company has .... over the place where I work and I might lose my job.
2 The boss came into the office when we were laughing and wanted to know what was .... on.
3 Do you think we could .... the meeting off until next Thursday?
4 The computer in my office broke down so they .... it away to fix it.
5 Many of the staff were ill with flu that week, so the director decided to .... off the meeting.
6 I'm tired because I had to .... up last night to finish some work.
7 My car belonged to the company, so when I lost my job I had to .... it back.
8 Janice is thinking of .... up her own restaurant.

Prepositional phrases

E Match to make sentences.

1 I'm afraid we're not looking for new workers at ....
2 They said on the news that bus drivers are on ....
3 In his new job, Paul is away travelling on ....
4 I was quite nervous the first time I was in ....
5 Anne works as a security guard and she's on ....
6 My boss said that if I wasn't on ....

A business a lot of the time so he's never at home for long.
B strike, so you might need to take a taxi to work.
C duty for about eight hours every night.
D charge of the whole department.
E the moment, but you could try again next month.
F time for work more often I would lose my

Word formation

F Complete by changing the form of the word in capitals.

He's a ....
BEG

He's an ....
. ASSIST

It's ....
SAFE

They're ....   He's ....   She's a police ....

EMPLOY   **RETIRE**   **OFFICE**

G | Each of the words in bold is wrong. Write the correct word.

1 The manager told me I was too **boss** and that I should discuss things with   ....
   my colleagues rather than telling them what to do all the time.

2 Being a firefighter is a very stressful **occupy**.   ....

3 It takes a lot of hard work to be **succeed** in this business.   ....

4 I wouldn't like to become so **fame** that I couldn't go out in public!   ....

5 Kate is 60 next week and she's leaving, so remember to wish her   ....
   'Happy **Retire**'.

6 It took Ralph a long time to find a new job – he was **employ** for nearly   ....
   two years.

Word patterns

H | Circle the correct word.

1 I don't know why but I've always wanted to work **as / of** a farmer.

2 They want a computer programmer at the office down the road and Fiona has applied
   about / for the job.

3 I'll look after the office while you're away – you can depend **on / with** me.

4 My mum is a neurologist, which is a kind **from / of** doctor.

5 I think it's time for a change. I'm fed up **on / with** working here.

6 Tessa is responsible **for / with** answering the phone and taking messages.

I | Write one word in each gap.

1 I wanted to become a vet, but the course was too difficult .... me.

2 Roberto got up late and only had ten minutes to get ready .... work.

3 When they informed me .... the hours I had to work, I couldn't believe it.

4 Please be careful .... my laptop. I need it for work.

5 Is it a good idea in the interview to refer .... your previous job?

6 I like working .... a large company because there are lots of opportunities.

Review 9

A Use the word given in capitals at the end of each line to form a word that fits in the gap in the same line.

My grandfather's career

My grandad had a long career. He started work as an (**1**) .... **ASSIST**
and worked his way to the top. He was very (**2**) .... and he **SUCCESS**
(**3**) .... the company from disaster many times. When he was **SAFE**
in charge he was never (**4**) .... He understood people and all **BOSS**
the (**5**) .... admired him. He was an engineer, which is quite **EMPLOY**
a difficult (**6**) .... , and for 40 years he worked on many **OCCUPY**
projects. Finally, he reached 65, which was the (**7**) .... **OFFICE**
age of (**8**) .... in his company. He was very well known to **RETIRE**
other engineers – you might even say he was (**9**) .... ! He was **FAME**
always very busy when he was working, but now he's (**10**) .... , **RETIRE**
he's got a lot more time to spend with his grandchildren!

(1 mark per answer)

B Match to make sentences.

11 Mr Robinson is responsible .... A on how long you've been working here.
12 We need to inform everyone .... B about the new time of the meeting.
13 Trisha seems to be fed up .... C to last year as 'a disaster'.
14 Your salary depends .... D of teacher, I suppose.
15 I would love to work .... E for a job to make a good impression.
16 During the meeting, the manager referred .... F for interviewing people applying for jobs.
17 I'm a swimming instructor, which is a kind .... G as a racing driver, or maybe a car mechanic.
18 It's important when you apply .... H with her job and is thinking of finding a new one.

(1 mark per answer)

C Complete each second sentence using the word given, so that it has a similar meaning to the first sentence. Write between two and five words.

19 It's so hot today that I can't work! **too**
It's .... me to work today!

20 I can't go to bed late because I've got to work in the morning. **up**
I can't .... late because I've got to work in the morning.

21 You're too young to join the army. **old**
You're .... to join the army.

22 Why did the boss cancel the meeting? **off**
Why did the boss .... the meeting?

23 Let's start our own business! **set**
    Let's .... our own business!

24 I have so much work at the moment that I have to work on Sundays. **such**
    I have .... work at the moment that I have to work on Sundays.

25 The manager wanted to know what was happening in the other office. **on**
    The manager wanted to know what was .... in the other office.

26 I didn't call early enough to speak to the manager. **too**
    I .... to speak to the manager.

(2 marks per answer)

D Choose the correct answer.

27 This job is much .... than the last one!
    A hard   C harder
    B hardest   D more hard

28 Charlotte earns .... much money that she can't spend it all!
    A such   C too
    B enough   D so

29 We have to work much longer each day .... in my old job.
    A from   C with
    B that   D than

30 I called as soon as I saw the job advert, but it was .... late.
    A enough   C too
    B such   D so

31 What's the .... job you've ever had?
    A most good   C better
    B best   D good

32 The office is .... a long way that I have to catch two buses.
    A too   C enough
    B such   D so

33 Ray works as an artist and doesn't earn .... to pay his bills each month.
    A too   C so
    B enough   D such

34 Our company is moving into a .... building next week.
    A larger   C more large
    B largest   D most large

(1 mark per answer)

E Choose the correct answer.

35 Anita works really hard and .... to be paid more.
    A worth   C deserves
    B values   D requires

36 It takes me about half an hour to get ready .... work each morning.
    A for   C about
    B on   D with

37 I'm going to stay at university and try to .... off getting a job for a few years!
    A stay   C move
    B put   D set

38 May I introduce you to my .... ?
    A worker   C relation
    B staff   D colleague

39 My main .... is to become a lawyer.
    A purpose   C ambition
    B emotion   D want

40 During the job .... they asked me lots of really difficult questions.
    A chat   C conversation
    B talk   D interview

41 *World Industries* is planning to .... over our business.
    A get   C move
    B take   D set

42 Our teachers are .... strike, so we don't have to go to school today!
    A for   C out
    B in   D on

(1 mark per answer)

Total mark: ..../50

117

Grammar

Conditionals 1: (zero, first, second)

Introduction to conditional

Some sentences with the word *if* are called conditional sentences.
With every conditional sentence, there are two parts: a situation and the result of that situation. It is the situation that starts with *if*.
There are different types of conditional sentence, depending on what the situation is.

Helpful hints

- When we start the sentence with *if*, we separate the situation and the result with a comma.
  ✓ *If you join a gym, I'll join too.*
- When we start the sentence with the result, we don't use a comma.
  ✓ *I'll join too if you join a gym.*

Zero conditional

Form

if + present simple, present simple

Use	Example
General or scientific facts	*If people **eat** too much, they often **get** fat.*

First conditional

Form

if + present simple, *will* + bare infinitive

Use	Example
Real or likely situations in the present or future and their results	*If you **take** these pills, you'**ll start** to feel better very soon.*

Helpful hints

- We can also use other modals instead of *will*, depending on the meaning.
  ✓ *If you get some rest, you **might** feel better tomorrow.*
- We can also use an imperative instead of *will* to give instructions.
  ✓ *If you don't feel well, **go** home!*

Second conditional

Form

if + past simple, *would* + bare infinitive

Use	Example
Impossible or unlikely situations in the present or future and their results	*If my legs **were** longer, I **would be** a much faster runner!*

Helpful hints

We can also use the second conditional to give advice. We use the phrases *If I were you …* or *If I was you …* for this. *If I were you …* is more formal than *If I was you …*
✓ *If I **were** you, I would eat less chocolate.* (more formal)
✓ *If I **was** you, I'd eat less chocolate!* (more informal)

A Look at the pictures and complete the sentences. Use the zero conditional.

1 If you heat water, it boils _____ .
   heat / water / it / boil

2 If you _____ .
   send / an e-mail / it / be / free

3 It _____ .
   be / dangerous / you / not / wear / a
   seatbelt

4 If you _____ .
   have / an injection / it / not / usually
   hurt

5 If you _____ .
   not / water / plants and flowers / they
   die

6 If the sea _____ .
   not / be / calm / not / be / safe / to swim

B The words and phrases in bold in each sentence are wrong. Write the correct
word or phrase.

1 If we **will go** shopping tomorrow, I'll probably buy a new top.   _____
2 If Mum is tired tonight, **I cook** dinner.   _____
3 John will tell us if there **will be** any news.   _____
4 If I **won't** get a good mark in the geography test, I'll be very annoyed!   _____
5 You **are** tired in the morning if you don't go to bed soon.   _____
6 If you see Karen, **do** you ask her to call me?   _____
7 **Does** Frank come with us if we go to the beach at the weekend?   _____
8 If you need help, **will tell** me!   _____

C Complete using the correct form of the verbs in brackets.

1 If I _____ (**do**) well in the exam, my parents will buy me an MP3 player.
2 If my sister borrows my clothes again, I _____ (**scream**)!
3 We'll leave at six o'clock if the weather _____ (**be**) bad.
4 They _____ (**not / mind**) if we're a bit late this afternoon.
5 Sarah will be very annoyed if Dave _____ (**not / call**) her this evening.
6 Will you still go to the concert if the tickets _____ (**cost**) 60 euros?
7 If Rania doesn't come to the party, _____ (**Greg / be**) upset?
8 I'll be surprised if Doug and Dana _____ (**not / get**) a new car soon.

D Circle the correct word or phrase.

1 If I **win / won** a million euros, I'd buy my mum and dad a new house.
2 If Steve paid more attention in class, he **will / would** learn more.
3 **They'll / They'd** go on a cruise if they had enough money.
4 You'd feel a lot healthier if you **don't / didn't** eat so much fast food.
5 If I **have / had** a bike, it wouldn't take me so long to get to school.
6 If you met Tom Hanks, what **will / would** you ask him?
7 **Will / Would** Bobby be upset if I didn't invite him?
8 If I **am / were** you, I'd get a haircut!

E Complete each second sentence so that it has a similar meaning to the first sentence. Write no more than three words.

1 Sylvia doesn't have enough money, so she can't buy a new computer.
   If Sylvia .... enough money, she'd buy a new computer.

2 The twins don't see their friends often because they're very busy.
   If the twins weren't so busy, they .... their friends more often.

3 I don't live in a city, so there's not much to do in the evening.
   If I .... in a city, there would be lots to do in the evening.

4 Grandma won't get a dog because she lives in a small flat.
   If Grandma .... in a small flat, she'd get a dog.

5 You use your mobile a lot, so you have large phone bills.
   If you didn't use your mobile so much, you .... large phone bills.

6 I think you should tell your parents the truth.
   If I .... you, I'd tell your parents the truth.

F Choose the correct answer.

Dear Marsha,
I'm not sure what to do. I'm thinking of becoming a vegetarian, but some of my friends say it's a bad idea. They say that if I (1) .... eating meat, my body won't get all the things it needs to stay healthy. Are my friends right?
Thanks,
Yuri, age 14

Dear Yuri,
Millions of people are vegetarians and they're perfectly healthy. You have to be careful, though. If you (2) .... up eating meat completely, and only (3) .... chocolate and crisps, that would obviously be very bad for you! If people don't eat properly, they (4) .... ill. It's that simple. If you eat lots of fruit and salad and beans, you (5) .... get all the things you need to stay healthy. But — you're only 14 years old. If you (6) .... at home with your parents — and you probably do — you'll have to ask them what they think too. If your mum cooks for you, (7) it .... be difficult for her to make you special meals. If I were you, I (8) .... think about this carefully and maybe wait until you're a bit older before making such a big decision.
Marsha

1	A stop	B stopped	5	A will	B would
2	A give	B gave	6	A live	B will live
3	A will eat	B ate	7	A will	B would
4	A get	B would get	8	A will	B would

Grammar

Conditionals 2: (third)

Third conditional

if + past perfect simple, *would* + *have* + past participle

Use	Example
Unreal situations in the past and their unreal past results	*If the chemist **had been** open, I **would have bought** some aspirin.* (= The chemist wasn't open, so I didn't buy any aspirin.)
	*If I **hadn't listened** to you, I **would have cooked** the chicken for too long.* (= I listened to you, so I didn't cook the chicken for too long.)
	*If he **had seen** the doctor, he **wouldn't have been** ill for such a long time.* (= He didn't see the doctor, so he was ill for a long time.)
	*If you **hadn't eaten** a giant pizza, you **wouldn't have been sick**!* (= You ate a giant pizza, so you were sick.)

Helpful hints

We can also use *could* and *might* instead of *would*, depending on the meaning.

✓ *If you had eaten a giant pizza, you **might** have been sick!*
(= It's possible, but not certain, that you would have been sick.)

✓ *If Mary had told me she was coming, I **could** have cooked a nice meal.*
(= I would have been able to cook a nice meal.)

- The third conditional is the only conditional that refers to the past.
  ✓ *If I **had had** a headache, I would have taken an aspirin.* (= in the past)

- We use past simple in the second conditional, but that does **not** refer to the past.
  ✓ *If I **had** a headache, I would take an aspirin.* (= now or generally)

- For more information on the second conditional, see Unit 28.

A Circle the correct answer.

> If Charles had had enough money, he'd have bought the CD.

1 Did Charles have enough money? **Yes / No**
2 Did he buy the CD? **Yes / No**

> Paul wouldn't have made a mistake if he'd listened to Lee.

7 Did Paul make a mistake? **Yes / No**
8 Did Paul listen to Lee? **Yes / No**

> Cilla would have called Andrea if she'd taken her mobile with her.

3 Did Cilla call Andrea? **Yes / No**
4 Did she take her mobile with her? **Yes / No**

> Jo wouldn't have gone to the party if she hadn't been invited.

9 Did Jo go to the party? **Yes / No**
10 Was Jo invited to the party? **Yes / No**

> If we hadn't been late, we'd have seen the start of the film.

5 Were they late? **Yes / No**
6 Did they see the start of the film? **Yes / No**

> Tom would have forgotten his keys if Lisa hadn't reminded him.

11 Did Tom forget his keys? **Yes / No**
12 Did Lisa remind him about his keys? **Yes / No**

B Complete using the correct form of the words in brackets.

1 If you .... (**tell**) me you were going to the beach, I'd have come with you.
2 If Dan had missed the plane, he .... (**be**) very annoyed.
3 I'd have got you a present if I .... (**know**) it was your birthday.
4 We .... (**not / get**) lost if we'd taken a map with us.
5 If the car .... (**not / break down**), I wouldn't have been late.
6 If you .... (**not / help**) me, I wouldn't have finished in time.
7 If Baz .... (**not / show**) you what to do, what .... (**you / do**)?

C Complete each second sentence so that it has a similar meaning to the first sentence. Write between two and five words.

1 It wasn't cold, so we didn't light a fire.
   If it .... cold, we'd have lit a fire.

2 John didn't come, so we didn't do any painting.
   If John .... , we'd have done some painting.

3 Claire didn't buy any clothes because she didn't see anything she liked.
   Claire .... some clothes if she'd seen something she liked.

4 The audience laughed because the joke was very funny.
   If the joke .... very funny, the audience wouldn't have laughed.

5 We decided to leave because it was really noisy.
   We .... to leave if it hadn't been really noisy.

D Look at the pictures and complete the sentences. Use the correct form of the verbs in the box. You may have to use some negative forms.

break • fall over • look • pick up • reply • see • stood

1 If Kevin hadn't just got a text message, he .... at his mobile phone.
2 If he hadn't looked at his mobile, he .... the banana skin.
3 If someone .... the banana skin earlier, it wouldn't have been there.
4 If Kevin had seen the banana skin, he .... on it.
5 If he hadn't stood on it, he ....
6 If he hadn't fallen over, he .... his mobile.
7 If he hadn't broken his mobile, he .... to the text message.

E Read the story and complete the sentences.

Vida loved to keep fit. Whenever she could, she went to the gym after work. But one evening, Vida got home late. 'It's too late to go to the gym now,' she said to herself. 'I'll just watch TV instead.'

She made herself a nice, fresh, healthy salad and sat down in front of the TV. Suddenly, she saw something on TV that caught her attention. It was an advert for an exercise bike called the Fitmaster 5000.

'That looks fantastic!' thought Vida. 'I think I'll buy that!'

She phoned the number and ordered the machine. It came the next day.

It was much bigger than it looked on TV, and the only place Vida could put it was at the top of the stairs.

She loved the Fitmaster 5000 so much, though, that from that day on, she only exercised at home. She didn't go to the gym any more. She spent hours every evening on her exercise bike, and every evening she went faster and faster. One evening, she was going so fast that the exercise bike began to move forwards. Before she knew what had happened, she – and the bike – fell down the stairs. All sixteen of them. Right to the bottom. Ouch!

The Fitmaster 5000 was broken, and so was Vida's leg.

'I think that's enough exercise for a while,' thought Vida, as she lay in her hospital bed. 'And that's enough watching adverts on TV too.'

1 If Vida had got home earlier, ...
....

2 If she'd gone to the gym that evening,
....

3 If she hadn't watched TV, ...
....

4 She wouldn't have bought the Fitmaster 5000 ....

5 She wouldn't have put it at the top of the stairs ....

6 She'd have continued going to the gym ......
....

7 If she hadn't gone so fast, ...
....

8 If she hadn't fallen down the stairs, ...
....

Vocabulary
Body and lifestyle

● Topic vocabulary

see page 195 for definitions

affect (v)	flu (n)	recover (v)
balance (v, n)	have an operation (v phr)	salty (adj)
benefit (v, n)	healthy (adj)	slice (v, n)
breathe (v)	ignore (v)	sour (adj)
chew (v)	infection (n)	spicy (adj)
chop (v)	ingredient (n)	stir (v)
contain (v)	injury (n)	suffer (v)
cough (v, n)	limit (v, n)	taste (v, n)
cure (v, n)	meal (n)	treatment (n)
exercise (v, n)	pill (n)	vitamin (n)

● Phrasal verbs

cut down (on)	do less of sth (smoking, etc)
fall down	trip and fall
get over	recover from (an illness, etc)
go off	no longer be fresh
lie down	start lying (on a bed, etc)
put on	gain (weight)
sit down	(start to) sit
stand up	(start to) stand

● Prepositional phrases

at night
at risk
in addition (to)
in comparison to/with
in shape
on a diet

● Word formation

bake	baker, bakery	**medicine**	medical
bend	bent	**pain**	painful, painless
cook	cooker, cookery	**reduce**	reduction
intend	intention, intentional	**sense**	sensible, sensitive
jog	jogging, jogger	**weigh**	weight

● Word patterns

adjectives	addicted to		die from/of
	allergic to		fight against
	covered in/with		recover from
	pleased with		smell of
verbs	combine sth with	*nouns*	a cure for
	complain (to sb) about		a recipe for

Topic vocabulary

A Choose the correct answer.

1 A chopping his food   B chewing his food
2 A chopping meat   B chewing meat
3 A slicing the bread   B chopping the bread
4 A stirring the soup   B tasting the soup
5 A stirring the soup   B tasting the soup

6 A the meal   B the ingredients
7 A the meal   B the ingredients
8 A It's very sour!   B It's very spicy!
9 A It's very sour!   B It's very salty!
10 A I like it spicy!   B I like it salty!

B Complete using the verbs in the box.

> affect • balance • benefit • contain • ignore • limit

1 If you .... the doctor's advice, you won't get well.
2 Drinking a lot of coffee can .... your mood and behaviour.
3 It's difficult to .... a healthy diet with a busy lifestyle.
4 I'd definitely .... from getting more exercise.
5 You should .... the amount of chocolate you eat to one bar a day.
   You're eating too much at the moment!
6 Does this cookery book .... any recipes for vegetarians?

C Complete using a word formed from the letters given.

1 Sandy hasn't been to school for a week because she's got .... **L U F**
2 Fruit contains lots of .... C. **M A T N I V I**
3 If you had to go to hospital to have an .... , would you be scared?
   N O T R O P E A I
4 Take one of these .... after every meal for three days. **S L I P L**
5 Ben couldn't play football for two months because of an .... **R U N J Y I**
6 I got some dirt in the cut and now I've got an .... **C O N F E T I I N**
7 Becky always looks really .... She must get lots of exercise. **L A Y E T H H**
8 What's the best .... for a bee sting? **T E N T R A T E M**
9 Have doctors finally found a .... for malaria? **U R E C**

D Each of the words in bold is in the wrong sentence. Write the correct word.

1 It can be difficult to **exercise** at the top of a very high mountain. ....
2 I know I should **recover** more often, but it's not easy to find the time. ....
3 It will take you a few weeks to completely **suffer** from your illness. ....
4 Both my grandparents **cough** from arthritis. ....
5 If you have to **breathe**, please put your hand in front of your mouth! ....

Phrasal verbs

E Write one word in each gap.

1 If you work in an office, you spend most of the day sitting ....
2 If you're a teacher, you spend a lot of your time standing ....
3 I fell .... on the way home from school and hurt my knee.
4 My dad has put .... two kilos since he gave up smoking.
5 Do you think I should cut .... on how much sugar I have in tea and coffee?
6 I've got a headache so I'm going to lie ....
7 My mum has had flu but she's getting .... it now.
8 This chicken smells awful. It must have gone ....

F Complete each second sentence so that it has a similar meaning to the first sentence. Use no more than two words.

1 I think I've gained weight in the last few months!
   I think I've .... weight in the last few months.

2 This milk isn't fresh any more.
   This milk .... off.

3 I hope James recovers from his illness soon.
   I hope James .... over his illness soon.

4 You should eat less chocolate!
   You should .... on the amount of chocolate you eat!

5 If you're tired, have a rest on the sofa for half an hour.
   If you're tired, ... down on the sofa for half an hour.

Prepositional phrases

G Complete each sentence using the word given. Write between two and three words.

1 When there's a flu epidemic, old people are particularly .... **risk**
2 I've put on a lot of weight recently so I'm thinking of going .... **diet**
3 I don't sleep well .... and I often feel tired during the day. **night**
4 .... most of my friends, I eat very healthy food. **comparison**
5 I'm thinking of running a marathon, so I'd better get myself .... ! **shape**
6 .... all the fruit I eat, I also have a vitamin pill once a day. **addition**

Word formation

H Complete by changing the form of the word in capitals when this is necessary.

1 I've never had a serious .... problem, thank goodness! **MEDICINE**
2 Toby is thinking of taking up .... **JOG**
3 My mum works in a .... so she brings home loads of lovely cakes. **BAKE**
4 We used to have an electric .... but now we've got a gas one. **COOK**
5 It's not very .... to eat such a large meal just before going to bed. **SENSE**
6 This spoon is .... I'll get another one. **BEND**
7 You look thinner. Have you lost .... ? **WEIGH**
8 It's not Karen's .... to give up eating meat completely. She just wants to eat it less often. **INTEND**
9 Over the last ten years, there's been a .... in the number of children being born in this country. **REDUCE**
10 I fell over and my knee is still a bit .... but it's slowly getting better. **PAIN**
11 Harry is quite .... so be careful what you say about his new haircut. **SENSE**
12 I've just bought a new .... book. It's got some great recipes in it. **COOK**
13 The injection is quite .... You won't even feel the needle going in. **PAIN**

Word patterns

I Write one word in each gap.

*M*r Grapley loved chocolate. In fact, he was addicted (**1**) .... chocolate. He ate more than thirty bars of chocolate a day. He had chocolate for breakfast, chocolate for lunch and chocolate for dinner. But he didn't just eat bars of chocolate. He also made delicious chocolate cakes. If anyone needed a recipe (**2**) .... the best chocolate cake in the world, they went to Mr Grapley.

People loved visiting Mr Grapley. His whole house smelt (**3**) .... chocolate and, when he had guests, Mr Grapley made the most amazing meals. He'd combine chocolate (**4**) .... everything. One of his best creations was chicken with chocolate sauce. Everyone was so pleased (**5**) .... this recipe that they built a statue of Mr Grapley in the town square.

One day, however, something terrible happened. Mr Grapley woke up and went to make himself a cup of hot chocolate. On his way to the kitchen, he passed a mirror. He was covered (**6**) .... spots. He quickly went to see Dr Getwellsoon.

'Oh dear,' said Dr Getwellsoon. 'I'm afraid I've got some bad news. You've become allergic (**7**) .... chocolate. If you continue to eat chocolate, you'll have these spots.'

'But that's not possible!' shouted Mr Grapley. 'I can't live without chocolate. There must be a cure (**8**) .... this allergy.'

'No,' said Dr Getwellsoon. 'I'm afraid there isn't. If you want to recover (**9**) .... this illness, you'll have to stop eating chocolate.'

'And if I don't stop?' asked Mr Grapley.

'Well, you're not going to die (**10**) .... an allergy to chocolate, but the spots won't go away. It's a straight choice. Spots ... or no chocolate.'

Mr Grapley spent the next three days complaining (**11**) .... everyone (**12**) .... what Dr Getwellsoon had said. 'He's a doctor. He's supposed to cure me. That's what doctors do!' shouted Mr Grapley to anyone who was listening. Mr Grapley was just discovering that, in the real world, things don't always happen the way we want them to. But he was determined to fight (**13**) .... the truth for as long as he could.

A Circle the correct word.

1 You don't need to go on a **diet / cure**. You're not fat!
2 **Chew / Chop** the meat into small pieces with a sharp knife.
3 What **infections / ingredients** do we need for this recipe?
4 **Stir / Slice** the soup with a wooden spoon.
5 If the grapefruit is too **sour / spicy**, add some sugar.
6 In **benefit / comparison** to me, you get lots of exercise!
7 Does this drink **limit / contain** any sugar?
8 Sam's in bed with **flu / cough**, so he's not going to school today.
9 Have you **suffered / recovered** from bad headaches for a long time?
10 You shouldn't **affect / ignore** the problem. See a doctor!

(1 mark per answer)

B Complete the sentences by changing the form of the word in capitals.

11 My skin is very .... (**SENSE**), so I shouldn't stay out in the sun all day.
12 Do you want to come .... (**JOG**) with me?
13 When I broke my arm, it was very .... (**PAIN**), but now it doesn't hurt at all.
14 There are lots of .... (**MEDICINE**) encyclopaedias on the Internet.
15 What's the best way to lose .... (**WEIGH**)?
16 I put salt in the coffee by mistake! It wasn't .... (**INTEND**)!
17 All the knives and forks are .... (**BEND**). We'll have to buy some new ones.
18 My mum prefers cooking on a gas .... (**COOK**).

(1 mark per answer)

C Complete the second sentence using the word given, so that it has a similar meaning to the first sentence. Write between two and five words.

19 I think I've gained a few kilos over the last few months! **on**
I think I've .... a few kilos over the last few months!

20 You should reduce the amount of fast food you eat. **down**
You should .... the amount of fast food you eat.

21 This milk isn't fresh, so I'll throw it away. **gone**
This milk .... , so I'll throw it away.

22 If I eat tomatoes, I get bad stomach problems. **allergic**
I .... tomatoes; if I eat them, I get bad stomach problems.

23 I hope your mum recovers from her illness soon. **over**
I hope your mum .... her illness soon.

24 There are red spots all over her body. **covered**
Her body .... red spots.

25 I like the new gym I'm going to. **pleased**
I .... the new gym I'm going to.

26 Could you tell me how to make a really good curry? **recipe**
Could you give me .... a really good curry?

(2 marks per answer)

D Complete using the correct form of the verbs in brackets.

27 If I'm still ill tomorrow, I .... (**miss**) the chemistry test!
28 If I was your doctor, I .... (**tell**) you to stop worrying!
29 It .... (**be**) awful if any of us had become ill on holiday.
30 If you .... (**go**) to the chemist's, can you get me some vitamin pills?
31 If you .... (**not / have**) a healthy diet, you get tired easily.
32 If he .... (**not / do**) some research on the Internet, he wouldn't have found out what was wrong with him.
33 It would be great if everyone in the world .... (**have**) enough to eat.
34 If you see the doctor, ... (**ask**) her when you can go back to school!

(1 mark per answer)

E Complete using the words in the box.

addition • balance • exercise • fight • injury • operation • shape • treatment

Help yourself to stay healthy

Doctors are useful. If you've had a/an (**35**) .... while doing sport, they can fix it. If you're ill, they can tell you what the best (**36**) .... is. If you're very ill, you might have to have a/an (**37**) .... in hospital. We need doctors for all of these things. But in (**38**) .... to what doctors do, there are things that you can do yourself in the (**39**) .... against ill health. Getting regular (**40**) .... at school or at a gym will help you to stay in (**41**) .... Having a healthy diet will also keep you strong. A healthy diet is all about (**42**) .... It doesn't mean never eating chocolate. It means not eating too much. And eating vegetables, too! The more we can look after ourselves, the less we'll need doctors to look after us. And that must be good!

Total mark: ..../50

Reported speech

Use	Example
To report what someone else said	*My dad said that he'd written a song.*

Form

Direct speech	Reported speech
present simple *'I **want** to build a new house,' said Jill.*	past simple *Jill said she **wanted** to build a new house.*
present continuous *'We **are making** a dress,' they said.*	past continuous *They said they **were making** a dress.*
present perfect continuous *'I **have been drawing** all day,' said Debbie.*	past perfect continuous *Debbie said she **had been drawing** all day.*
past simple *'Jim **made** a card for me yesterday,' Amy said.*	past perfect simple *Amy said Jim **had made** a card for her the day before.*
past continuous *'I **was writing** a poem,' said Tina.*	past perfect continuous *Tina said she **had been writing** a poem.*
will *'I **will** make you a scarf,' my grandma said.*	would *My grandma said she **would** make me a scarf.*
am/is/are going to *'They **are going to** make a new one,' said Joe.*	was/were going to *Joe said they **were going to** make a new one.*
can *'I **can** draw quite well,' Emma said.*	could *Emma said she **could** draw quite well.*
must / have to *'You **have to** visit the fashion show,' she said.*	had to *She said we **had to** visit the fashion show.*
may *'I **may** visit the White House next week,' said Polly.*	might *Polly said she **might** visit the White House the following week*

⃝Helpful hints

We often have to change other words apart from the verb form.

pronouns
- I ➜ he/she
- you ➜ I/me/they/them
- we ➜ they
- us ➜ them
- my ➜ his/her
- your ➜ my/their

time and place
- here ➜ there
- now ➜ then/at that moment
- tomorrow ➜ the next day
- tonight ➜ that night

- next week ➜ the following week
- yesterday ➜ the day before
- last week ➜ the week before
- ago ➜ before

- We only make tense changes when the reporting verb (*say*, etc) is in the past.
  - ✓ Tony **says** he **is going** to study architecture.
  - ✗ ~~Tony **says** he **was going** to study architecture.~~
- We don't change the past perfect simple and the past perfect continuous.
  - ✓ *'I **had seen** the picture before.'* ➜ *He said **he had** seen the picture before.*
- We also don't change *would*, *should*, *could* and *might*.
  - ✓ *'I **might** take up painting.'* ➜ *She said she **might** take up painting.*
- We can use verbs like *apologise*, *deny*, *promise*, *refuse* and *suggest* in reported speech.
  - ✓ Jan **apologised for** losing the picture.
  - ✓ He **denied** breaking the statue.
  - ✓ Terence **promised to** help me decorate the house.
  - ✓ Charlotte **refused to** let me see her painting.
  - ✓ My dad **suggested** going to an art gallery.

A Choose the correct answer.

1 'I'm a big fan of U2,' Derek said.
   Derek said he .... a big fan of U2.
   A was
   B has been
   C had been

2 'We're watching TV,' said the twins.
   The twins said they .... TV.
   A watched
   B were watching
   C had watched

3 'You've been annoying me all day!' my mum said.
   My mum said I .... her all day.
   A annoyed
   B was annoying
   C had been annoying

4 'The dog ate my homework!' said Ivan.
   Ivan said the dog .... his homework.
   A was eating
   B had eaten
   C has eaten

5 'At one o'clock, I was having lunch,' said Molly.
   Molly said she .... lunch at one o'clock.
   A had been having
   B has had
   C is having

6 'You'll get wet without an umbrella,' Dad said.
   Dad said I .... wet without an umbrella.
   A will be getting
   B got
   C would get

7 'He can juggle five balls!' said Angie.
   Angie said he .... five balls.
   A juggled
   B would juggle
   C could juggle

8 'You must give me your essays,' Mrs Vine said.
   Mrs Vine said we .... give her our essays.
   A were having to
   B had to
   C would have to

B Complete using the words and phrases in the boxes.

| his • their • them • there | before • that night • the day before • the next day |

1 'I'm seeing Simon tomorrow,' Mary said.
   Mary said she was seeing Simon ....

2 'We moved into the area two years ago,' Bella said.
   Bella said they had moved into the area two years ....

3 'Our teacher is giving us a test!' said Michelle.
   Michelle said their teacher was giving .... a test.

4 'My dad gave me fifty pounds!' said Neil.
   Neil said .... dad had given him fifty pounds.

5 'I scored a great goal yesterday,' Marina said.
   Marina said she had scored a great goal ....

6 'We saw our cousin at the fair,' said Ben.
   Ben said they had seen .... cousin at the fair.

7 'I left my wallet here,' Frank said.
   Frank said he had left his wallet ....

8 'I'll sleep well tonight!' said Arnie.
   Arnie said he would sleep well ....

C Underline the mistake in each second sentence and write the correct words.

1 'There's a mouse in the kitchen!' said Martha.
Martha said there had been a mouse in the kitchen. ....

2 'We've won every match this year,' Amy said.
Amy said they won every match that year. ....

3 'I broke my leg two weeks ago,' said Spencer.
Spencer said he had broken his leg two weeks ago. ....

4 'We'd heard the song before,' Rory said.
Rory said he had heard the song before. ....

5 'I've been working since four o'clock,' said Dad.
Dad said he was working since four o'clock. ....

6 'We're spending tomorrow by the swimming pool,' Belinda said.
Belinda said they have spent the next day by the swimming pool. ....

D Complete each second sentence using the word given, so that it has a similar meaning to the first sentence. Write between two and five words.

1 'I'm going to bake a cake,' said Mum. **she**
Mum said .... to bake a cake.

2 'Richard has passed his driving test,' Andy said. **passed**
Andy said .... his driving test.

3 'We're staying in tonight to watch TV,' Jim said. **that**
Jim said they .... to watch TV.

4 'I'm thinking of going on a diet,' said George. **he**
George said .... of going on a diet.

5 'My sister lived in Russia for a year,' Carol said. **lived**
Carol said .... in Russia for a year.

6 'I went snowboarding last year,' Jill said. **year**
Jill said she .... before.

7 'I'll call you tomorrow,' Karl said to me. **next**
Karl said he .... day.

8 'We're flying home next week,' said Arthur. **the**
Arthur said they .... week.

E Rewrite the sentences in reported speech using the verb given.

1 'I'm sorry I told everyone your secret,' my sister said. **apologised**
....

2 'I didn't give the money to John,' said Ali. **denied**
....

3 'I'll love you forever!' Francis said to Elizabeth. **promised**
....

4 'No, I won't open the door!' said Mandy. **refused**
....

5 'Why don't we give Jenny a call?' Albert said. **suggested**
....

Grammar
Reported questions, orders, requests

Reported questions, orders, requests

Use	Example
To report what someone else asked/ordered/requested	*Pat asked me if I had tried the jeans on in the shop.*

Form

Direct question/order/request	Reported question/order/request
questions beginning with *have, do* or *be* '**Have** you **been** to the gallery?' *he asked her.* '**Do** you **want** a sweater?' *my mum asked.* '**Are** you **making** a skirt?' *I asked Anne.*	*He asked her **if** she **had been** to the gallery.* *My mum asked **if** I **wanted** a sweater.* *I asked Anne **if** she **was making** a skirt.*
questions beginning with a modal '**Can** you paint?' *Mary asked her friend.* '**Will** you make me one?' *I asked Terry.* '**Shall** I wear a jacket?' *I asked Mum.* '**May** I borrow your coat?' *Mr Jones asked me.*	*Mary asked her friend **if** he **could** paint.* *I asked Terry **if** he **would** make me one.* *I asked Mum **if** I **should** wear a jacket.* *Mr Jones asked me **if** he **might** borrow my coat.*
questions beginning with a question word '**What** kind of shoes are in fashion now?' *my mum asked me.* '**Who** did you see at the fashion show?' *asked Ben.* '**Which** one do you want?' *Sarah asked Liam.* '**When** will they finish the house?' *I asked.* '**Why** did you say that?' *my sister asked me.* '**How** much did your hat cost?' *Ed asked Carl.*	*My mum asked me **what** kind of shoes **were** in fashion at that moment.* *Ben asked **who** I **had seen** at the fashion show.* *Sarah asked Liam **which** one he **wanted**.* *I asked **when** they **would** finish the house.* *My sister asked me **why** I **had said** that.* *Ed asked Carl **how** much his hat **had cost**.*
orders '**Put** your clothes in the drawer,' *Mum said.* '**Don't wear** the red one,' *Alice said.*	*Mum **told** me **to put** my clothes in the drawer.* *Alice **told** me **not to wear** the red one.*
requests '**Will** you **make** me one?' *I asked Terry.* '**Please don't move** my pictures,' *said Olga.*	*I **asked** Terry **to make** me one.* *Olga **asked** me **not to move** her pictures.*

Helpful hints

We can also use *whether* instead of *if* in reported questions.
✓ *He asked her **whether** she had been to the gallery.*

Watch out! Remember not to use question word order in reported questions.
✓ *I asked when **they would finish the house**.*
✗ ~~I asked when **would they finish the house**.~~

A Circle the correct answer.

1 'Has your brother gone out?' Mum asked me.
Mum asked me if my brother **has gone / had gone** out.

2 'Do you know the answer?' Miss Smith asked Ruby.
Miss Smith asked Ruby if she **knew / had known** the answer.

3 'Is this your car?' the police officer said to the man.
The police officer asked the man if it **is / was** his car.

4 'Have you been to see the exhibition?' I asked Benjamin.
I asked Benjamin if he **went / had been** to see the exhibition.

5 'Does your laptop need a new battery?' Jerry asked me.
Jerry asked me if my laptop **needed / will need** a new battery.

6 'Are you having a barbecue?' I asked the Browns.
I asked the Browns if they **were having / had been having** a barbecue.

B Write one word in each gap.

1 'Will you be at the party?' Richard asked me.
Richard asked me if I .... be at the party.

2 'May I ask you a few questions?' the woman asked Ted.
The woman asked Ted if she .... ask him a few questions.

3 'Can we go to the zoo tomorrow?' Jane asked her father.
Jane asked her father if they .... go to the zoo the following day.

4 'Shall I study maths or English?' Sally asked her best friend.
Sally asked her best friend whether she .... study maths or English.

5 'Can you write with your left hand?' Val asked me.
Val asked me whether I .... write with my left hand.

6 'Shall we play tennis or volleyball?' Debbie asked her sister.
Debbie asked her sister if they .... play tennis or volleyball.

7 'May I leave the table?' Samantha asked her parents.
Samantha asked her parents if she .... leave the table.

8 'Will our bus leave on time?' Mum asked the driver.
Mum asked the driver whether our bus .... leave on time.

C Complete each second sentence so that it has a similar meaning to the first sentence. Write between two and five words.

1 'When did your brother join the army?' Rudy asked me.
Rudy asked me .... the army.

2 'How was your trip to Turkey?' I asked Katherine.
I asked Katherine how .... been.

3 'How will we find your keys in the dark?' Ashley asked Susie.
Ashley asked Susie .... keys in the dark.

4 'Why was Rob on TV?' Denise asked me.
Denise asked me .... on TV.

5 'Who saw you at the park?' the police officer asked me.
The police officer asked me .... at the park.

6 'Who did you see at the park?' the police officer asked me.
The police officer asked me .... at the park.

D Look at the pictures and complete the sentences.

1 My mum told ....

2 I ....

3 The man ....

4 The parrot ....

5 Jenny's grandma ....

6 The magician ....

E Choose the correct answer.

1 'Could you pass me the salt, please?' I asked the man next to me.
   I asked the man next to me .... me the salt.
   A pass   B if he passes   C to pass

2 'Would you mind waiting a moment?' the shop assistant asked the woman.
   The shop assistant asked the woman .... for a moment.
   A to wait   B waiting   C she wait

3 'Please don't leave your dirty football boots in the hall,' Mum said to Doug.
   Mum told Doug .... his dirty football boots in the hall.
   A that he doesn't leave   B not to leave   C don't leave

4 'Could you tell us where you were at six o'clock?' the police officers asked Barry.
   The police officers asked Barry .... he had been at six o'clock.
   A telling them where   B where he tells them   C to tell them where

5 'Could I have your e-mail address?' I asked Mariella.
   I asked Mariella .... e-mail address.
   A to give me her   B give me your   C give me her

6 'Can I have a new Xbox for my birthday?' I asked my mum.
   I asked my mum .... a new Xbox.
   A that she get me   B get me   C to get me

F If the word or phrase in bold is correct, put a tick (✓). If it is wrong, write the correct word or phrase.

1 I asked Toni why **had she taken** my CD without asking me.   ....

2 Roger told Isabelle **don't make** any plans for the weekend.   ....

3 Madison asked me how much my new jeans **had cost**.   ....

4 Alexander asked his dad **giving** him some money for his school trip. ....

5 I told Jeremy **you don't move** while I took his photograph.   ....

6 Annie told her dog **to sit**, but it didn't.   ....

Vocabulary
Creating and building

see page 196 for definitions

Topic vocabulary

ancient (adj)	maintain (v)	sleeve (n)
checked (adj)	match (v)	smooth (adj)
cotton (n)	material (n)	stretch (v)
create (v)	notice (v, n)	striped (adj)
design (v, n)	pattern (n)	style (n)
fix (v)	pile (n)	suit (v, n)
fold (v)	practical (adj)	suitable (adj)
gallery (n)	rough (adj)	tear (v, n)
improvement (n)	shape (n)	tight (adj)
loose (adj)	silk (n)	tool (n)

Phrasal verbs

cut off	completely remove by cutting
do up	button/zip up a piece of clothing
fill up	make sth completely full
have on	wear (a piece of clothing)
leave out	not include
put on	start wearing (a piece of clothing)
take off	remove (a piece of clothing)
try on	put on (a piece of clothing) to see how it looks and if it fits

Prepositional phrases

at the back (of)
at the end (of)
in fashion/style
in front (of)
in the corner (of)
out of fashion/style

Word formation

art	artist, artistic	**hand**	handful, handle
break	broke, broken, (un)breakable	**imagine**	imagination, imaginative
compose	composition, composer	**intelligent**	intelligence
exhibit	exhibition	**perfect**	perfection, imperfect
free	freedom	**prepare**	preparation

Word patterns

adjectives	amazed at/by		describe sth as
	disappointed with		explain sth to
	familiar with		remind sb of
	involved in		remove sth from
	similar to	*nouns*	an influence on
verbs	change sth (from sth) into		a picture of

Topic vocabulary

A Match the pictures with the verbs in the box.

> create • design • fix • fold • match • stretch • tear

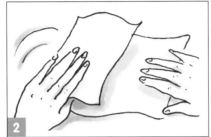

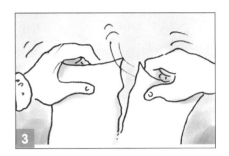

....

....

....

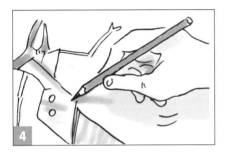

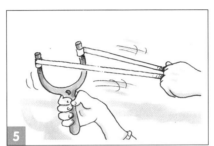

....

....

....

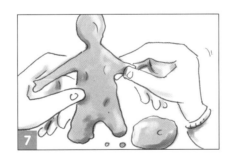

....

B Each of the words in bold is in the wrong sentence. Write the correct word.

1 These jeans are too **ancient**. Do you have a smaller size? ....
2 I don't like your **smooth** dress. It makes you look like a zebra! ....
3 It's good to have **rough** skills, like being able to make your own clothes. ....
4 Ouch! These shoes are far too **checked**. Have you got any in a bigger size? ....
5 Wear that **suitable** shirt, the one with the red and white squares. ....
6 The woman asked the assistant if they had any jackets **loose** for a one-year-old girl. ....
7 This woollen jumper is really **striped**. I don't like wearing it because it makes me itch! ....
8 The **practical** Egyptians almost always wore white clothes. ....
9 Feel this material. It's so soft and **tight**. I bet it's really expensive. ....

C Circle the correct word.

1 They've got some fantastic paintings in the local art **gallery / style**.
2 Amy asked me if I had seen her **silk / shape** blouse.
3 We pay someone to **maintain / notice** the block of flats we live in.
4 The latest fashion is short **piles / sleeves** with lots of bright colours.
5 The assistant said the T-shirts were made out of **cotton / suit**.
6 I asked my mum what **tools / improvements** I needed to fix the car.
7 Oscar bought some **material / pattern** to make a costume for the fancy-dress party.

Phrasal verbs

D Write one word in each gap.

Dress to impress

Do you think carefully about what you (**1**) .... on each morning when you get dressed? What do the clothes that you (**2**) .... on say about you? If you want to make the right impression, try these easy tips.

When you buy clothes, always (**3**) .... them on. Ask a friend's opinion if you're not sure. And check that what you buy is the right size! If it's a jacket, for example, make sure that you can (**4**) .... it up properly. And make sure it's easy to put on and (**5**) .... off.

Clear out your wardrobe. Take everything out and only put back those things you actually like. (**6**) .... out all the things you never wear. It will create space for new clothes and you'll be able to (**7**) .... it up with things that suit you.

Finally, try making your old clothes more fashionable. You could (**8**) .... the sleeves off an old shirt or change the colour. Have fun, and always dress to impress!

Prepositional phrases

E In each sentence there is a word missing. Put an arrow (↑) to show where the missing word should go and write the word.

1 My parents said they wanted to build a play area at the back our house.
2 Those silver boots are really fashion at the moment!
3 Jan said it would look nice if we put some candles the corner of the room.
4 We need to design a new sign to go in front the shop to attract customers.
5 What's going to happen at end of your story?
6 Things become fashionable and then go out style very quickly.

Word formation

F Complete by changing the form of the word in capitals when this is necessary.

1 She must have a lot of .... to think of ideas like that. **IMAGINE**
2 I love the way they've designed this cup without a .... **HAND**
3 Kevin said he loved classical music and his favourite .... **COMPOSE**
  was Mozart.
4 When you look at his notebooks, you can see that Leonardo da Vinci was really **INTELLIGENT**
  ....
5 Todd is really .... He loves painting, playing music and **ART**
  writing poetry.
6 Would it be safer if all houses had windows made out of .... **BREAK**
  glass?
7 It took a lot of .... to get the show right, but it was worth it. **PREPARE**
8 Mum asked if I wanted to go to the Dali .... and I said yes. **EXHIBIT**
9 You might create something that's wonderful, but remember that it's impossible **PERFECT**
  to achieve ....
10 Our art teacher gives us a lot of .... to paint what we want to. **FREE**

Word patterns

G Circle the correct word.

1 Tina is only two, so I was amazed **by / with** the picture she drew.
2 Picasso has been a huge influence **in / on** me as a painter.
3 Writing poetry is similar **to / with** writing a song in some ways.
4 Look at this wonderful still life – it's a picture **from / of** fruit in a bowl.
5 I like Stephen King's books, but I was a bit disappointed **from / with** his last one.
6 There's a lot involved **in / on** writing a symphony. It takes a lot of hard work.
7 Derek asked if I was familiar **on / with** an artist called Titian and I said yes.

H Complete using a form of the verbs from the box. Add any other words you need.

change • describe • explain • remind • remove

1 We need to .... the old wallpaper .... the walls before we put the new
  one up.
2 Could you .... how you make concrete .... me?
3 I would .... this style of painting .... quite modern.
4 This piece of music always .... me .... long summer evenings.
5 My drawing of a horse went a bit wrong so I .... it .... a camel!

A Write one word in each gap.

Dear Gemma,

Hi! How are you? I finally persuaded my mum to take me shopping yesterday. It was great! I tried (**1**) .... lots of clothes and I was amazed (**2**) .... the choice in all the shops. It reminded me (**3**) .... the time we went shopping when you came to stay. We had a lot of fun, didn't we?

Anyway, I found one of those jackets that are (**4**) .... fashion at the moment — but I couldn't do it (**5**) .... ! I needed a bigger size, but they didn't have any. Oh, well. Maybe I'll have another look (**6**) .... the end of this week. I bought some shoes, though — they're similar (**7**) .... the ones you've got, the pink ones. I have them (**8**) .... at the moment and they look great!

Oh, and you know that old blouse I had? Well, I've changed it (**9**) .... a T-shirt! I cut the sleeves (**10**) .... and now it'll be perfect for the summer.

I have to go now. Write soon and tell me all your news.

Lots of love,

Olivia

(1 mark per answer)

B Match to make sentences.

11 She described the picture she was painting ....   A in designing buildings.

12 My sister's an architect, so she's involved ....   B to Martin, but he didn't understand.

13 I like Picasso's paintings, but I'm not familiar ....   C from the exhibition because it was damaged.

14 I tried to explain how to use oil paints ....   D from a winter scene into a spring scene.

15 They had to remove one of the paintings ....   E of a horse and it was brilliant.

16 Vincent Van Gogh has had an influence ....   F on many other painters.

17 Darren drew a picture ....   G as modern, but it looked quite old-fashioned to me.

18 Adding flowers to my picture changed it ....   H with his sculptures.

(1 mark per answer)

C Complete the second sentence using the word given, so that it has a similar meaning to the first sentence. Write between two and five words.

19 'I want to learn how to paint,' Janet said. **said**
   Janet .... to learn how to paint.

20 'We're building a house outside town,' said Mrs Turner. **they**
   Mrs Turner .... a house outside town.

21 'We're working on our website tomorrow,' Keith said. **day**
   Keith said they were working on their website ....

22 'Will you draw me a picture?' Jenny asked. **draw**
   Jenny asked .... a picture.

23 'We have to paint a picture for art class,' John said. **they**
John .... to paint a picture for art class.

24 'Can I see your drawing?' I asked Amy. **if**
I asked Amy .... see her drawing.

25 'You'll enjoy the show,' Belinda said to me. **I**
Belinda said .... the show.

26 'Please don't take my photograph,' Hans said. **take**
Hans asked me .... photograph.

(2 marks per answer)

D Choose the correct answer.

27 I asked her when .... finish making her model.
A will she
B she will
C would she
D she would

28 Don said he had an art lesson .... night.
A that
B the
C this
D those

29 My mum told .... my paints.
A that I move
B me to move
C to move to me
D to move me

30 Tom apologised .... ink on my picture.
A for getting
B that he got
C to get
D for he gets

31 Molly denied .... my camera.
A to lose
B for losing
C losing
D on losing

32 Gary promised .... me paint the outside of the house.
A helping
B to help
C that he helps
D for helping

33 My brother refused .... me use his digital camera.
A to let
B that he let
C letting
D for letting

34 I suggest .... a new architect who will understand what you want.
A to find
B you to find
C for finding
D finding

(1 mark per answer)

E Choose the correct answer.

35 Just put the statue .... the corner of the room for now.
A on
B in
C at
D over

36 Do these shoes .... my new skirt?
A suit
B go
C match
D look

37 Don't get that colour – green went out .... fashion last year!
A from
B of
C with
D on

38 This shirt is too .... around the neck. I can't breathe!
A tight
B smooth
C rough
D practical

39 The gallery was too big to see it all in one day, so we .... out the modern paintings.
A put
B left
C went
D made

40 Why don't you .... your clothes in half before you put them in the drawer?
A fix
B stretch
C create
D fold

41 My new shirt has a .... like a Chinese dragon on the back.
A tear
B pile
C design
D cotton

42 I filled the bucket .... with water.
A out
B on
C in
D up

(1 mark per answer)

Total mark: ..../50

Grammar

Direct and indirect objects

Verbs without an object

Some verbs only need a subject. They don't need an object.

Form	Example
subject + verb	**The flowers** grew. **The dog** got up.

These verbs include:

fall down	happen	sit down	stand up
get up	laugh	sleep	walk
grow	run away	speak	work

Verbs with one object

Many verbs can be followed by an object.

Form	Example
subject + verb + object	We picked up **the rubbish**. I've planted **a tree**.

These verbs include:

borrow	drink	have	paint
close	drive	invite	pick up
draw	eat	open	plant

Verbs with two objects

Some verbs can be followed by two objects. One is called the 'direct object' and the other is called the 'indirect object'. The indirect object is usually a person.
In both the examples below, *some flowers* is the direct object and *Jill* is the indirect object.

Form	Example
subject + verb + indirect object + direct object	Simon gave **Jill some flowers**.
subject + verb + direct object + preposition + indirect object	Simon gave **some flowers to Jill**.

These verbs include:

bring	give	owe	send	teach
buy	lend	pass	show	tell
cost	make	pay	sing	throw
get	offer	read	take	write

Helpful hints

- There are two prepositions which often go between the direct object and the indirect object: *to* and *for*.
  - ✓ I bought an umbrella **for** George.
  - ✓ I gave the umbrella **to** George.

- Some of the verbs above can also be used in the passive.
  - ✓ Jill was given some flowers.
  - ✓ Some flowers were given to Jill.

 Watch out! We don't use a preposition if the indirect object comes before the direct object.
✗ Simon gave **to** Jill some flowers.

A   Match to make sentences. If a phrase 1–8 cannot be matched with a phrase
A–F, put a cross (✗) on the line.

1 I've never driven   ....   A the window!
2 We're going to have   ....   B some money.
3 Don't close   ....   C a lovely picture.
4 Have you invited   ....   D a tractor.
5 Our rabbit has run away   ....   E lots of people?
6 Of course you can borrow   ....   F a party on Saturday.
7 Clare has drawn   ....
8 I think I'll sit down   ....

B   Circle the extra word in each sentence.

1 My mum often makes for the old lady who lives next door some soup.
2 I won't tell to anyone your secret.
3 Sing to us a song!
4 Could you bring for me some crisps when you come?
5 I think I'll buy for Carl a computer game for his birthday.
6 That CD cost to me fifteen euros.
7 Dan showed to me his autograph book.

C   Rewrite the sentences with the direct object at the end.

1 I owe ten euros to Danny.
   I owe Danny ten euros.

2 Susan hasn't bought a birthday present for her mum yet.
   ....

3 You should show your new guitar to Mike.
   ....

4 Did you give that CD to Liz?
   ....

5 I'd like to teach English to young teenagers.
   ....

6 Are you going to write a letter to your grandparents?
   ....

7 Could you take this magazine to your dad?
   ....

D Rewrite the sentences with the indirect object at the end.

1 I'm going to read the kids a story.
I'm going to read a story to the kids.

2 Could you pass Ed the potatoes?
....

3 Throw the dog that bone!
....

4 Why are you sending Aunty June those clothes?
....

5 Steve sang us his new song.
....

6 I'll lend Doug the money.
....

7 I've never told my mum a lie.
....

E Write one word in each gap. If no word is necessary, put a dash (–).

1 My mum is going to write a letter .... the editor.
2 I paid the money .... the shop assistant and then left.
3 Let's get a birthday card .... your dad.
4 I'm not going to tell .... you the answer!
5 I've made some sandwiches .... you.
6 We'll bring .... you that DVD tonight.
7 Tony has bought a book .... Jake.
8 A prize was given .... the best student.

F If a line is correct, put a tick (✓). If there is an extra word in a line, write the word.

My new hobby

1 .... My uncle loves astronomy. It's his hobby. My aunt recently bought for
2 .... him a new telescope for his birthday, so he gave his old one to me! It's a
3 .... very good telescope. When he bought it, it cost to him over two hundred
4 .... euros! Last weekend, he taught to me the basics. He showed me how to
5 .... look through it, and told to me the names of all the planets. He said he'll
6 .... bring to me a book with more information about the night sky next time
7 .... he comes. Now astronomy is my hobby too. I think I'm going to enjoy it!

144

Grammar
wish

wish

We use the verb *wish* to talk about situations which are not real, but which we would like to be real.
We use *wish* with different tenses and modals depending on what we want to say.

Use	Tense / modal	Example
To express wishes about now or generally	*wish* + past simple	*Carl* **wishes** *he* **had** *a telescope.* *I wish I* **wasn't** *scared of spiders.*
To express wishes about the past	*wish* + past perfect simple	*Tracy* **wishes** *she* **'d seen** *that programme about the moon last night.* *I wish they* **hadn't cut down** *so many trees.*
To criticise other people, or to complain about something	*wish* + *would* + bare infinitive	*I* **wish** *people* **would throw** *their litter in the bin and not on the ground!* *I* **wish** *you* **wouldn't smoke** *in here.*
To express wishes about ability and permission now or in the future	*wish* + *could* + bare infinitive	*I* **wish** *I* **could travel** *through time!* *David* **wishes** *he* **could come** *with us, but his parents won't let him.*

Helpful hints

- When we use *wish* + past simple, we can say *I/he/she/it was …* or *I/he/she/it were …* *Were* is more formal than *was*.
  - ✓ *I wish I* **was** *an astronaut.* (more informal)
  - ✓ *I wish I* **were** *an astronaut.* (more formal)
- We can use the phrase *if only* in the same way as *wish*.
  - ✓ *If only I* **was/were** *an astronaut.*

 Watch out!
- We don't use *would* for wishes about ourselves.
  - ✓ *I wish I* **lived** *on Mars.*
  - ✗ ~~I wish I **would live** on Mars.~~

- We use *wish* for situations that aren't real. If there is a possibility that something will happen in the future, we don't use *wish*, but we can use *hope*.
  - ✓ *I* **hope** *it doesn't snow tomorrow.*
  - ✗ ~~I **wish** it doesn't snow tomorrow.~~

A Complete using the correct form of the verbs in brackets.

1 I wish I .... (**have**) a million euros! I'd buy lots of great things.
2 I wish we .... (**live**) in a bigger house. This one is too small.
3 Becca wishes she .... (**be**) old enough to drive a car.
4 Do you wish you .... (**feel**) more confident about the exam tomorrow?
5 I wish my computer .... (**not / be**) broken. I can't check my e-mail.
6 I wish I .... (**not / like**) chocolate so much! I eat three bars a day!
7 Grant wishes he .... (**not / make**) so many mistakes all the time.
8 Look what they're wearing! I bet they wish they .... (**not / look**) so silly!

B Complete using the correct form of the verbs in the box. You may have to use some negative forms.

> feel • give • have • live • spend • wear

1 I wish I .... in the countryside. The city is so noisy!
2 Tracy has got curly hair but she often wishes she .... straight hair.
3 I wish our teachers .... us less homework every day, but there's nothing I can do about it.
4 I wish I .... so scared, but I do!
5 Do you wish you .... contact lenses or are you happy with glasses?
6 Jake's mum wishes he .... so much money on clothes whenever he goes shopping.

C Look at the pictures and complete the sentences.

1 I wish I .... (**win**).

2 I wish I ....
(**listen**) to my mother.

3 I wish we ....
(**bring**) a camera with us.

4 I wish I ....
(**study**) a bit harder for this test.

5 I wish I ....
(**not / make**) so many phone calls last month!

6 I wish he ....
(**not / choose**) me!

D The words in bold in each sentence are wrong. Write the correct word or phrase.

1 I wish I **can** speak German, but I never learnt it at school. ....

2 I wish you **will** put your toys away! It's not difficult! ....

3 Do you sometimes wish you **can** fly? ....

4 I wish you **won't** lie to me all the time! ....

5 I wish the neighbours **won't** make so much noise. ....

6 If only she **will** ask me to go to the disco with her! ....

7 If only you **can** come with us! ....

E Choose the correct answer.

1 I wish I .... an MP3 player.
   A have   B had   C would have

2 We all wish Tim .... with the housework.
   A helps   B will help   C would help

3 I wish I .... to buy a lottery ticket last night.
   A remember   B remembered   C had remembered

4 I wish you .... live so far away.
   A don't   B didn't   C won't

5 I wish they .... keep changing the time of this programme.
   A couldn't   B wouldn't   C don't

6 Do you wish you .... to help Michael in the shop last weekend?
   A hadn't offered   B didn't offer   C haven't offered

F Circle the correct word or phrase.

26th April 3500

I wish today (**1**) **has / had** never happened! If only I (**2**) **could / would** start the day again, I'd do everything differently. Why did I forget to set the alarm last night? I really wish I (**3**) **haven't / hadn't** done that! I also wish I (**4**) **live / lived** nearer the Earth. It takes such a long time to get there from Mars – especially when the traffic is bad. (**5**) **If only / Only if** I (**6**) **have / had** a faster spaceship. Anyway, the point is, I was late for my job interview. The first question they asked was why I wanted to be an Environmental Officer on the moon. Do you know what I said? Because I really wanted to look at the aliens in the Super Alien Zoo. Oh, I wish I (**7**) **didn't say / hadn't said** that. Why am I so stupid? I (**8**) **wish / hope** now that I'd never applied for the job in the first place. I'm sure I won't get the job. I just (**9**) **wish / hope** tomorrow is better than today was.

Topic vocabulary

see page 197 for definitions

amazing (adj)	lightning (n)	recycle (v)
climate (n)	litter (v, n)	reptile (n)
countryside (n)	local (adj)	rescue (v, n)
environment (n)	locate (v)	satellite (n)
extinct (adj)	mammal (n)	shower (n)
forecast (v, n)	mild (adj)	solar system (n phr)
freezing (adj)	name (v, n)	species (n)
global (adj)	origin (n)	thunder (n)
heatwave (n)	planet (n)	wild (adj)
insect (n)	preserve (v)	wildlife (n)

Phrasal verbs

blow up	explode
build up	increase
clear up	tidy
go out	stop burning
keep out	prevent from entering
put down	stop holding
put out	make something stop burning
put up	put something on a wall (eg, a picture)

Prepositional phrases

at most
at the top/bottom (of)
in the beginning
in the distance
in total
on top (of)

Word formation

centre	central	**fog**	foggy
circle	circular	**garden**	gardener, gardening
danger	dangerous	**invade**	invasion, invader
deep	deeply, depth	**nature**	natural, naturally
destroy	destruction, destructive	**pollute**	pollution, polluted

Word patterns

adjectives	afraid of		prevent sb from
	aware of		save sth from
	enthusiastic about		think about
	serious about		worry about
	short of	*nouns*	damage to
verbs	escape from		an increase in

Topic vocabulary

A Complete using the words in the boxes.

climate • forecast • heatwave • lightning • shower • thunder

1 Have you heard what the weather .... is for tomorrow?
2 Britain is experiencing a .... at the moment. It's unusually hot and it hasn't rained for several weeks.
3 It's not going to rain much, but there might be the occasional ....
4 During the thunderstorm, the .... was so loud I hid under the bed!
5 .... hit a tree in the garden during the thunderstorm and a branch came off.
6 I wish I lived in a country with a warmer ....

insect • mammal • reptile • species • wildlife

7 I don't see a lot of .... because I live in a big city.
8 It's very unusual to see this .... of bird round here at this time of year.
9 If it's got six legs, it's probably a/an ....
10 Humans and monkeys are different types of ....
11 Snakes and lizards are different kinds of ....

B Write one word in each gap. The first letter is given to help you.

1 If we all **r**... our paper, fewer trees would be cut down.
2 The castle is perfectly **p**... , so it's just like it was four hundred years ago.
3 If only we could go to the **c**... to get some fresh air.
4 Many plants and animals are in danger of becoming **e**... . If they do, we'll never see them again.
5 Zoos give us the opportunity to see **w**... animals up close.
6 The weather is quite **m**... here, even in the winter. It rarely snows.
7 The **l**... weather forecast is usually much more accurate than the national one.
8 I wish you wouldn't drop your **l**... on the ground. Put it in the bin!
9 Scientists have **n**... the new planet 'Sedna'.
10 Looking down at the Earth from space must be an **a**... experience.
11 It's **f**... in here! Let's put the heating on.
12 The wildlife park is **l**... 15 km outside the town.
13 If you get lost in the desert, there will be no one around to **r**... you!
14 Climate change is a **g**... problem. Every country in the world is affected.

C Each of the words in bold is in the wrong sentence. Write the correct word.

1 The sun is at the centre of the solar **origin**. ....

2 The Earth is the **satellite** that we live on. ....

3 The moon goes round the Earth so it's a/an **planet**. ....

4 The **system** on the moon is very different to the one on Earth. For example, there are no plants on the moon. ....

5 Scientists aren't sure of the **environment** of the moon, but they think that maybe it was once part of the Earth. ....

Phrasal verbs

D Match to make sentences.

1 They're going to blow	....	A up a sign to tell people not to drop any litter.
2 Let's clear	....	B down and then I'll help you with the tent.
3 I'm going to put	....	C up the old bridge with dynamite.
4 There was a sign saying 'Keep	....	D up a lot round here over recent years.
5 How long did it take to put	....	E Out' on the gate.
6 I'll just put this box	....	F up this rubbish and put it in the bin.
7 The traffic has built	....	G out unless we put some more wood on.
8 The fire will go	....	H out the forest fire?

Prepositional phrases

E Complete using the word given. Write between two and four words.

1 A beautiful golden eagle was sitting .... the tree. **top**

2 I could just see the top of the mountain .... **distance**

3 It will take an hour .... to pick up this rubbish. **most**

4 .... , there are over eighty different types of animal in the zoo. **total**

5 .... , I didn't think I'd enjoy camping in the snow, but it was actually great fun! **beginning**

6 There are lots of strange fish .... the sea. **bottom**

Word formation

F One of the words in each sentence is in the wrong form. Write the correct word.

1 This path looks a bit danger to me.   ....
2 This submarine only goes to a deep of 500 metres.   ....
3 Scientists worry about the destroying of the Amazonian rainforests.   ....
4 Garden must be a very interesting hobby.   ....
5 Air pollute is a serious problem, especially in cities.   ....
6 What's it like living in centre London?   ....
7 We should let animals live in their nature environment rather than keep   ....
   them in zoos.
8 It's so fog that I can't see where I'm going.   ....
9 What would you do if there was an invade of the Earth by aliens?   ....
10 The island is almost completely circle.   ....

Word patterns

G Write one word in each gap.

EarthWatch

the environmental organisation that cares

Are you worried (**1**) .... our planet?

We at *EarthWatch* care about the damage that's being done (**2**) .... our environment. We're aware (**3**) .... the problems that this damage will cause in the future, and we believe that we're extremely short (**4**) .... time. If we don't act soon, it will be too late!

There's been an increase (**5**) .... all kinds of pollution in the past hundred years. This pollution is destroying the ozone layer, and creating global warming. We've got to prevent people (**6**) .... polluting the planet further. It's not going to be easy to save the Earth (**7**) .... destruction, but we have to try.

If you're afraid (**8**) .... what might happen if we don't all change our ways, if you're serious (**9**) .... helping to save the world, if you're enthusiastic (**10**) .... fighting for the only planet we've got, then we want to hear from you!

Think (**11**) .... it! You can't escape (**12**) .... the facts. The Earth is in danger and it's going to take every single one of us to help save it. Join us today!

A Complete using the words in the box.

| extinct • freezing • global • local • mild • wild |

1 Britain generally has very .... winters. It never gets very cold.
2 It's .... ! Do you think it might snow tonight?
3 Save the polar bears before they become ....!
4 A .... problem is a problem that affects the whole world.
5 What kind of .... animals live in the mountains round here?
6 There are several large forests in the .... area.

(1 mark per answer)

B Complete by changing the form of the word in capitals.

7 They closed the airport because it was so .... (**FOG**).
8 High winds can be very .... (**DESTROY**).
9 Lots of .... (**NATURE**) things are poisonous to humans.
10 Air .... (**POLLUTE**) isn't really a serious problem where we live.
11 Isn't .... (**GARDEN**) a bit of a boring hobby?
12 The submarine went down to a .... (**DEEP**) of 200 metres.
13 The island isn't square – it's almost completely .... (**CIRCLE**).
14 Is it .... (**DANGER**) to swim in that lake?

(1 mark per answer)

C Complete each second sentence using the word given, so that it has a similar meaning to the first sentence. Write between two and five words.

15 Not more than a thousand people live in the village. **most**
A thousand people .... live in the village.

16 In the film, the car explodes and we don't know if Murray is alive or not. **up**
In the film, the car .... and we don't know if Murray is alive or not.

17 There are lots of strange fish on the sea bed. **bottom**
There are lots of strange fish .... the sea.

18 The fire stopped burning in the middle of the night. **out**
The fire .... in the middle of the night.

19 Could you help me hang this 'DO NOT LITTER' sign? **up**
Could you help me .... this 'DO NOT LITTER' sign?

20 We need to increase people's awareness about the environment. **build**
We need to .... people's awareness about the environment.

21 One small sign isn't going to stop people from entering the wood! **keep**
One small sign isn't going to .... of the wood!

22 Please extinguish that cigarette right now! **out**
Please .... that cigarette right now!

23 Are you okay carrying that box or do you want to stop carrying it for a while? **down**
Are you okay carrying that box or do you want to .... for a while?

24 Let's tidy these clothes before Mum gets home. **clear**
Let's .... before Mum gets home.

(2 marks per answer)

D | If the word or phrase in bold is correct, put a tick (✓). If it is wrong, write the correct word or phrase.

25 Could you show **to me** your book about the moon? ....

26 Do you sometimes wish you **have** a bigger boat? ....

27 I wish people **didn't cause** so much damage to the environment. ....

28 Harry wishes that he **has studied** astrophysics instead of Latin when he was at university. ....

29 I wish you **wouldn't throw** rubbish out of the car window! ....

30 Laura sometimes wishes she **can** breathe underwater for hours. ....

31 I bought a new telescope **for my** dad. ....

32 I **wish** it snows during the night! ....

(1 mark per answer)

E | If a line is correct, put a tick (✓). If there is an extra word in a line, write the word.

Saving the rainforests of South America

	Every day, thousands and thousands of trees are cut down in the Amazonian
33	rainforest. This does enormous damage to the local environment, and also
34	possibly affects the world's climate. But how can we save up the rainforests
35	from destruction? First of all, we have to make the local people aware that of
36	the damage to they're doing. Secondly, there need to be more police in the
37	area preventing people from cutting down trees. A lot of the people who cut
38	them down do it illegally. If they were more afraid for of getting caught, they
39	might stop. It's a very serious about problem, and there's no easy solution,
40	but we're short of time. It won't be long before the rainforests disappear
	completely.

(1 mark per answer)

Total mark: ..../50

Grammar
-ing and infinitive

-ing

Some verbs are sometimes followed by -ing.

*He enjoys **making** other people laugh.*

These include:

admit	deny	dislike	feel like	give up	mind	suggest
avoid	discuss	enjoy	finish	mention	practise	take up

 Helpful hints

After a preposition, we usually use -ing.

✓ *I'm afraid **of** fly**ing**.*

Watch out!
- Some phrases end in the preposition *to*. These are also followed by -ing, not an infinitive.
  ✓ *I look forward **to hearing** from you.*   ✗ ~~I look forward **to hear** from you.~~
- We can also use the -ing form as the subject of a sentence.
  ✓ ***Cooking** is great fun!*

Infinitive

Some verbs are sometimes followed by the full infinitive.   *I decided **to apologise** to Emma.*

These include:

advise	choose	help	learn	plan	refuse	tell
afford	decide	hope	manage	pretend	seem	want
agree	expect	invite	offer	promise	teach	would like

Some verbs are usually followed by an object + bare infinitive (without *to*). These include: *let*   *make*

 Watch out!
- *Make* in the passive is followed by the full infinitive.
  ✓ *Michael **was made to apologise** by his mother.*
- Some verbs are followed by the full infinitive alone and some can be followed by an object + full infinitive.
  ✓ *He **wants me to tell** him a joke.*

-ing or infinitive

Some verbs can be followed by either -ing or the full infinitive.
*I started **liking / to like** James after he helped me with my problem.*

With some verbs, the meaning is the same or nearly the same.

These include:

begin	continue	hate	like	love	prefer	start

With some verbs, the meaning changes. These verbs include:

	+ -ing	+ full infinitive
remember	have a memory in your mind Do you **remember seeing** that comedy?	do something you are/were planning to Did you **remember to say** sorry to James?
forget	not be able to remember a past event I'd **forgotten hearing** that joke.	not do something you are/were planning to do Oh, no! I **forgot to invite** Shelly!
stop	stop an action **Stop crying** – it's not that bad.	interrupt an action to do something else I was on my way to see Maria and I **stopped to get** her some flowers.
try	do something to try and solve a problem Have you **tried talking** to her?	make an effort to do something I'm **trying to say** I'm sorry, but you won't listen!

A Circle the correct word or phrase.

1 My dad finally gave up **smoking / to smoke** at the age of forty-nine.
2 I really enjoyed **listening / to listen** to those MP3s you sent me. Thanks.
3 Can you afford **buying / to buy** so many presents?
4 You should practise **juggling / to juggle** every day or you'll never learn.
5 How did you learn **speaking / to speak** Japanese so well?
6 I thought we discussed **going / to go** to India and now you want to go to China!
7 We finally managed **finding / to find** my passport and then left for the airport.
8 I look forward to **seeing / see** you when I come next week!
9 It was very kind of Jack to offer **to baby-sit / baby-sitting** this weekend.
10 No! I refuse **waiting / to wait** a moment longer!

B If the verb in bold in each sentence is correct, put a tick (✓). If it is wrong, write the correct form of the verb (-*ing*, full or bare infinitive).

1 I hope to start **driving** as soon as I'm seventeen.   ....
2 Stop pretending **being** asleep. I saw you open your eyes!   ....
3 My mum suggested **to go** bowling, but I didn't think that was a good idea.   ....
4 Quentin will do anything to avoid **to walk** to school. He's so lazy!   ....
5 I'd really like **visiting** New York one day.   ....
6 Do you like watching TV or do you prefer **play** computer games?   ....
7 The weather seems **being** better. What about a picnic this weekend?   ....
8 I expect **to be** home at nine o'clock, so have dinner without me.   ....
9 Our head teacher makes us all **to wear** jackets – even in summer!   ....
10 Don't let the dog **sitting** on the sofa!   ....

C Choose the correct answer.

1 He tried to deny .... the money, but no one believed him.
   A take   B to take   C taking

2 I hope .... a pilot when I grow up.
   A become   B to become   C becoming

3 Mr Foster has decided .... , so we're going to have a party.
   A retire   B to retire   C retiring

4 Do you remember .... to Germany when you were two years old?
   A go   B to go   C going

5 You can make the dog .... to you by shouting 'come'.
   A come   B to come   C coming

6 There's no answer at the office. Let's try .... Roger's mobile.
   A call   B to call   C calling

D Complete each second sentence using the word given, so that it has a similar meaning to the first sentence. Write between two and five words.

1 They finally succeeded in escaping from the room. **managed**
They finally .... from the room.

2 I bought a new notebook on the way to school. **stopped**
On the way to school, I ....
.... a new notebook.

3 We're staying in Milan for a night before flying home. **planning**
We .... in Milan for a night before flying home.

4 I don't want to cook tonight – let's have a takeaway. **feel**
I don't .... tonight – let's have a takeaway.

5 I'm going to get annoyed if you don't stop making that noise! **continue**
If you ....
that noise, I'm going to get annoyed!

6 Could you ask Francis to come into my office, please? **mind**
Do you ....
Francis to come into my office, please?

E Complete using the correct form of the verbs in the box. Add any other words you need.

ask • be • bring • tidy • turn • win

1 Oh, no! I forgot .... my homework!

2 I remember .... on holiday.

3 I tried .... my room, but I couldn't find it!

4 Did you remember .... the tap off?

5 I'll never forget .... the lottery.

6 Try .... her to take it off!

F Circle the correct word or phrase.

Laughter is the best medicine!

The next time you're feeling ill, try (**1**) **watching / to watch** a comedy instead of just doing nothing. At least, that's what some doctors suggest (**2**) **doing / to do**. If you want (**3**) **getting / to get** better, there's nothing like laughter. First of all, an activity you enjoy (**4**) **doing / to do** takes your mind off your illness. Time seems (**5**) **passing / to pass** more quickly and you stop (**6**) **worrying / to worry** about how you feel.

Grammar

Both, either, neither, so, nor

both

Form

both + noun + *and* + noun
both + adjective + *and* + adjective

Use	Example
To emphasise that each of two things is true	**Both** Adam **and** Vicky said Colin was very kind. Simon is **both** rude **and** unkind.
To say the same thing about two things	My sister and I were **both** shocked by what you said. Jack and Jill **both** know lots of jokes.

Helpful hints

We sometimes use *of* with *both*. We always use this when it comes before a pronoun.

✓ I used to be good friends with Lisa and Mike, but I've had an argument with **both of** them.

either

Form

either + noun + *or* + noun
either + adjective + *or* + adjective
either + verb + *or* + verb

Use	Example
To talk about a choice between two things	I think I'll buy a Valentine's card with **either** a puppy **or** a kitten on it. I'm not sure how Tom will react – he'll be **either** happy **or** shocked! You can **either** tell him how you feel **or** hope he notices.

Helpful hints

We sometimes use *of* with *either*. We always use this when it comes before a pronoun.

✓ I really like Robert and Martin – I'll go out with **either of** them!

neither

Form

neither + noun + *nor* + noun
neither + adjective + *nor* + adjective
neither + verb + *nor* + verb

Use	Example
To emphasise that each of two negative things is true	I've got **neither** the time **nor** the energy to take up a new hobby at the moment. What you said to Lucy was **neither** true **nor** fair.

Helpful hints

We sometimes use *of* with *neither*. We always use this when it comes before a pronoun.

✓ **Neither of** us found Jason's joke funny.

so, nor

Form

so + do/have/be/modal + subject
nor + do/have/be/modal + subject

Use	Example
To add more information to a positive statement	Lisa is really unkind, and **so** is Angela. You're good at listening to people, and **so** am I.
To add more information to a negative statement	My brother hasn't been invited to the party, and **nor** has his friend. Tom wouldn't forgive Jenny if she told everyone his secret, and **nor** would I.

Helpful hints

You can also use these structures on their own in a conversation.

✓ 'I like Hannah's sense of humour.'
'So do I.'

✓ 'I don't find Mark funny.'
'Nor do I.'

A If the phrase in bold in each sentence is correct, put a tick (✓). If it is wrong, write the correct phrase.

1 I was surprised that **both and Mary and Oliver** were late for the meeting. ....
2 My mum said she was **both of** proud and nervous when I appeared in the school play. ....
3 Why don't **both of you** wait here while I go and see if Stuart is in? ....
4 **Both of books** have got pages missing. ....
5 Can I throw **and both** these magazines away, Derek? ....
6 When I won the race, I was **and exhausted and** happy. ....
7 Edward and Nigel **both of them** wanted to go on holiday, but they couldn't afford it. ....
8 Did **both you and** Sylvia grow up in the south of France? ....

B Join the two sentences using *either ... or*.

1 You can have ice cream for dessert. You can also have fruit.
You can ....
2 I'm considering studying maths at university and I'm considering studying physics.
I'm considering ....
3 I might play chess tonight. I might read a book.
I might ....
4 Perhaps John has forgotten about our meeting. Perhaps he's got lost.
John has ....
5 Some nights my dad cooks. Some nights he washes up.
Every night, my dad ....
6 We can order a pizza. We can order a Chinese takeaway.
We can ....
7 I might have lost the piece of paper with Dave's number on it. I might have thrown it away.
I've ....
8 You could write to your cousin. You could give her a call.
You could ....

C Circle the correct word.

1 Neither Alex **or / nor** Gareth knew that I'd seen them take the money.
2 I thought it was strange when both Ian **and / or** Anne left at the same time.
3 We could order either a chicken salad **and / or** a green salad.
4 Evi was neither embarrassed **and / nor** angry when Victoria told her to shut up.
5 Passengers can both watch recent movies **and / or** listen to great albums on many of our flights.
6 I have neither the money **or / nor** the time to go on holiday right now.

D Join the two sentences using *neither ... nor.*

1 Jim wasn't surprised by what I said. He wasn't shocked by what I said.
Jim ....
2 Carol doesn't have a car. She also doesn't have a motorbike.
Carol ....
3 Al doesn't play tennis. He doesn't watch it on TV.
Al ....
4 The manager wasn't very helpful. The receptionist wasn't very helpful.
Neither ....
5 Pauline couldn't read until she was seven. She also couldn't write until she was seven.
Pauline ....
6 I haven't been to Poland before. Boris hasn't been to Poland before.
Neither ....

E Write one word in each gap.

June: ... and so we went to see that new Tim Banks comedy last week.
Polly: Oh, so (**1**) .... we. What did you think? We weren't very impressed.
June: (**2**) .... were we. It wasn't very funny.
Polly: I didn't want to go, but Kevin likes that cinema. So (**3**) .... I, actually. We've
been there hundreds of times.
June: The one in town? Oh, so (**4**) .... we. The ice cream there is great, and
(**5**) .... is the popcorn! I could eat it all night.
Polly: Yes! So (**6**) .... I! I don't like their drinks, though.
June: Oh, no. (**7**) .... do I. Anyway, we're thinking of going to see what's on this evening.
Polly: (**8**) .... are Jack and I. Let's meet up. I don't finish work until seven.
June: (**9**) .... do I. I'll see what's on and give you a ring. I'm looking forward to it already.
Polly: So (**10**) .... I. Okay, speak to you later.

F Write what they say using the words given in the correct form. Add any other
words you need and use your imagination.

1 both / enjoy / run
....
2 have / either
....

3 neither / like
....
4 she / go home / so / I
....

Vocabulary
Laughing and crying

Topic vocabulary

see page 199 for definitions

amusing (adj)	embarrassing (n)	react (v)
annoy (v)	emotion (n)	regret (v, n)
attitude (n)	enthusiastic (adj)	ridiculous (adj)
bad-tempered (adj)	feeling (n)	romantic (adj)
behave (v)	glad (adj)	rude (adj)
bully (v, n)	hurt (v, adj)	sense of humour (n phr)
calm (adj)	miserable (adj)	shy (adj)
celebrate (v)	naughty (adj)	stress (n)
character (n)	noisy (adj)	tell a joke (v phr)
depressed (adj)	polite (adj)	upset (v, adj)

Phrasal verbs

calm down	become/make calmer
cheer up	become/make happier
come on	be quicker
go on	continue happening or doing sth
hang on	wait
run away (from)	escape by running
shut up	stop talking, stop making a noise
speak up	talk more loudly so sb can hear you

Prepositional phrases

at first
at least
at times
in secret
in spite of
in tears

Word formation

bore	boring, bored	**feel**	felt, feeling(s)
comedy	comedian	**happy**	unhappy, (un)happiness
emotion	emotional	**hate**	hatred
energy	energetic	**noise**	noisy, noisily
excite	excitement, exciting, excited	**sympathy**	sympathise, sympathetic

Word patterns

adjectives	ashamed of		sorry about/for
	embarrassed about		surprised at/by
	frightened of		tired of
	happy about/with	*verbs*	congratulate sb on
	nervous about		laugh at
	scared of	*nouns*	a joke about

Topic vocabulary

A Complete the crossword.

Across

5 My younger brother can be really .... and he often gets into trouble. (7)
9 Ben is really serious and I don't think he has a .... (5, 2, 6)
11 I passed my exam! Let's go out and .... (9)

Down

1 Harry isn't very good at volleyball, but he's really .... He puts a lot of energy into it. (12)
2 Jack is quite confident now, but he used to be really .... and didn't like meeting new people. (3)
3 You look .... with that hat on. Take it off! (10)
4 I didn't have enough money to pay for the meal! It was really .... (12)
6 I'm trying to work, and that loud music is beginning to .... me! (5)
7 The Petersons moved house because living on a main road was very .... (5)
8 You gave Jane a dozen roses on her birthday? Oh, that's so .... ! (8)
10 It was very .... of Nicky not to thank you for her present. (4)

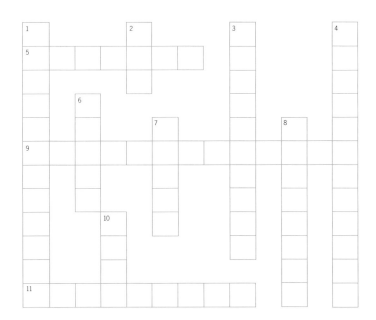

B Match to make dialogues.

1 'Alice seems a bit depressed.' ....   A 'Oh, yes. Nothing ever upsets her.'
2 'Mary is very polite.' ....   B 'I know. She always makes me laugh.'
3 'Diane seems like a calm person.' ....   C 'Well, maybe I should apologise, then.'
4 'Gemma seems a bit bad-tempered today.' ....   D 'Maybe she's had some bad news.'
5 'Megan is amusing.' ....   E 'I think it's because she's won some money.'
6 'Janice looks glad about something.' ....   F 'Yes. She's definitely angry about something.'
7 'Nina was hurt by what you said.' ....   G 'Yes, she always says 'thank you'.'

C Circle the correct word.

1 My grandfather had a very strong **bully / character** and everyone respected him.
2 Have you noticed that Caroline has started to **behave / regret** a bit strangely recently?
3 Dad has been under a lot of **feeling / stress** at work, so try not to annoy him.
4 Whenever I try to **react / tell** a joke, I can never remember it!
5 My **attitude / emotion** towards life is that you should enjoy yourself and not worry too much about the future.
6 After three weeks of rain and wintry weather, we were all starting to feel a bit **miserable / upset**.

Phrasal verbs

D Complete using a phrasal verb in the correct form to replace the words in bold.

1 You'll have to .... I can't hear what you're saying. **talk more loudly**
2 Let's try to .... Jimmy .... by having a surprise party! **make happier**
3 Could you please tell the children to .... ? I'm trying to sleep! **stop making a noise**
4 If you're upset, try taking long, deep breaths to .... **become calmer**
5 Roger first .... from home when he was only thirteen years old. **escaped by running**
6 After drying her eyes, Molly .... telling us why she was so unhappy. **continued**
7 And then the man said … oh, ... a second! I've forgotten the ending to the joke! **wait**
8 .... and get ready or we're going to be late. **be quicker**

Prepositional phrases

E Complete using the phrases in the box.

> at first • at least • at times • in secret • in spite of • in tears

1 We moved to a new town and I like it here a lot, but .... I miss my old friends.
2 Kate found Peter .... and asked him what was wrong.
3 I didn't like Ted .... , but after a while I realised that he was a really nice person.
4 Rob and Christine's parents didn't approve of their relationship, so they had to meet ....
5 I've told that joke .... ten times and everyone always laughs at it!
6 Alfie seemed quite happy, ... failing the exam.

Word formation

F Use the word given in capitals at the end of each line to form a word that fits in the gap in the same line.

Charlie Chaplin

During the First World War, at a time when there was lots of (**1**) .... **HATE**

in the world, one man did more than anyone else to spread (**2**) .... **HAPPY**

That man was the (**3**) .... , Charlie Chaplin. Audiences around the **COMEDY**

world watched his films and each new one caused a lot of (**4**) .... **EXCITE**

Chaplin created the character of the little tramp and people (**5**) .... **SYMPATHY**

with this poor man. Up until then, film comedies had been (**6**) .... **NOISE**

and very fast. Although they were fun and (**7**) .... , the audiences **ENERGY**

became (**8**) .... with seeing the same situations. Chaplin produced **BORE**

a different kind of comedy. It was slower and more (**9**) .... His **EMOTION**

films both made people laugh and touched their (**10**) .... Even **FEEL**

today, his films are enjoyed by many people of all ages.

Word patterns

G Write one word in each gap.

Hans: Hello?

Sam: Hans? It's Sam.

Hans: Oh, hi, Sam! How are you?

Sam: I was thinking about the exam next week. I'm a bit nervous (**1**) .... it, to be honest.

Hans: So am I. But you? I'm surprised (**2**) .... that. I thought you studied a lot.

Sam: I do. But my parents put so much pressure on me that I'm scared (**3**) .... failing.

Hans: I don't think you should be frightened (**4**) .... failure. Just you wait. In a month's time, I'll be congratulating you (**5**) .... passing with flying colours!

Sam: I guess you're right. I'm sure I'll look back and laugh (**6**) .... myself. Anyway, what have you been doing today?

Hans: Me? Oh, you know, a bit of revision …

H Each of the words in bold is wrong. Write the correct word.

1 Look at Jenny! She's either happy **from** her exam results, or she's won the lottery!   ....

2 Jodie and Marshall are splitting up because they're tired **from** arguing so much.   ....

3 There's no need to be embarrassed **in** crying. Everyone does it.   ....

4 Kathy was ashamed **with** herself for stealing the money.   ....

5 Debbie is sorry **on** what we said to you, and so am I.   ....

6 Have you heard the joke **for** the man with a frog on his head?   ....

163

A Use the word given in capitals at the end of each line to form a word that fits in the gap in the same line.

How are you?

People don't always show their true (**1**) .... Somebody with   **FEEL**

a big smile on their face might actually be (**2**) .... One of the   **HAPPY**

reasons for this is that our (**3**) .... life is very personal. Not   **EMOTION**

everyone is (**4**) .... to our problems, so we have to protect   **SYMPATHY**

ourselves. Some people, particularly teenagers, appear (**5**) ....   **BORE**

by everything, even things that they actually find (**6**) .... This   **EXCITE**

may be because they think it's not very cool to be (**7**) ....   **EXCITE**

about things, or to be too (**8**) .... and enthusiastic.   **ENERGY**

(1 mark per answer)

B Write one word in each gap.

9 Come .... , or we're going to be late!

10 Just hang .... one second while I find my mobile phone.

11 Peter is so noisy! I wish he would just shut .... !

12 It annoyed me that Jason just went .... talking when he could see I was crying.

13 Try to calm .... and tell us exactly what has happened.

14 You'll have to speak .... because I can't hear what you're saying.

15 Did you know that Sarah ran .... from home when she was fourteen?

16 I was feeling sad, but seeing my cousins really cheered me ....

(1 mark per answer)

C Complete each second sentence using the word given, so that it has a similar meaning to the first sentence. Write between two and five words.

17 I'm depressed because I don't have enough money to buy a new pair of jeans. **afford**
    I'm depressed because I .... a new pair of jeans.

18 Pam looked like she was happy, but I knew she was sad. **pretended**
    Pam .... happy, but I knew she was sad.

19 Toby made me feel bad about what I'd done. **made**
    I .... bad by Toby about what I'd done.

20 I made up my mind to apologise to Mary. **decided**
    I .... to Mary.

21 We finally succeeded in cheering Michael up. **managed**
    We finally .... Michael up.

22 I don't argue with friends if I can avoid it. **avoid**
    I .... with friends if I can.

23 I don't care what other people think any more. **stopped**
I've .... what other people think.

24 Claudia dislikes arguments and so do I. **both**
Claudia .... dislike arguments.

25 Martha isn't very kind and neither is Vicky. **nor**
Neither Martha .... very kind.

(2 marks per answer)

D Choose the correct answer.

26 I want .... me what's wrong, but she won't.
A Lisa to tell   C Lisa telling
B to tell Lisa   D Lisa to telling

27 Matt hates people who tell lies and .... do I.
A nor   C neither
B so   D both

28 I feel like .... out tonight. What about you?
A to go   C we go
B going   D to going

29 Jane and I listened to Guy's explanation, but .... of us believed him.
A both   C none
B either   D neither

30 Do you remember .... excited the first time you went on a train?
A to feel   C to feeling
B you feel   D feeling

31 You need to either ask Neil to apologise .... forget it.
A or   C either
B both   D nor

32 Be quiet and let me .... you how I feel!
A telling   C tell
B to tell   D to telling

33 I'm really looking forward .... you next week.
A to see   C seeing
B to seeing   D see

(1 mark per answer)

E Choose the correct answer.

34 I was quite nervous .... starting at a new school, but it was okay.
A on   C with
B about   D in

35 The newspapers congratulated the writer .... producing a very funny show.
A with   C on
B for   D of

36 Oscar and Pauline met .... secret to discuss the surprise party.
A in   C at
B with   D on

37 Are you scared .... snakes?
A with   C for
B on   D of

38 Isaac .... us a really funny joke, but I can't remember it!
A said   C spoke
B told   D mentioned

39 You should be ashamed .... yourself!
A with   C of
B on   D in

40 It's important to have a sense of .... or it's easy to get depressed.
A laughter   C comedy
B amusement   D humour

41 Marina was .... tears after the lesson, so I asked her what was wrong.
A to   C at
B on   D in

(1 mark per answer)

Total mark: ..../50

Grammar
Connectives

Time words and phrases

With some time words and phrases, we use the present simple to talk about the future. We don't use *will* or *be going to*.

after	I'll call you **after** we **solve** the problem.
as soon as	I'll call you **as soon as** we **solve** the problem.
before	It'll be a few days **before** we **find** the solution.
until / till	I won't call you **until** we **find** the solution.
when	It'll be great **when** we **find** the solution.
while	I'll be in the office **while** I **deal** with this problem.

 We can also put these time words and phrases at the beginning of the sentence.
✓ **As soon as** we solve the problem, I'll call you.

Although

We use the word *although* to express contrast.

Although + subject + verb, subject + verb	**Although** my homework was difficult, I finished it before bed.

 We can also put *although* in the middle of the sentence.
✓ I finished my homework before bed, **although** it was difficult.

In spite of / Despite

We use *in spite of* and *despite* to express contrast. They mean the same thing.

In spite of / despite + -ing form, subject + verb	**In spite of revising** for hours, I didn't do well in the test.
In spite of / despite + noun, subject + verb	**Despite my revision**, I didn't do well in the test.

 We can also put *in spite of* and *despite* in the middle of the sentence.
✓ I didn't do well in the test, **despite** revising for hours.

However

We use *however* to express contrast.

Subject + verb. *However*, subject + verb.	We believed that we would find a solution. **However**, we were wrong.

 We can also put *however* at the end of the second sentence.
✓ We believed that we would find a solution. We were wrong, **however**.

Unless

The word *unless* means *if … not* or *except if*.

✓ **Unless** you hurry up, we'll be late. (= **If** you do**n't** hurry up, we'll be late.)
For more information about conditional sentences, see Units 28 and 29.

A The phrases in bold are wrong. Write the correct phrases.

1 We'll have something to eat when we **will get** home. ....

2 I won't book the tickets until you **will tell** me to. ....

3 I'll come home as soon as the concert **will finish**. ....

4 After you **are going to do** this test, we'll play a game. ....

5 He'll send you a text message before he **is going to leave**. ....

6 Will you go to St. Petersburg while you **will be** in Russia? ....

B Complete using the correct form of the verbs in the box.

be • come • finish • have • leave • return • take

1 Call me as soon as you .... any news.

2 She'll have to do a lot of revision before she .... the exam.

3 Are they going to visit you while they .... in the UK?

4 Do you want to go to university after you .... school?

5 Claire won't have a break until she .... all her homework.

6 The lesson can't start till the teacher ....

C Circle the correct word.

1 **Although / Despite** the water was cold, we still went swimming.

2 **Although / Despite** my mum's got a mobile, she never uses it.

3 **Although / Despite** looking for hours, I couldn't find a nice pair of jeans.

4 **Although / Despite** taking a map, we still got lost.

5 I don't like sweets, **although / despite** I do like chocolate.

6 We enjoyed the picnic **although / despite** the bad weather.

D Choose the correct answer.

1 .... it was expensive, the CD wasn't very good quality.
   A Although   B In spite of   C However

2 .... being expensive, the CD wasn't very good quality.
   A Although   B In spite of   C However

3 .... the cost, the CD wasn't very good quality.
   A Although   B In spite of   C However

4 The CD was expensive. .... , it wasn't very good quality.
   A Although   B In spite of   C However

5 The CD was expensive. It wasn't very good quality, ...
   A although   B despite   C however

6 The CD wasn't very good quality, ... being expensive.
   A although   B despite   C however

7 The CD wasn't very good quality, ... it was expensive.
   A although   B in spite of   C however

8 The CD wasn't very good quality, ... the cost.
   A although   B despite   C however

167

E Complete each second sentence so that it has a similar meaning to the first sentence.

1 If the traffic isn't bad, she'll be here at six o'clock.
Unless the traffic .... bad, she'll be here at six o'clock.

2 If it doesn't rain, we'll go to the beach.
Unless it .... , we'll go to the beach.

3 If I'm not tired, I'll come to the party.
Unless .... tired, I'll come to the party.

4 If Mrs Potts doesn't come, we won't have a test.
Unless Mrs Potts .... , we won't have a test.

5 If Sarah comes, we'll watch the video.
We'll watch the video unless Sarah ....

6 If Mum gives me some pocket money, I'll buy a new pair of jeans.
I won't buy a new pair of jeans unless Mum .... some pocket money.

F Choose the correct answer.

> ### *One* door leads to freedom, but which one? *One* guard tells the truth, but which one? I can ask *one* question, but what?
>
> Here's a problem for you. Imagine you're in a prison cell with two doors. There's a guard at each door. You can ask one of the guards one question, and then you can go through one door. (**1**) .... you choose the right door, you can go free. (**2**) .... , if you choose the wrong door, you have to stay in prison forever!
> And it gets worse! (**3**) .... one of the guards always tells the truth, the other one always lies. And you don't know which one tells the truth.
> It's an impossible situation – isn't it? No, it's not. But (**4**) .... you're extremely careful, you might choose the wrong door. And you shouldn't choose a door (**5**) .... you're absolutely sure it's the door to freedom. And you'll only know it's the right door (**6**) .... you ask the right question. So – if you ever find yourself in that situation, here's what you do.
> Say to one of the guards, 'If I asked the other guard which door leads to freedom, what would he say?' (**7**) .... of not knowing if the guard always tells the truth or always lies, you'll always get an answer that will help you. (**8**) .... you get the answer, go through the *other* door. You'll be free!

1	A Unless	B If	C Before	D As soon
2	A In spite of	B Despite	C Although	D However
3	A However	B Although	C Despite	D In spite of
4	A unless	B when	C if	D as soon as
5	A until	B if	C when	D while
6	A unless	B as soon as	C before	D when
7	A Although	B However	C In spite	D Despite
8	A Before	B Although	C As soon as	D Unless

Grammar
The causative

Form

The causative

subject + *have* in the correct form + object + past participle

Use

To show that someone arranges for someone else to do something for them

Tense / modal	Example
present simple	*Mrs Taylor **has her car cleaned** once a month.*
present continuous	*She **is having the tyres checked** at the moment.*
present perfect simple	*She **has had the windscreen replaced**.*
present perfect continuous	This is not usually used in the causative.
past simple	*She **had the car filled up** with petrol yesterday.*
past continuous	*She **was having the car repaired** when I last saw her.*
past perfect simple	*She **had had the engine checked**.*
past perfect continuous	This is not usually used in the causative.
will and other modals	*She **will have a car alarm fitted** when she can afford it.* *She **would have air bags put in** but it's too expensive.*
be going to	*She **is going to have a new car radio installed**.*
-ing form	*She might stop **having the car cleaned** so often.*

Helpful hints

- Look at the differences between a normal active sentence and a sentence in the causative.

  Normal active sentence: <u>Someone</u> <u>cleans</u> <u>Mrs Taylor's</u> <u>car</u> **every week.**

  In the causative: <u>Mrs Taylor</u> <u>has</u> <u>her car</u> <u>cleaned</u> **every week.**

- We can also use *get* instead of *have*. *Get* is more informal than *have*.
  ✓ *I'm going to **have** my hair cut tomorrow.* (more formal)
  ✓ *I'm going to **get** my hair cut tomorrow.* (more informal)

- Just as with the passive (see Unit 11), we can use *by* to show who does the action.
  ✓ *We're having a family photo taken **by** a local photographer.*

 Watch out!

- With the causative, *have* always comes **before** the noun and the past participle always comes **after** the noun.

- When we ask questions using the causative, the past participle stays after the noun.
  ✓ *Did you have the furniture **delivered** yesterday?*
  ✗ *Did you have **delivered** the furniture yesterday?*

- Some verbs have irregular past participle forms. See page 182.

A Complete each second sentence using the correct form of *have* so that it has a similar meaning to the first sentence.

1 Let's arrange for someone to knock that wall down.
   Let's .... that wall knocked down.

2 We paid someone to deliver the furniture.
   We .... the furniture delivered.

3 I'm going to pay someone to paint this wall.
   I'm .... this wall painted.

4 Has anyone printed the invitations for you yet?
   .... you .... the invitations printed yet?

5 You should arrange for someone to fix your mobile.
   You should .... your mobile fixed.

6 When did you dye your hair?
   When .... you .... your hair dyed?

7 A vet is looking at Lucy at the moment.
   They .... Lucy looked at by a vet at the moment.

8 I haven't taken my suit to the dry-cleaner's yet.
   I .... my suit dry-cleaned yet.

B Complete using the correct form of the verbs in the box.

clean • cut • deliver • paint • repair • sign

1 I have my teeth .... by a dentist every six months.
2 My mum has just had her hair .... by a hairdresser in the town centre.
3 The car broke down, so we had it .... by a mechanic.
4 Let's get a pizza .... before the film starts.
5 Did you get your book .... by the author?
6 Garry is going to have his face .... blue for the party!

C If the phrase in bold is correct, put a tick (✓). If it is wrong, write the correct phrase.

1 Mandy **is having cut her hair** at the moment. ....
2 I might **have the house redecorated** next summer. ....
3 Our dog loves **having his back scratching**. ....
4 The receptionist **had the suitcases brought up** to the room. ....
5 We're not going to **have costumes make** for the play. ....
6 How often do you **have checked your teeth**? ....
7 You don't like **having your photo taken**, do you? ....

D Look at the pictures and complete the sentences. Use the causative.

1 Three times a day, a giraffe called Gloria does the washing-up for Mr Lazylion.
Three times a day, Mr Lazylion <u>has the washing-up done by a giraffe called Gloria</u> .

2 At the moment, Harry Hippo is cleaning Mr Lazylion's car.
At the moment, Mr Lazylion ....

3 Later, the Mice Sisters will cook Mr Lazylion's supper.
Later, Mr Lazylion ....

4 Ellie Phant has just brushed Mr Lazylion's hair.
Mr Lazylion ....

5 Mr Lazylion loves it when Marty Monkey tickles his feet.
Mr Lazylion loves ....

6 George is making a suit for Mr Lazylion.
Mr Lazylion ....

E Circle the correct word or phrase.

Mr Lazylion had a problem. The animals were refusing to help him.

Mr Lazylion had had things (**1**) **doing / done** for him (**2**) **by / with** the other animals for so long that he didn't know what to do. He (**3**) **hadn't had / hadn't** his meals prepared for him for two days now, and he was starting to get hungry.

So, he had some Chinese food (**4**) **delivering / delivered** – all the way from China. That filled him up, but it's not easy to (**5**) **get / be** food delivered in the jungle. He couldn't do that every day. What was he going to do?

He felt very sad. He really wanted to have (**6**) **brushed his hair / his hair brushed** by Ellie and his feet (**7**) **tickling / tickled** by Marty, but they just said 'No'.

There was only one solution, and Mr Lazylion didn't like it at all. He would have to start doing things for himself.

Unit 42 — Vocabulary
Problems and solutions

see page 200 for definitions

Topic vocabulary

accident (n)	encourage (v)	purpose (n)
assume (v)	get rid of (v phr)	refuse (v)
cause (v, n)	gossip (v, n)	result (v, n)
claim (v)	ideal (adj)	rumour (n)
complain (v)	insult (v, n)	sensible (adj)
convince (v)	investigate (v)	serious (adj)
criticise (v)	negative (adj)	spare (adj)
deny (v)	positive (adj)	theory (n)
discussion (n)	praise (v, n)	thought (n)
doubt (v, n)	pretend (v)	warn (v)

Phrasal verbs

hang up	put clothes in a wardrobe, etc
pick up	lift something from the floor, a table, etc
put back	return something to where it was
run out (of)	not have any left
share out	give a part of sth to a group of people
sort out	solve a problem
watch out	be careful
work out	find the solution to a problem, etc

Prepositional phrases

by accident/mistake
in a mess
in danger (of)
in my view
in trouble
under pressure

Word formation

advice	advise, adviser	**prefer**	preference, preferable
confuse	confused, confusion	**recommend**	recommendation
except	exception	**refuse**	refusal
help	(un)helpful, helpless	**solve**	solution
luck	(un)lucky, (un)luckily	**suggest**	suggestion

Word patterns

adjectives	sure about/of		happen to
verbs	advise against		hide sth from sb
	agree (with sb) about		insist on
	approve of		rely on
	believe in	*nouns*	an advantage of
	deal with		a solution to

Topic vocabulary

A Match the statements with the verbs in the box.

complain • criticise • deny • encourage • gossip • insult • praise • refuse • warn

1 'I didn't take your jacket!'   ....
2 'Well done! You did that really well.'   ....
3 'No, I'm not going to help you clean your room.'   ....
4 'Be careful or you'll cut yourself.'   ....
5 'Mum, that's not fair!'   ....
6 'I thought his singing was awful!'   ....
7 'Did you hear what Becca told Lizzy about Robert?'   ....
8 'Go on! You can do it! I know you can!'   ....
9 'You stupid lazy idiot!'   ....

B Circle the correct word.

1 Don't **pretend / claim** to be asleep. I know you're awake really!
2 I've been trying to **doubt / convince** Kathy that Jacob isn't a liar, but she doesn't believe me.
3 Police are investigating the **cause / purpose** of the accident.
4 I've just had a **thought / theory**. Why don't we have the party at your place?
5 There's a **discussion / rumour** going round the school that Mrs Tibbs is leaving at the end of term. I wonder if it's true.
6 I'm going to **get / become** rid of these shoes. They're really old.
7 The **result / accident** of the experiment wasn't what I'd expected at all.
8 The detective **assumed / investigated** that the burglar had got in through an open window.

C Complete using a word formed from the letters given.

1 I think we should all go in the same car and save petrol. That's the most .... idea. **B L E S S I N E**
2 Angie has got a .... problem with her motorbike. It's going to take at least a week to fix. **R E S S I U O**
3 I think this is the .... place to camp – it's dry and flat and has a stream to get water from. **L A D E I**
4 Don't be so .... ! I'm sure everything will be fine. **G E N T A V I E**
5 I had the .... tyre on the car pumped up at the garage. **R A S P E**
6 Your teachers all said lots of .... things about you. Well done! **S E P T I O I V**

Phrasal verbs

D Match the pictures with the statements.

A Watch out!
B Let's share this out.
C I'll hang this up.
D I'd better pick this up.
E I can't work this out.

F I think we've run out.
G I'll just put this back.
H Thanks for sorting that out.

Prepositional phrases

E Write one word in each gap.

1 If Mum and Dad find out, you'll be .... big trouble!
2 I bought the wrong CD .... mistake.
3 .... my view, nobody has really seen a ghost.
4 Sue is .... quite a lot of pressure at work at the moment.
5 You're .... danger of making a terrible mistake!
6 Your room is .... a terrible mess. Go and tidy it at once!

Word formation

F   Use the word given in capitals to form a word that fits in the gap.

Personal shoppers

Do you get (**1**) .... (**CONFUSE**) about what to buy when you go clothes shopping? Do you feel (**2**) .... (**HELP**) when you have to choose between two pairs of jeans? Are you fed up with rude and (**3**) .... (**HELP**) sales assistants? Has the (**4**) .... (**REFUSE**) of your credit card caused you embarrassment? Everyone, without (**5**) .... (**EXCEPT**), finds shopping stressful at times.

But you don't need to worry any more! (**6**) .... (**LUCK**), now there's a (**7**) .... (**SOLVE**). You can have your own personal shopper. Personal shoppers work in several different ways. If you want someone to come shopping with you, they'll do that. They'll (**8**) .... (**ADVICE**) you about the best bargains and make (**9**) .... (**SUGGEST**) and (**10**) .... (**RECOMMEND**) about what to buy. However, many people who have personal shoppers find it (**11**) .... (**PREFER**) not to go to the shops at all. They let their personal shopper do all the shopping for them. They trust their personal shopper to know their (**12**) .... (**PREFER**) and to make the right decisions.

Word patterns

G   Match to make sentences.

1 Jim doesn't believe   ....   A about that at all.
2 I completely agree   ....   B on Craig.
3 I'm not sure   ....   C in ghosts.
4 Dominic doesn't approve   ....   D to Tara.
5 I've got no idea what happened ....   E of people smoking.
6 You can always rely   ....   F with you.

H   Choose the correct answer.

1 What's the best way to deal .... a disobedient child?
   A for   B with   C about

2 I'd definitely advise .... getting a snake for a pet.
   A against   B from   C without

3 I don't know what the solution .... this problem is.
   A about   B for   C to

4 Our teacher insists .... us waiting in silence outside the class before the lesson.
   A for   B on   C about

5 The advantage .... having brothers and sisters is that you get more birthday presents!
   A of   B from   C for

6 You can't hide the truth .... me!
   A across   B against   C from

A   Complete using the correct form of the verbs in the box.

complain • convince • criticise • deny • doubt • praise • refuse • warn

1   It took a long time to .... Lee that poetry isn't boring.
2   My dad has just .... to increase my pocket money again. It's not fair!
3   Stop .... about how much work you have and just get on with it!
4   I .... it'll be warm enough to go to the beach tomorrow.
5   We all .... you not to trust Jerry, but you didn't listen!
6   Paul Fletcher, do you .... stealing €1,000 from Leicester Stores on 24th September?
7   You should always .... a puppy when it does something good.
8   I wish Alex wouldn't .... me all the time. It makes me feel useless.

(1 mark per answer)

B   Write one word in each gap.

9   .... my view, every problem has a solution.
10   Your room is .... a terrible mess! Tidy it up!
11   My mum is .... a lot of pressure at work at the moment.
12   Oh no! Are you .... trouble with the police again?
13   We weren't .... any real danger, I promise!
14   I got on the wrong train .... mistake!

(1 mark per answer)

C   Complete each second sentence using the word given, so that it has a similar meaning to the first sentence. Write between two and five words.

15   Let's throw these old clothes away. **rid**
     Let's .... these old clothes.

16   I don't think people should drive fast through the town centre. **approve**
     I don't .... fast through the town centre.

17   Do you think that ghosts exist? **believe**
     Do you .... ghosts?

18   You should solve that problem as quickly as you can. **sort**
     You should .... as quickly as you can.

19   I'm afraid we haven't got any sandwiches left. **run**
     I'm afraid .... sandwiches.

20   How should teachers handle badly-behaved students? **deal**
     How should teachers .... badly-behaved students?

21   If you're not careful, you'll fall! **watch**
     If you .... , you'll fall!

22   I wouldn't buy that computer if I were you. **advise**
     I would .... that computer.

176

23 I can't understand why Jake would have said that. **work**

I can't .... why Jake would have said that.

24 You can always trust Souli. **rely**

You can always .... Souli.

(2 marks per answer)

D Choose the correct answer.

25 I'll buy a ticket as soon as I .... my pocket money.
A will get   C get
B would get   D got

26 The food was great, ... it was very expensive.
A although   C however
B despite   D in spite

27 I'll get my dad a book for his birthday .... I find something better.
A if   C although
B until   D unless

28 I'll send you a text message .... I'm on the bus.
A before   C until
B while   D as soon

29 We're going to have .... down.
A knocked that wall   C knocking that wall
B that wall knocking   D that wall knocked

30 We decided to go for a walk .... of the rain.
A although   C however
B despite   D in spite

31 I .... the windows cleaned about twice a year.
A get   C am
B put   D do

32 Most students did very well. .... , a few students did very badly.
A Although   C However
B Despite   D In spite of

(1 mark per answer)

E Use the word given in capitals at the end of each line to form a word that fits in the gap in the same line.

Careers advice

Do you know what job or career you want to do when you leave school? Maybe you know exactly what you want to do. If so, you're (**33**) .... ! For   **LUCK**

most teenagers, thinking about future jobs can lead to (**34**) ....   **CONFUSE**

That's what careers (**35**) .... are for. They're people who ask you   **ADVICE**

questions about your (**36**) .... and help you with your choices.   **PREFER**

They can make (**37**) .... about jobs which might suit you, and can   **SUGGEST**

also make (**38**) .... about where to find more information. They're   **RECOMMEND**

not there to tell you what to do, they're just there to be (**39**) ....   **HELP**

Choosing the right career can be a problem, but you don't need to search for the

(**40**) .... on your own!   **SOLVE**

(1 mark per answer)

Total mark: ..../50

Progress Test 2

A Choose the correct answer.

1 I'm not old enough to .... in this election.
  A commit   B protest   C vote   D admit

2 Is it really your .... to be a professional footballer?
  A application   B profession   C ambition   D contract

3 What we eat .... how much energy we have during the day.
  A balances   B contains   C benefits   D affects

4 These jeans are too .... I think I need a bigger pair.
  A tight   B loose   C rough   D smooth

5 Britain's .... is fairly mild – it's never very hot or very cold.
  A forecast   B climate   C environment   D heatwave

6 I fell over in front of everyone at lunch. It was so .... !
  A embarrassing   B naughty   C romantic   D depressed

7 I asked Jim to help me with the project, but he ....
  A doubted   B denied   C refused   D warned

8 Jeanne, ... us that joke about the guy who knocks on the door.
  A say   B speak   C make   D tell

(1 mark per answer)

B Write one word in each gap.

A prisoner's view

Although I hate (**9**) .... in prison, I know it's my own fault. If I hadn't committed several burglaries, I wouldn't (**10**) .... been sent here to prison. I really (**11**) .... I hadn't done the things I did. But you can't change the past, (**12**) .... you? So I'm here.

My cell is tiny – it's not much bigger (**13**) .... a cupboard! It's (**14**) .... small that I can touch the door and the window at the same time! I share it with one other prisoner, called Dave. Both (**15**) .... us get on well, which is good.

My family live a long way from here, so none of them can visit me very often, but they write (**16**) .... me every week. I always look forward to their letters.

There's a chance I'll be allowed out later this year. If I get out, I (**17**) .... never commit another crime. That's for sure! It'll be (**18**) .... a great feeling to be free again!

(1 mark per answer)

C Complete each second sentence using the word given, so that it has a similar meaning to the first sentence. Write between two and five words.

19 Henry was three when he first performed in public. **age**
Henry first performed in public .... three.

20 Why don't you start a youth club? **set**
You should .... a youth club.

21 How long did it take you to recover from your illness? **over**
How long did it take you to .... your illness?

22 Are you helping to organise the celebrations? **involved**
Are you .... the celebrations?

23 We don't have enough time. **short**
We .... time.

24 She carried on playing despite her injury. **spite**
She carried on playing .... her injury.

25 They haven't got any bread at the supermarket. **run**
They .... bread at the supermarket.

26 It's illegal to take a gun onto a plane in most countries. **against**
Taking a gun onto a plane .... in most countries.

27 We had to cancel the meeting because Paul was ill. **called**
The meeting had to .... because Paul was ill.

28 Spiders don't frighten me! **afraid**
I .... spiders!

(2 marks per answer)

D Use the word given in capitals at the end of each line to form a word that fits in the gap in the same line.

A new painter

Were you (**29**) .... enough to be invited to the opening of the **LUCK**
Winchester Art Gallery last Thursday evening? I was, and therefore had
the pleasure of seeing the new (**30**) .... of Daniella Warner's **EXHIBIT**
paintings. Daniella Warner is not (**31**) .... – yet – but she's **FAME**
clearly an (**32**) .... who has a very bright future. **ART**
All Daniella Warner's paintings – without (**33**) .... – are **EXCEPT**
(**34**) .... She very often paints areas of outstanding **IMAGINE**
(**35**) .... beauty, such as lakes and forests, but she makes **NATURE**
them (**36**) .... , lively places. Her paintings often focus on **EXCITE**
the subjects of (**37**) .... and peace. It's certainly not easy to **FREE**
be a (**38**) .... artist these days, but if anyone deserves it, **SUCCESS**
Daniella Warner does. Daniella Warner's paintings will be on show at the Winchester
Art Gallery until Saturday 25th March.

(1 mark per answer)

E Write one word in each gap.

39 You shouldn't criticise people .... the way they look.

40 I'm really fed up .... studying all the time!

41 My brother is allergic .... milk.

42 Would you describe her .... a shy person?

43 Nothing is going to prevent me .... coming to the concert!

44 Congratulations .... passing your driving test!

45 I don't approve .... young children wearing earrings.

46 Have you ever been accused .... doing something you didn't do?

47 I think I might apply .... that job at the local shop.

48 This song reminds me .... our holiday last summer.

(1 mark per answer)

F Match to make sentences.

49 What's going .... A up this morning?

50 What time did you get .... B off your jacket?

51 When are you going to give me .... C out or is it still burning?

52 Has this milk gone .... D on here?

53 Why don't you take .... E into the building?

54 Has the fire gone .... F back my book?

55 How did the burglars break .... G up until the film finishes?

56 Mum, can I stay .... H off or is it okay?

(1 mark per answer)

G One word in each sentence is in the wrong form. Write the correct form.

57 I think we're all in agree about this. ....

58 Carl is so boss – he's always telling us what to do. ....

59 My dad is a very good cooker. ....

60 Mozart is my favourite compose. ....

61 Motorbikes cause a lot of noise pollute. ....

62 Thank you for being so sympathy. ....

63 He's one of the funniest comedies I've ever seen. ....

64 Could I make a suggest? ....

65 That shop assist wasn't very helpful, was he? ....

66 That's a very sense idea. ....

(1 mark per answer)

H Complete using the words in the box.

diet • distance • fashion • least • mistake • strike • tears • touch

67 Do you think I need to go on a .... ?

68 John was in .... earlier. Do you know why he was crying?

69 Wearing clothes that are in .... isn't very important to me.

70 We could just see Doug a long way ahead in the ....

71 I failed the history test, but at .... I passed the geography test.

72 I did the wrong exercise by ....

73 Are you still in .... with your friends from your old school?

74 The bus drivers are on .... today, so there are no buses.

(1 mark per answer)

I Write one word in each gap.

75 I wonder who's going to move .... next door.

76 We'll have to put the match .... until next Saturday.

77 I'm going to cut .... on the amount of coffee I drink.

78 We filled the car .... with petrol before leaving.

79 Excuse me, can I try these shoes .... , please?

80 I'm going to put that poster .... on my bedroom wall.

81 Hang .... ! I'm not quite ready yet.

82 Watch .... ! There's a car coming!

(1 mark per answer)

J Choose the correct answer.

83 I'm going to have a part in the play, ... I?
A am not   B don't   C haven't   D aren't

84 Sophie .... have been ill today because she didn't come to school.
A can't   B should   C must   D would

85 I'm .... to go on holiday on my own! I'm nineteen!
A so old   B such an old   C too old   D old enough

86 My MP3 player is better .... yours!
A from   B to   C than   D that

87 If you .... helped me, I would never have finished on time.
A hadn't   B haven't   C don't   D wouldn't

88 Carol asked me if you .... the film.
A already see   B had already seen   C already saw   D has already seen

89 I wish you .... be quiet for five minutes!
A must   B would   C can   D should

90 We were made .... up all the mess we'd made.
A clear   B to clear   C clearing   D cleared

(1 mark per answer)

Total mark: ..../100

Irregular present forms

be

I	am ('m)	am not ('m not)
you/we/they	are ('re)	are not (aren't)
he/she/it	is ('s)	is not (isn't)

have

I/you/we/they	have ('ve)	have not (haven't)
he/she/it	has ('s)	has not (hasn't)

Verbs ending in -o

do

I/you/we/they	do	do not (don't)
he/she/it	do**es**	does not (doesn't)

go

I/you/we/they	go	don't go
he/she/it	go**es**	doesn't go

Verbs ending in consonant + -y

fly

I/you/we/they	fly	don't fly
he/she/it	fl**ies**	doesn't fly

Verbs ending in -s, -z, -ch, -sh, -x

pass

I/you/we/they	pass	don't pass
he/she/it	pass**es**	doesn't pass

buzz

I/you/we/they	buzz	don't buzz
he/she/it	buzz**es**	doesn't buzz

watch

I/you/we/they	watch	don't watch
he/she/it	watch**es**	doesn't watch

wish

I/you/we/they	wish	don't wish
he/she/it	wish**es**	doesn't wish

mix

I/you/we/they	mix	don't mix
he/she/it	mix**es**	doesn't mix

Irregular verbs

Bare infinitive	Past simple	Past participle	Bare infinitive	Past simple	Past participle
be	was, were	been	build	built	built
beat	beat	beaten	burn	burnt / burned	burnt / burned
become	became	become	buy	bought	bought
begin	began	begun	catch	caught	caught
bite	bit	bitten	choose	chose	chosen
blow	blew	blown	come	came	come
break	broke	broken	cost	cost	cost
bring	brought	brought	cut	cut	cut

Bare infinitive	Past simple	Past participle	Bare infinitive	Past simple	Past participle
deal	dealt	dealt	pay	paid	paid
dig	dug	dug	put	put	put
do	did	done	read	read	read
draw	drew	drawn	ride	rode	ridden
dream	dreamt / dreamed	dreamt / dreamed	ring	rang	rung
drink	drank	drunk	rise	rose	risen
drive	drove	driven	run	ran	run
eat	ate	eaten	say	said	said
fall	fell	fallen	see	saw	seen
feed	fed	fed	sell	sold	sold
feel	felt	felt	send	sent	sent
fight	fought	fought	set	set	set
find	found	found	shake	shook	shaken
fly	flew	flown	shine	shone	shone
forget	forgot	forgotten	shoot	shot	shot
forgive	forgave	forgiven	show	showed	shown
freeze	froze	frozen	shut	shut	shut
get	got	got / gotten	sing	sang	sung
give	gave	given	sit	sat	sat
go	went	gone / been	sleep	slept	slept
grow	grew	grown	smell	smelt / smelled	smelt / smelled
have	had	had	speak	spoke	spoken
hear	heard	heard	spend	spent	spent
hide	hid	hidden	spill	spilt / spilled	spilt / spilled
hit	hit	hit	stand	stood	stood
hold	held	held	steal	stole	stolen
hurt	hurt	hurt	sting	stung	stung
keep	kept	kept	swim	swam	swum
know	knew	known	take	took	taken
lead	led	led	teach	taught	taught
learn	learnt / learned	learnt / learned	tear	tore	torn
leave	left	left	tell	told	told
lend	lent	lent	think	thought	thought
let	let	let	throw	threw	thrown
lie	lay	lain	understand	understood	understood
light	lit	lit	wake	woke	woken
lose	lost	lost	wear	wore	worn
make	made	made	win	won	won
mean	meant	meant	write	wrote	written
meet	met	met			

Topic vocabulary

beat (v)	to defeat someone in a game, competition, election, or battle	England needed to beat Germany to get to the final.
board game (n phr)	any game in which you move objects around on a special board	I think that Trivial Pursuit is my favourite board game.
captain (n)	the person who is in charge of a team or organisation	She was captain of the Olympic swimming team.
challenge (v)	to invite someone to compete or fight	The girls challenged the boys to a cricket match.
challenge (n)	something that needs a lot of skill, energy, and determination to deal with or achieve	I felt I needed a new challenge at work.
champion (n)	someone who has won an important competition, especially in sport	He finally became the world heavyweight boxing champion.
cheat (v)	to behave dishonestly, or to not obey rules	Kids have always found ways of cheating in school exams.
classical music (n phr)	serious music that is played on instruments such as the piano and the violin	I love classical music, like Beethoven.
club (n)	an organisation for people who take part in a particular activity, or the building that they use	Why don't you join a chess club?
coach (n)	someone who trains a sports player or team	After playing for ten years, Barry became a baseball coach.
competition (n)	an organised event in which people try to win prizes by being better than other people	He'd entered a competition in the local newspaper.
concert (n)	an event at which an orchestra, band, or musician plays or sings in front of an audience	Did you hear that the Rolling Stones did a concert in China?
defeat (v)	to win against someone	France defeated Italy 3–1.
defeat (n)	failure to win a competition or to succeed in doing something	England suffered a 2–0 defeat.
entertaining (adj)	enjoyable or interesting	I saw a really entertaining programme on TV last night.
folk music (n phr)	traditional music from a particular country or region, or music played in a traditional style	What I like about folk music is the sound of the guitar.
group (n)	a small set of musicians who play pop music	My brother has got his own group and they play in our local area.
gym (n)	a room or club with equipment for doing physical exercises	I'm thinking of joining a gym.
have fun (v phr)	get enjoyment from an activity that is not important or serious	We haven't had such fun for years.
interest (v)	to make someone want to know about or take part in something	Photography has always interested me.
interest (n)	an activity that you enjoy doing when you are not working	Tell us about your interests and hobbies.
member (n)	someone who belongs to a group or an organisation: a trade union member	Are you a member of the golf club?
opponent (n)	someone who is competing against you	His opponent received only 36 per cent of the vote.
organise (v)	to prepare or arrange an activity or event	Who's organising the conference?
pleasure (n)	a feeling of happiness, enjoyment, or satisfaction	He smiled with pleasure when she walked in.
referee (n)	someone whose job is to make sure that players in a game obey the rules	The referee blew his whistle and the game began.

rhythm (n)	a regular pattern of sounds in music	This song has got a really great rhythm.
risk (v)	to do something although you know that something that is bad could happen as a result	He risked a lot of money on the company.
risk (n)	the possibility that something unpleasant or dangerous might happen	There's a serious risk of an accident on this road.
score (v)	to get a point in a game or sport	No one scored in the first half.
score (n)	the number of points that someone gains in a game or test	The final score was 4–3 to United.
support (v)	to like a particular sports team and always want them to win	I support West Ham – who do you support?
support (n)	help that you give to a particular idea, organisation, etc	I hope all the students will support our plans to rebuild the school.
team (n)	a group of people who play a sport or game against another group	Are you in the hockey team this year?
train (v)	to practise a sport regularly before a match or competition	The players train five days a week.
video game (n phr)	a game in which players use electronic controls to move images on a television or computer screen	I don't like video games – I'd rather play outside.

Unit 6

achieve (v)	to succeed in doing or having something	We've achieved what we wanted to do.
brain (n)	the organ inside your head that allows you to think and feel, and controls your body	The illness had affected his brain.
clever (adj)	good at learning or understanding things	I'd like to be a doctor, but I'm not clever enough.
concentrate (v)	to give all your attention to the thing that you are doing	Just concentrate on your work.
consider (v)	to think about something carefully before you make a decision	At one time I seriously considered leaving.
course (n)	a series of lessons in an academic subject or a practical skill	You could do a language course abroad.
degree (n)	a course of study at a university, or the qualification that you get after completing the course	She's doing a degree at Exeter University.
experience (v)	if you experience a problem or situation, you have that problem or are in that situation	I'd love to experience being in a submarine.
experience (n)	knowledge and skill that you get by doing a particular job or activity	Do you have any previous experience with children?
expert (n)	someone who has a particular skill or knows a lot about a particular subject	She's a computer expert.
expert (adj)	having special skills in or knowledge about something	He's an expert painter.
fail (v)	to be unsuccessful in something	I failed the maths exam.
guess (v)	to say or decide what you think is true, without being certain about it	Whoever guesses correctly will win two tickets to the show.
guess (n)	an occasion when you say what you think is true without being certain	Have a guess and then check it on your calculator.
hesitate (v)	to pause before doing something because you are nervous or not certain about it	He hesitated for a moment and then knocked on the door.
instruction (n)	a statement of something that must be done, or an explanation of how to do or use something	I tried to follow her instructions, but I got confused.
make progress (v phr)	to develop or improve	My guitar teacher says I'm making a lot of progress.
make sure (v phr)	to check something, so that you can be sure about it	I just wanted to make sure you knew where to go.

mark (v)	to judge the quality of a student's work and write a mark on it	I spent the evening marking essays.
mark (n)	a score or grade that you are given for school work or for how you perform in a competition	What mark did you get for your essay?
mental (adj)	existing in the mind, or relating to the mind	Scientists know a lot about the mental development of children.
pass (v)	to be successful in an examination or test	She passed her driving test.
qualification (n)	something such as a degree or a diploma that you get when you successfully finish a course of study	Simon left school with no qualifications.
remind (v)	to help someone to remember something	Remind Jenny to bring my CD when she comes.
report (n)	a spoken or written description of a particular subject, situation, or event	We have to write a short report on the conference.
revise (v)	to study your notes and information again in order to prepare for an examination	I've got a test tomorrow, so I have to revise tonight.
search (v)	to try to find something or someone by looking carefully	After three days searching, I gave up.
search (n)	an attempt to find something	The police have carried out an extensive search of the area.
skill (n)	the ability to do something well, usually as a result of experience and training	Being a doctor demands a lot of skill.
smart (adj)	intelligent	Sophie is a very smart student.
subject (n)	something that you learn or teach at a school, for example English, mathematics, or biology	What's your favourite subject?
take an exam (v phr)	to have an important test	I'm taking the exam in June.
talented (adj)	very good at something	She's a talented singer.
term (n)	one of the periods of time that the year is divided into for students	How many weeks is it till the end of term?
wonder (v)	to think about something because you want to know more facts	I was wondering about the best place for a holiday.

Unit 9

abroad (adv)	in or to a foreign country	We try to go abroad at least once a year.
accommodation (n)	a place for someone to stay, live, or work in	The hotel provides accommodation for up to 100 people.
book (v)	to arrange to have or use something at a particular time in the future	Shall I book a room for you?
break (n)	a period of time when you are not working and can rest or enjoy yourself	OK, let's take a fifteen-minute break.
cancel (v)	to say that something that has been arranged will not now happen	The 4.05 train has been cancelled.
catch (v)	to get on a train, bus, plane, or boat that is travelling somewhere	I caught the next train to London.
coach (n)	a comfortable bus for long journeys	Let's take the coach to Brighton this weekend.
convenient (adj)	easy for you to do, or suitable for your needs	Travelling underground is fast and convenient.
crash (v)	if a vehicle crashes, or if someone crashes it, it hits something	Three people were killed when their car crashed into a tree.
crash (n)	an accident that happens when a vehicle hits something	He was seriously injured in a car crash.
crowded (adj)	containing a lot of people or things	Was the pool crowded?
cruise (n)	a journey on a ship for pleasure, often visiting a series of places	I would love to go on a cruise round the Mediterranean.

delay (v)	to do something later than is planned or expected	They delayed the decision for as long as possible.
delay (n)	a situation in which something happens later or more slowly than you expected	After a long delay, the plane finally took off.
destination (n)	the place where someone or something is going	After eight hours on the road, we finally reached our destination.
ferry (n)	a boat that makes short regular journeys between two or more places	They took the ferry to Dover.
flight (n)	a journey in a plane	The flight from New York to Heathrow took about five hours.
foreign (adj)	from another country, or in another country	Do you speak any foreign languages?
harbour (n)	an area of water next to the land where boats can stop	There were about twenty boats in the harbour.
journey (n)	an occasion when you travel from one place to another, especially over a long distance	We had a long journey ahead of us.
luggage (n)	bags and suitcases that you take on a journey	We have to get our luggage when we get off the plane.
nearby (adj)	a nearby place is not far away	Let's go to a nearby restaurant, shall we?
nearby (adv)	not far from where you are	My cousin lives nearby.
pack (v)	to put your things into a bag, case, or box so that you can take or send them somewhere	He was still packing his suitcase when the taxi came.
passport (n)	an official document that contains your photograph and shows which country you are a citizen of	Bill has a Canadian passport.
platform (n)	an area next to a railway track where passengers get onto and off trains	The train to Brussels will depart from platform 3.
public transport (n phr)	the system that is used for travelling or for moving goods from one place to another	Auckland's public transport system is excellent.
reach (v)	to arrive somewhere	We hoped to reach the camp before dark.
resort (n)	a place where people go for a holiday	We stayed in a lovely ski resort.
souvenir (n)	something that you buy to remind you of a place that you visited on holiday or of a special event	This T-shirt with Big Ben on it will make a great souvenir.
traffic (n)	the vehicles that are travelling in an area at a particular time	At that time of night, there was no traffic on the roads.
trip (n)	an occasion when you go somewhere and come back again	The whole family went on a trip to Florida.
vehicle (n)	a machine that you travel in or on, especially one with an engine that travels on roads, for example a car, bus, etc	Four vehicles were involved in the accident.

Unit 12

apologise (v)	to tell someone that you are sorry for doing something wrong	You should apologise to your brother.
boyfriend (n)	a man or boy that you are having a romantic relationship with	She's got a new boyfriend.
close (adj)	connected by shared feelings such as love and respect	My brother and I are very close.
confident (adj)	certain about your abilities and not nervous or frightened	I was starting to feel more confident about the exam.
cool (adj)	a cool person is one that you like or admire, or is very fashionable	Jake is really cool!
couple (n)	two people who are married to each other, or who have a romantic relationship with each other	Bill and Melissa make a great couple.

decorate (v)	to put new paint or paper on the walls of a room	We decorated the kitchen last weekend.
defend (v)	to say things to support someone or something	We will defend their right to free speech.
divorced (adj)	no longer married because your marriage has been legally ended	After they got divorced, she never remarried.
flat (n)	a set of rooms for living in, usually on one floor of a large building	The family live in a fourth-floor flat.
generous (adj)	giving people more of your time or money than is usual or expected	She is a warm and generous human being.
girlfriend (n)	a girl or woman that you are having a romantic relationship with	Have you got a girlfriend?
grateful (adj)	the feeling that you want to thank someone because they have given you something or done something for you	Thanks for coming with me. I'm really grateful.
guest (n)	someone that you have invited to your home or your party	He was a guest at our wedding.
independent (adj)	not depending on other people	Michelle is young, independent and confident.
introduce (v)	to tell someone another person's name when they meet for the first time	I'd like to introduce you to my friend Martin.
loving (adj)	feeling or showing love	Cats are really loving animals.
loyal (adj)	someone who is loyal continues to support a person or organisation, or idea in difficult times	These are people who have remained loyal to the company for years.
mood (n)	the way that someone is feeling, or the way that a group of people is feeling at a particular time	I had never seen Ann in such a good mood before.
neighbourhood (n)	a particular area of a town	We live in a quiet neighbourhood.
ordinary (adj)	normal or average, and not unusual or special	It was just an ordinary Saturday morning.
patient (adj)	someone who is patient is able to wait for a long time or deal with a difficult situation without becoming angry or upset	Susan is very patient with the children.
private (adj)	a private person does not talk to other people about their personal life or feelings	Damian is a very private person.
recognise (v)	to know someone or something because you have seen, heard, or met them before	I thought I recognised your voice!
relation (n)	a member of your family	All our relations are coming to the party.
rent (v)	to pay money regularly to use a house, room, office, etc that belongs to someone else	How long have you been renting this place?
rent (n)	an amount of money that you pay regularly for using a house, room, office, etc that belongs to someone else	After she'd paid her rent, Jan had no money left for food.
respect (v)	to treat someone in a way that shows that you think they are important and should be admired	People will respect you for telling the truth.
respect (n)	the attitude that someone is important and should be admired, and that you should treat them politely	She's worked hard to gain the respect of her colleagues.
single (adj)	not married, or not in a romantic relationship or divorced.	Please state whether you are single, married,
stranger (n)	someone who you do not know stranger.	I didn't want to share a room with a complete
trust (v)	to believe that someone or something is good, honest, or reliable	You can trust Dana.
trust (n)	a feeling that you trust someone or something	The doctor-patient relationship has to be based on trust.

Unit 15

advertisement (n)	an announcement in a newspaper, on television, on the Internet, etc that is designed to persuade people to buy a product or service, go to an event, or apply for a job	I saw an advertisement for a new kind of camera.
afford (v)	to have enough money to pay for something	I'm not sure how they're able to afford such expensive holidays.
bargain (n)	something you buy that costs much less than normal	Her dress was a real bargain.
brand (n)	a product or group of products that has its own name and is made by one particular company	I tried using a new brand of soap.
catalogue (n)	a book that contains pictures of things that you can buy	Do you have a catalogue with all your products in it?
change (n)	coins rather than notes	I'm sorry, I haven't got any change.
coin (n)	a flat round piece of metal used as money	Put a coin into the slot.
cost (v)	if something costs an amount of money, you need that amount to pay for it or to do it	A new computer costs around €1,000.
cost (n)	the amount of money that you need in order to buy something or to do something	What's the total cost of these three pairs of shoes?
customer (n) or services	a person or company that buys goods customers.	Supermarkets use a variety of ways to attract
debt (n)	an amount of money that you owe	By this time we had debts of over €15,000.
demand (v)	to say strongly that you want something	The teacher demanded an explanation for all the water on the floor.
export (v)	to send a product to another country so that it can be sold there	Their flowers are exported around the world.
fee (n)	money that you pay to a professional person or institution for their work	He will have to pay school fees of €2,000.
fortune (n)	a large amount of money	They must have spent a fortune on flowers.
import (v)	to buy a product from another country and bring it to your country	We import most of our coal from other countries.
invest (v)	to use your money with the aim of making a profit from it	Banks invested €20 million in the scheme.
obtain (v)	to get something that you want or need	She has to obtain her father's permission before she does anything.
owe (v)	to have to give someone a particular amount of money because you have bought something from them or have borrowed money from them	Pam still owes me €5.
own (v)	to legally have something, especially because you have bought it	Who owns that house by the lake?
profit (n)	money that you get when you sell something for a price that is higher than the cost of making it or buying it	Investors have made a 14 per cent profit in just three months.
property (n)	the things that you own	The books are my personal property.
purchase (v)	to buy something	She purchased a new lamp for her bedroom.
purchase (n)	something that you buy	Her latest purchase was a long black coat.
receipt (n)	a document that you get from someone showing that you have given them money or goods	Make sure you get a receipt for the taxi.
require (v)	to need someone or something	Working with these children requires a great deal of patience.
sale (n)	an event or period of time during which a shop reduces the prices of some of its goods	The Easter sales start tomorrow.
save (v)	to regularly put money in a bank, or to invest it so that you can use it later	Don't wait until you're 40 to start saving for retirement.
select (v)	to choose someone or something from a group	You can select one of four colours.

supply (v)	to provide someone or something with something that they need or want	*Our shop supplies things to people all over the country.*
supply (n)	an amount or quantity of something that is available to use	*We have a good supply of fresh water here.*
variety (n)	a number of different people or things	*Adults study for a variety of reasons.*
waste (v)	to use more of something than is necessary, or to use it in a way that does not produce the best results	*Don't waste water like that – turn the tap off when you're not using it!*
waste (n)	the failure to use something that is valuable or useful in an effective way	*All this uneaten food – what a waste!*

Unit 18

artificial (adj)	not natural or real, but made by people	*There was a vase of artificial flowers on the table.*
automatic (adj)	an automatic machine can work by itself without being operated by people	*It's an automatic door.*
complicated (adj)	difficult to do, deal with, or understand	*This is a complicated problem.*
decrease (v)	to become less	*The number of visitors has decreased significantly.*
decrease (n)	the amount by which something is less	*There's been a decrease in the number of visitors.*
digital (adj)	storing information such as sound or pictures as numbers or electronic signals	*It's a digital recording.*
discover (v)	to find something that was hidden or that no one knew about before	*William Herschel discovered Uranus in 1781.*
effect (n)	a change that is produced in one person or thing by another	*Scientists are studying the chemical's effect on the environment.*
equipment (n)	the tools, machines, or other things that you need for a particular job or activity	*A computer is the most important piece of equipment you will buy.*
estimate (v)	to guess or calculate an amount or value by using available information	*It is impossible to estimate how many of the residents were affected.*
exact (adj)	done, made, or described with all the details correct	*The exact number of people there was unknown.*
experiment (v)	to perform scientific tests in order to find out what happens to someone or something in particular conditions	*This lab does not experiment on animals.*
experiment (n)	a scientific test to find out what happens to someone or something in particular conditions	*Researchers now need to do more experiments.*
gadget (n)	a small tool or piece of equipment that does something that is useful or impressive	*That's a very useful gadget!*
hardware (n)	computer equipment	*Printers and modems are examples of hardware.*
invent (v)	to design or create something that did not exist before	*Alfred Nobel invented dynamite.*
involve (v)	to include something as part of an activity, event, or situation	*The course involves a lot of hard work.*
laboratory (n)	a building or large room where people do scientific research	*This is our new research laboratory.*
lack (v)	to not have something, or to not have enough of something	*He lacked the skills required for the job.*
lack (n)	a situation in which you do not have something, or do not have enough of something	*The match was cancelled because of lack of support.*
laptop (n)	a small computer that you can carry with you	*I'm going to buy a new laptop.*
maximum (adj)	the largest in amount, size, or number that is allowed or possible	*The maximum amount of cash you can withdraw is €500.*
minimum (adj)	the smallest in amount, size, or number that is allowed or possible	*What's the minimum voting age in your country?*

operate (v)	if equipment operates, or if you operate it, you use or control it and it works in the way it should	*Do not operate machinery after taking this medication.*
plastic (n)	a very common light, strong substance that is produced by a chemical process and used for making many different things	*This pen is made of plastic.*
plastic (adj)	made of plastic	*Have you got a plastic bag?*
program (v)	to make a computer or other piece of equipment do something automatically	*Can you program the PC to come on in the morning?*
program (n)	a series of instructions that makes a computer do something	*It's a complicated computer program.*
research (n)	the detailed study of something in order to discover new facts	*Scientists have carried out lots of research into the effects of these drugs.*
run (v)	if you run a computer program, or if it runs, you start it or use it	*The software will run on any PC.*
screen (n)	the flat surface on a computer, television, or piece of electronic equipment where words and pictures are shown	*Suddenly the screen went blank.*
software (n)	the programs used by computers for doing particular jobs	*You log onto our website, then download and install the software.*
sudden (adj)	happening very quickly and without any sign that it is going to happen	*She felt a sudden pain in her leg.*
technology (n)	advanced scientific knowledge that is used for practical purposes	*Technology is improving all the time.*
unique (adj)	not the same as anything or anyone else	*Every person is unique.*

Unit 21

accent (n)	a way of pronouncing words that shows what country, region, or social class you come from	*Tom hasn't lost his broad Irish accent.*
announcement (n)	a public statement that gives people information about something	*The head teacher made an announcement about the school holidays.*
broadcast (v)	to send out messages or programmes to be received by radios or televisions	*The BBC will be broadcasting the match live from Paris.*
broadcast (n)	a programme that is broadcast	*They mentioned the problem on Channel 5's main news broadcast.*
channel (n)	a television station and the programmes that it broadcasts	*What's on the other channel?*
clear (adj)	easy to understand	*Clear instructions are provided.*
click (v)	to make a computer do something by pressing a button on the mouse	*To send the message, click on the 'send' button.*
contact (v)	to communicate with someone by phone, e-mail, letter, etc	*Please contact us if you have any information.*
contact (n)	communication between people, countries, or organisations	*Do you and Jo still keep in contact?*
file (n)	a set of information that is stored on a computer and that is given a particular name	*I can't find the file on my computer.*
formal (adj)	suitable for serious situations or occasions	*'Ameliorate' is a more formal way of saying 'improve'.*
image (n)	a picture, especially one in a mirror or on a computer, television, or cinema screen	*Images of Germany appeared on the screen.*
informal (adj)	suitable for relaxed friendly situations *tomorrow.*	*You should wear informal clothes to the party*
Internet (n)	a computer system that allows people in different parts of the world to exchange information	*Do you have access to the Internet?*
interrupt (v)	to say or do something that stops someone when they are speaking or concentrating on something	*Please don't interrupt her while she's working.*

link (v)	if people, things, or events are linked, they are related to each other in some way	Police think that the two robberies are linked.
link (n)	a connection between two or more people, places, facts, or events	Is there any link between this and what we were talking about yesterday?
media (n)	radio, television, newspapers, the Internet and magazines, considered as a group	The story has been widely reported in the media.
mobile phone (n phr)	a small phone that you can carry around with you	Don't forget to take your mobile phone with you when you go out.
online (adj)	connected to or available through the Internet	I bought it from an online bookshop.
online (adv)	connected to the Internet	Let's go online and check your e-mail.
pause (v)	to stop moving or doing something for a short time before starting again	She paused at the door and then left.
pause (n)	a short time when someone stops moving or doing something before starting again	There was a short pause before the orchestra continued to play.
persuade (v)	to make someone agree to do something by giving them reasons why they should	He did finally come with us, although it took a long time to persuade him.
pronounce (v)	to say the sounds of words	I find some Japanese words very difficult to pronounce.
publish (v)	to produce many copies of a book, magazine, or newspaper for people to buy	Their company publishes a wide selection of books.
report (v)	to provide information about something, especially to people in authority	You should report the accident to the police.
report (n)	a spoken or written description of a particular subject, situation, or event	A new report shows crime is on the increase.
request (v)	to ask for something, or to ask someone to do something, in a polite or formal way	I would like to request a meeting with the manager, please.
request (n)	an act of asking for something in a polite or formal way	Evening meals are available on request.
ring (v)	to call someone on the telephone	Ring me at home later.
signal (n)	a movement or sound that is made by someone and has a special meaning for another person	We waited for them to give us the signal to move.
swear (v)	to use words that are deliberately offensive, for example because you are angry	That's the first time I've ever heard him swear.
type (v)	a group of people or things with similar qualities that make them different from other groups	What type of dog have you got?
viewer (n) programmes	someone who watches television *Double Money!*	Our regular viewers will know that it's time for
website (n)	a place on the Internet where information is available about a particular subject, company, university, etc	I'm thinking of starting a website for people from our school.
whisper (v)	to speak very quietly to someone, so that other people cannot hear you	Stop whispering, you two!
whisper (n)	a very quiet way of saying something to someone so that other people cannot hear you	'Be careful!' she said in a whisper.

Unit 24

admit (v)	to say that you have done something wrong	In court he admitted that he had lied about the accident.
arrest (v)	if the police arrest someone, they take that person to a police station because they think that he or she has committed a crime	The police entered the building and arrested six men.
charity (n)	an organisation that gives money and help to people who need it; money or food that is given to people who need it	The event raised €59,000 for charity.
commit (v)	to do something that is illegal	What makes people commit crimes?

community (n)	the people who live in an area	*I wanted to work somewhere where I could serve the community.*
court (n)	a place where trials take place and legal cases are decided	*The man will appear in court on Monday.*
criminal (n)	someone who has committed a crime	*Some criminals take exams in prison.*
criminal (adj)	relating to illegal acts	*That's criminal behaviour!*
culture (n)	a society that has its own set of ideas, beliefs and ways of behaving	*There were people from lots of different cultures at the meeting.*
familiar (adj)	well known to you, or easily recognized by you	*The name Harry Potter will be familiar to many readers.*
government (n)	the people who control a country or area and make decisions about its laws and taxes	*The government has announced plans to raise the minimum wage next year.*
habit (n)	something that you do often	*Biting your fingernails is a very bad habit!*
identity card (n phr)	an official document that shows who you are	*The police officer asked to see my identity card.*
illegal (adj)	not allowed by the law	*Robbing banks is illegal!*
politics (n)	the ideas and activities that are involved in getting power in an area or governing it	*She's heavily involved in local politics.*
population (n)	the number of people who live in a particular area	*Los Angeles has a population of over 3 million.*
prison (n)	an institution where people are kept as a punishment for committing a crime	*He's currently in prison.*
protest (v)	to show publicly that you oppose something	*Workers are protesting against high unemployment.*
protest (n)	an occasion when people show strong public opposition to something	*Students will hold a protest this weekend outside Parliament.*
resident (n)	someone who lives in a particular place	*Many local residents have objected to the new road.*
responsible (adj)	if you are responsible for something that has happened, you caused it, or you deserve to be blamed for it; in charge of someone or something	*He was responsible for the accident.*
rob (v)	to take money or property from someone illegally	*They were planning to rob the museum.*
routine (n)	your usual way of doing things	*It shouldn't take too long to return to our old routine.*
routine (adj)	ordinary and not interesting or special	*This is just routine work.*
schedule (n)	a plan of activities or events and when they will happen	*What's your schedule for today?*
situation (n)	the set of conditions that exist at a particular time in a particular place	*I found myself in an embarrassing situation.*
social (adj)	relating to society and to people's lives in general	*There are lots of social problems, such as unemployment.*
society (n)	people in general living together in organised communities, with laws and traditions controlling the way that they behave towards each other	*Society has to support its old people.*
steal (v)	to take something that belongs to someone else without permission	*She was caught stealing food from the supermarket.*
tradition (n)	a very old custom, belief, or story	*His son followed the family tradition and entered politics.*
typical (adj)	like most things of the same type	*His opinions are typical of people of his generation.*
vote (v)	to decide something, or to choose a representative or winner, by officially stating your choice, for example in an election	*I'm going to vote for Jackson.*
vote (n)	an official choice you make between two or more issues, people, etc, for example in an election	*My vote will go to the candidate who promises lower taxes.*

youth club (n phr)	a place where young people can go to meet and take part in activities	Let's go to the youth club after school!

Unit 27

ambition (n)	something that you very much want to achieve	His ambition was to become a successful writer.
application (n)	a formal request to do something or have something, for example a job	His application for membership was rejected.
bank account (n phr)	an arrangement with a bank that allows you to keep your money there	We'll pay the money into your bank account.
boss (n)	the person who is in charge of you at work	I'll ask my boss for a day off next week.
career (n)	a job or profession that you work at for some time	Rosen had decided on an academic career.
colleague (n)	someone who works in the same organisation or department as you	Friends and colleagues will remember him as a kind man.
company (n)	an organisation that sells services or goods	Max works for a large oil company.
contract (n)	a written legal agreement between two people or organisations	After six months she was offered a contract of employment.
department (n)	a section in a government, organisation, or business that deals with a particular type of work	You need to speak to our sales department.
deserve (v)	if you deserve something, it is right that you get it, because of the way that you are or the way that you have behaved	After five hours on your feet you deserve a break.
earn (v)	to receive money for work that you do	Most people here earn about €30,000 a year.
fame (n)	the state of being famous	Albert Finney rose to fame in the British cinema of the early Sixties.
goal (n)	the action of putting a ball into a goal in a game such as football	Nielsen scored two goals in the last ten minutes.
impress (v)	if someone or something impresses you, you admire them	Her ability to deal with problems impresses me.
income (n)	money that someone gets from working or from investing money	What is your approximate annual income?
industry (n)	all the businesses involved in producing a particular type of goods or services	How long have you worked in the oil industry?
interview (v)	to ask someone, especially someone famous, questions about themselves, their work, or their ideas	He was interviewed on the radio this morning.
interview (n)	a meeting in which someone asks another person, especially a famous person, questions about themselves, their work, or their ideas	This is her first interview since becoming Olympic champion.
leader (n)	someone who is in charge of a group, organisation, or country	Victoria became a manager because she's a good leader.
manager (n)	someone whose job is to organise and control the work of a business, a department, or the people who work there	I'd like to speak to the manager.
pension (n)	an amount of money that someone receives regularly when they no longer work because of their age or because they are ill	My grandma stopped working three years ago and now she gets a pension.
poverty (n)	a situation in which someone does not have enough money to pay for their basic needs	Half the world's population is living in poverty.
pressure (n)	attempts to persuade or force someone to do something	My parents put me under a lot of pressure at school.
previous (adj)	a previous event, period, or thing happened or existed before the one that you are talking about	All the other guests had arrived the previous day.
profession (n)	a job that you need special skills and qualifications to do	Her father discouraged her from going into the legal profession.

retire (v)	to stop working permanently, especially when you are old	He retired from the army last month.
salary (n)	a fixed amount of money that you earn each month or year from your job	Lisa gets an annual salary of €30,000.
staff (n)	the people who work for a particular company, organisation, or institution	She joined the staff in 1996.
strike (n)	a period of time during which people refuse to work, as a protest	There's a train strike in the city.
tax (v)	to make someone pay money to the government	Everyone in my country pays 20 per cent tax on any money they earn.
tax (n) to the government	an amount of money that you have to pay after the election.	The government has promised to lower taxes
wealthy (adj)	rich	Ian became a very wealthy businessman.

Unit 30

affect (v) in a negative way	to change or influence something, often of the election?	Did the newspapers really affect the outcome
balance (v)	to create or preserve a good or correct balance between different features or aspects	We have to balance the needs and tastes of all our customers.
balance (n)	a situation in which different aspects or features are treated equally or exist in the correct relationship to each other	A healthy diet is about getting the correct balance of a variety of foods.
benefit (v)	to get an advantage, or to give someone an advantage	Thousands of people could benefit from the invention.
benefit (n)	an advantage that you get from a situation	He has had the benefit of the best education money can buy.
breathe (v)	to take air into your lungs through your nose or mouth and let it out again	Doctors said he was having difficulty breathing.
chew (v)	to use your teeth to bite food in your mouth into small pieces	She chewed her food slowly.
chop (v)	to cut something such as food or wood into pieces	Chop the meat into small pieces.
contain (v)	to have something inside	The envelope contained a few old photographs.
cough (v)	to force air up through your throat with a sudden noise, especially when you have a cold or when you want to get someone's attention	My chest felt painful, and I was coughing uncontrollably.
cough (n)	the action of coughing, or the sound that you make when you cough; an illness in which you cough a lot and your throat hurts	I've got a bad cough.
cure (v)	to stop someone from being affected by an illness	Only an operation will cure her.
cure (n)	a medicine or treatment that makes someone who is ill become healthy	Doctors say there are several possible cures.
exercise (v)	to do a physical activity in order to stay healthy and to make your body stronger	Do you eat properly and exercise regularly?
exercise (n)	physical activity that you do in order to stay healthy and make your body stronger	I get plenty of exercise being an aerobics instructor.
flu (n)	a very common infectious disease that lasts for a short time and makes you feel weak and tired	My dad has got flu.
have an operation (v phr)	the process of cutting into someone's body for medical reasons	The baby had to have an operation.
healthy (adj)	physically strong and not ill	I feel very healthy at the moment.
ignore (v)	to not consider something, or to not let it influence you	We had ignored the fact that it was getting darker.
infection (n)	a disease that is caused by bacteria or by a virus	I've got a throat infection.

ingredient (n)	one of the foods or liquids that you use in making a particular meal	Mix all the ingredients together carefully.
injury (n)	physical harm	All the passengers in the vehicle escaped injury.
limit (v)	to prevent a number, amount, or effect from increasing past a particular point	We want to limit classes to a maximum of 30 pupils.
limit (n)	the greatest amount of something that is possible or allowed	The speed limit here is 40 miles an hour.
meal (n)	an occasion when you eat, such as breakfast or lunch, or the food that you eat at that time	He cooked us a delicious meal.
pill (n)	a small piece of solid medicine that you swallow with water	Did you remember to take your pills this morning?
recover (v)	to become fit and healthy again after an illness or injury	I haven't fully recovered from the flu.
salty (adj)	containing salt, or tasting like salt	This soup is very salty.
slice (v)	to cut something into flat pieces	I'll slice some bread.
slice (n)	a flat piece of food that has been cut from something larger	Cut the bread into thick slices.
sour (adj)	with a taste like a lemon	If it's too sour, add some sugar.
spicy (adj)	with a strong hot flavour	Curry should be spicy!
stir (v)	to move food or a liquid around using a spoon or other object	Stir the sauce gently over a low heat.
suffer (v)	to feel pain in your body or your mind; to have a particular illness or physical problem	I'm suffering from a cold at the moment.
taste (v)	to have a particular flavour; to eat or drink something and experience its flavour	The dinner was one of the best meals I've ever tasted.
taste (n)	the flavour that something creates in your mouth when you eat or drink it	I love the taste of chocolate.
treatment (n)	the process of providing medical care, or a particular type of medical care	What's the best treatment for this disease?
vitamin (n)	a natural substance in food that is necessary to keep your body healthy	Oranges contain lots of vitamin C.

Unit 33

ancient (adj)	very old	They've found an ancient city at the bottom of the sea.
checked (adj)	printed or woven in a pattern of squares	I got a new red and blue checked shirt.
cotton (n)	cloth made from the white fibres of a plant called a cotton plant	Is this shirt made out of cotton?
create (v)	to make something new exist or happen	How do I create a new file?
design (v)	to decide how something will be made, how it will work, or what it will look like, and often to make drawings of it	The bride wore a dress that she'd designed herself.
design (n)	the way that something is made so that it works and looks a certain way, or a drawing that shows what it will look like	The car has a new design.
fix (v)	to repair something	Jessica fixed my watch.
fold (v)	to bend a piece of paper or cloth and press one part of it over another part	Fold the paper in half.
gallery (n)	a public building where you can look at paintings and other works of art	We could go to a museum or a gallery this weekend.
improvement (n)	the state of being better than before, or the process of making something better than it was before	There has been an improvement in relations between the two countries.
loose (adj)	loose clothes are large and do not fit your body tightly	These jeans are a bit loose, so maybe I need a smaller size.
maintain (v)	to make regular repairs to something, so that it stays in good condition	The car had been very well maintained.

match (v)	if one thing matches another, or they match, they form an attractive combination	*She wore a green dress and a hat to match.*
material (n)	cloth	*What sort of material is your dress made from?*
notice (v)	to become conscious of someone or something by seeing, hearing, or feeling them	*After a few days here you hardly notice the rain!*
notice (n)	a written sign or announcement that gives information or that warns people about something	*They put up a notice on the door saying they'd gone out of business.*
pattern (n)	a set of lines, shapes, or colours that are repeated regularly	*I like the pattern on your carpet.*
pile (n)	a number of things that are put on top of each other in an untidy way	*Rubbish lay in piles in the street.*
practical (adj)	involving, or relating to, real situations rather than theories or ideas alone	*Practical experience can be as valuable as academic qualifications.*
rough (adj)	with a surface that is not smooth	*The walls were built of dark rough stone.*
shape (n)	the form of something	*Trace the shape onto the card and cut it out.*
silk (n)	a thin smooth cloth made from the fibres produced by insects called silkworms	*I love your new silk shirt!*
sleeve (n)	the part of a piece of clothing that covers your arm	*Oh, no! I've got a hole in one of my sleeves.*
smooth (adj)	completely even with no rough areas	*How do you keep your skin so smooth?*
stretch (v)	if you stretch something, or if it stretches, it becomes longer or wider when you pull it	*Can you stretch the material a little?*
striped (adj)	with a pattern of coloured lines on the table.	*There was a blue and white striped tablecloth*
style (n)	the way that something is made or done that is typical of a particular group, time, or place	*I don't like the style of dresses that are out now.*
suit (v)	if a style or something you wear suits you, it makes you look good	*The new hairstyle really suits her.*
suit (n)	a set of clothes made from the same cloth, usually a jacket with trousers or a skirt	*He was wearing a dark suit and a tie.*
suitable (adj)	right for a particular purpose, person, or situation	*This film is not suitable for young children.*
tear (v)	to pull something so that it separates into pieces or gets a hole in it, or to become damaged in this way	*He'd torn his raincoat.*
tear (n)	a hole in something where it has been torn	*There was a tear in her coat.*
tight (adj)	fitting closely around your body or part of your body	*These shoes are too tight.*
tool (n)	a piece of equipment that you hold to do a particular type of work	*Do you know where my gardening tools are?*

Unit 36

amazing (adj)	very good, surprising, or impressive	*Her story was quite amazing.*
climate (n)	the climate of a country or region is the type of weather it has	*Mexico is well known for its hot climate.*
countryside (n)	areas away from towns and cities, with farms, fields and trees	*Let's get out of the city and go to the countryside.*
environment (n)	the natural world, including the land, water, air, plants and animals	*Industries are causing a lot of damage to the environment.*
extinct (adj)	if something such as a type of animal or plant is extinct, it no longer exists	*Dinosaurs are extinct.*
forecast (v)	to make a statement about what is likely to happen, often relating to the weather	*Is it difficult to forecast the weather?*
forecast (n)	a statement about what is likely to happen, often relating to the weather	*Have you heard the weather forecast for tomorrow?*
freezing (adj)	very cold; the temperature at which water freezes and becomes ice	*It's absolutely freezing in here.*

global (adj)	including or affecting the whole world	This is a global problem – it affects every country.
heatwave (n)	a continuous period of very hot weather	Britain has been having a heatwave for the last three weeks.
insect (n)	a small animal that has six legs and often has wings	Flies and mosquitoes are insects.
lightning (n)	the bright flashes of light that you see in the sky during a storm	The ship was struck by lightning soon after it left the port.
litter (v)	to drop litter	The sign said 'No littering!'
litter (n)	things that people have dropped on the ground in a public place, making it untidy	Pick up that litter and put it in the bin.
local (adj)	in or related to a particular area, especially the place where you live	Ask for the book in your local library.
locate (v)	to find out the exact place where someone or something is; be located: to exist in a particular place	The hotel is located in Wolverhampton town centre.
mammal (n)	an animal that is born from its mother's body, not from an egg, and drinks its mother's milk as a baby	Humans and monkeys are mammals.
mild (adj)	mild weather is warm and pleasant	It was a mild winter.
name (v)	to know and say what the name of someone or something is; to give someone or something a name	How many world capitals can you name?
name (n)	a word or set of words used for referring to a person or thing	What's the name of this flower?
origin (n)	the place or moment at which something begins to exist	Meteorites may hold clues about the origin of life on Earth.
planet (n)	a very large round object that moves around the Sun or around another star	Mars is sometimes known as the red planet.
preserve (v)	to take care of something in order to prevent it from being harmed or destroyed	We work hard to preserve historic buildings.
recycle (v)	to treat waste materials so that they can be used again	Let's recycle those old bottles.
reptile (n)	a type of animal such as a snake or lizard that lays eggs, and whose body is covered in scales	Crocodiles are reptiles.
rescue (v)	to save someone from a dangerous or unpleasant situation	The crew of the ship were rescued just before it sank.
rescue (n)	an act of saving someone or something from danger or from an unpleasant situation	Firefighters carried out the dangerous rescue.
satellite (n)	an object that is sent into space to travel round the Earth in order to receive and send information; a natural object such as a moon that moves around a planet	There are lots of satellites above the Earth.
shower (n)	a short period when it rains	Tonight there's a 50 per cent chance of showers.
solar system (n phr)	the sun and the group of planets that move around it	How many planets are there in our solar system?
species (n)	a plant or animal group whose members all have similar general features and are able to produce young plants or animals together	Over 120 species of birds have been recorded in this national park.
thunder (n)	the loud noise that you sometimes hear in the sky during a storm	Listen to that thunder!
wild (adj)	a wild animal or plant lives or grows on its own in natural conditions and is not raised by humans	This behaviour is common in both domestic and wild dogs.
wildlife (n)	animals, birds and plants that live in natural conditions	A lot of the local wildlife is in danger.

Unit 39

amusing (adj)	funny or entertaining	*Jan sent me an amusing birthday card.*
annoy (v)	to make someone feel slightly angry or impatient	*I don't dislike her – she just annoys me sometimes.*
attitude (n)	opinions or feelings that you show by your behaviour	*We can win if we keep a positive attitude.*
bad-tempered (adj)	made annoyed or angry very easily	*Relax and try not to be so bad-tempered.*
behave (v)	to do things in a particular way	*The children behaved very badly.*
bully (v)	to frighten or hurt someone who is smaller or weaker than you	*You shouldn't bully the other children in your class.*
bully (n)	someone who uses their strength or status to threaten or frighten people	*Leave him alone and don't be such a bully!*
calm (adj)	not affected by strong emotions	*'Don't move and the snake won't attack,' he said in a calm voice.*
celebrate (v)	to do something enjoyable in order to show that an occasion or event is special	*Let's have a party to celebrate.*
character (n)	the qualities that make up someone's personality	*Amy has got a really nice, friendly character.*
depressed (adj)	very unhappy and without any feelings of hope or enthusiasm	*She got very depressed after her husband left her.*
embarrassing (n)	making you feel nervous, ashamed, or stupid	*What's the most embarrassing thing you've ever done?*
emotion (n)	a feeling that you experience, for example love, fear, or anger	*Jealousy is an uncomfortable emotion.*
enthusiastic (adj)	very interested in something, or excited by it	*For a while, we were enthusiastic about the idea.*
feeling (n)	an emotional state, for example anger or happiness	*He found it difficult to express his feelings.*
glad (adj)	happy and pleased about something	*Maggie was glad to be home.*
hurt (v)	to feel pain somewhere in your body	*Fred's knees hurt after skiing all day.*
hurt (adj)	injured, or feeling physical pain	*Two young men were badly hurt in the accident.*
miserable (adj)	extremely unhappy	*He looked cold and miserable.*
naughty (adj)	a naughty child behaves badly	*Sally was often naughty and got into trouble at school.*
noisy (adj)	making a lot of noise, or full of noise	*We have really noisy neighbours.*
polite (adj)	behaving towards other people in a pleasant way that follows all the usual rules of society	*It's not polite to talk with your mouth full of food.*
react (v)	to behave in a particular way because of things that are happening around you or things that other people are doing to you	*I wasn't sure how you would react.*
regret (v)	to feel sorry or sad about something that has happened, or about something that you have done	*We regret any problems because of the delay.*
regret (n)	a feeling of sadness about something that has happened or something that you have done	*Do you have any regrets about what you did?*
ridiculous (adj)	silly or unreasonable and deserving to be laughed at	*She looks absolutely ridiculous in that hat.*
romantic (adj)	involving love, or making you have feelings of love	*We had a romantic dinner in an expensive restaurant.*
rude (adj)	not polite	*I don't want to seem rude, but I'd rather be alone.*
sense of humour (n phr)	the ability to laugh at things and recognize when they are funny	*Kev has got a great sense of humour and he makes me laugh all the time.*
shy (adj)	nervous and embarrassed in the company of other people, especially people who you do not know	*I'd love to meet her, but I'm too shy to introduce myself.*

stress (n)	a worried or nervous feeling that makes you unable to relax, or a situation that makes you feel like this	*Carol's been under a lot of stress lately.*
tell a joke (v phr)	say a short story with a funny ending to make people laugh	*The kids were telling jokes.*
upset (v)	to make someone feel sad, worried, or angry	*I'm sorry, I didn't mean to upset you.*
upset (adj)	sad, worried, or angry about something	*It's nothing to get upset about.*

Unit 42

accident (n)	something that happens without being planned	*I didn't do it on purpose – it was an accident!*
assume (v)	to believe that something is true, even though you cannot be certain	*I assume everyone here has an e-mail address.*
cause (v)	to make something happen, usually something bad	*Bad weather continues to cause problems for travellers.*
cause (n)	an event, thing, or person that makes something happen	*We had to write an essay on the causes of the First World War.*
claim (v)	to say that something is true, even though there is no definite proof	*He claims he is innocent.*
complain (v)	to say that you are not happy about something	*She complained that it was too hot.*
convince (v)	to make someone believe that something is true; to persuade someone to do something	*He failed to convince the judge that he was innocent.*
criticise (v)	to say what you think is wrong or bad about something or someone	*Why are you always criticising me?*
deny (v)	to say that something is not true	*He still denies stealing the money.*
discussion (n)	a conversation about something important	*We need to have a discussion about your schoolwork.*
doubt (v)	to think that something is probably not true, probably does not exist, or probably will not happen	*'Do you think they'll win?' 'I doubt it.'*
doubt (n)	a feeling of not being certain about something	*There's no doubt about it – we're in trouble.*
encourage (v)	to give someone confidence or hope	*Mum always encouraged us when we took part in competitions.*
get rid of (v phr)	to throw away, give away, or sell something that you no longer want or need	*We're moving, so we have to get rid of a lot of our furniture.*
gossip (v)	to talk about other people or about things that are not important	*You shouldn't gossip about people.*
gossip (n)	talk or a conversation about things that are not important or about people's private lives	*Here's an interesting piece of gossip for you!*
ideal (adj)	perfect	*Upgrading your computer seems the ideal solution.*
insult (v)	to say or do something that is offensive	*You'll insult the cook if you don't at least taste the meal.*
insult (n)	an offensive remark	*I've never heard such a dreadful insult.*
investigate (v)	to try to find out all the facts about something in order to learn the truth about it	*We sent a reporter to investigate the rumour.*
negative (adj)	harmful or bad	*Does TV have a negative effect on children?*
positive (adj)	a positive experience, situation, result, etc is a good one	*School was a totally positive experience for me.*
praise (v)	to express strong approval or admiration for someone or something	*If you never praise your kids, how can they know when they're doing something right?*
praise (n)	an expression of strong approval or admiration	*I never got much praise as a child.*
pretend (v)	to behave in a particular way because you want someone to believe that something is true when it is not	*She closed her eyes and pretended to be asleep.*
purpose (n)	an aim or use	*The purpose of this dictionary is to help students of English.*
refuse (v)	to say that you will not do or accept something, or will not let someone do something	*I asked him to apologise, but he refused.*

result (v)	to cause or produce something	*The fight resulted in three people being hurt.*
result (n)	something that is caused directly by something else	*He said the argument was the result of a misunderstanding.*
rumour (n)	something that people are saying that may or may not be true	*A student had been spreading rumours about the teachers.*
sensible (adj)	reasonable and practical	*This seems to be a sensible way of dealing with the problem.*
serious (adj)	bad or dangerous enough to make you worried	*It's not a serious problem.*
spare (adj)	kept in addition to other similar things, so that you can use it if you need it	*Bring a towel and some spare clothes.*
theory (n)	an idea that you believe is true, although you have no proof	*I have my own theory about why he left.*
thought (n)	a word, idea, or image that comes into your mind	*I've just had an interesting thought.*
warn (v)	to tell someone about a possible problem or danger, so that they can avoid it or deal with it	*Police are warning everyone in the area to take extra care when going out alone.*

Phrasal verbs

add up	to find the total of	The shop assistant added up what I'd bought and told me the total.
blow up	to explode	Luckily, the bomb didn't blow up.
break down	to stop working (for a machine, etc)	Our car broke down on the motorway.
break in(to)	to enter illegally	A house in Brecon Place was broken into last night.
bring up	to take care of a child until he or she becomes an adult	She brought up three sons on her own.
build up	to increase	These exercises are good for building up leg strength.
call back	to ring again on the phone	I'll call you back later when you're not so busy.
call off	to cancel	The concert has been called off because of the weather.
calm down	to become/make calmer	The woman finally calmed down and explained what had happened.
carry on	to continue	The phone rang, but Mark just carried on watching TV.
catch up (with)	to reach the same point/level as	He's missed so much school that he's going to find it hard to catch up.
cheer up	to become/make happier	I started to cheer up when the sun came out.
clear up	to tidy	I'll clear up if you want to go to bed.
come across	to find something by chance	I came across a word I'd never seen before.
come back (from)	to return (from)	Give me a call when you come back from Greece.
come on	to be quicker	Come on, or we'll be late!
come out	to be published	When does her new book come out?
cross out	to draw a line through something written	Just cross it out and rewrite it correctly.
cut down (on)	to do less of something (smoking, etc)	I'm trying to cut down on the amount of sugar I eat.
cut off	to disconnect (phone, electricity, etc)	Pay the electricity bill tomorrow or they might cut us off.
cut off	to completely remove by cutting	Keep your roses healthy by cutting off any dead flowers.
do up	to button/zip up a piece of clothing	It's very windy, so do your coat up.
eat out	to eat at a restaurant	Would you like to stay in or eat out tonight?
fall down	to trip and fall	I fell down and hurt my knee.
fall out (with)	to have an argument with someone and stop being friends	Have you two fallen out?
fill in a form, etc	to add information in the spaces on	Just fill in this application form, please.
fill up	to make something completely full	Just fill this bowl up with sugar and put it on the table.
find out	to discover information, etc	I don't want Jerry to find out about this.

get away with	to escape punishment for	*They have repeatedly broken the law and got away with it.*
get in(to)	to enter a car	*I hurt my head as I was getting into the car.*
get off	to leave a bus/train/etc	*You need to get off the bus opposite the supermarket.*
get on (with)	to have a good relationship (with)	*She seems to get on with everybody.*
get on(to)	to enter a bus/train/etc	*You can buy a ticket when you get on the bus.*
get out (of)	to leave a car/building/room/etc	*Quick! Get out of the car!*
get over	to recover from (an illness, etc)	*It can take weeks to get over an illness like that.*
get up	to leave your bed	*He never gets up before nine.*
give away	to give something free of charge	*They're giving away free tickets at the cinema!*
give back	to return something you've taken/borrowed	*Could you give my CDs back because you've had them for two weeks.*
give up	to stop doing something you do regularly	*You should give up smoking.*
go away	to leave a place/someone	*Why don't you just go away and leave me alone?*
go back (to)	to return (to)	*I can't wait to go back to Italy.*
go off	to no longer be fresh	*Has this milk gone off?*
go on	to continue happening or doing something	*Please go on with your work while I speak to the head teacher.*
go on	to happen	*There isn't much going on in this town in the evening.*
go out	to stop burning	*The fire must have gone out during the night.*
go out with	to be the boyfriend/girlfriend of	*Greg used to go out with Katy.*
grow up	to become older (for children)	*He rarely saw his father while he was growing up.*
hang on	to wait	*Just hang on – I'll be ready in a minute.*
hang up	to put clothes in a wardrobe, etc	*The women hung up their coats and sat down.*
hang up	to put the receiver down to end a phone call	*I can't believe that Jessica hung up without saying goodbye!*
have on	to wear (a piece of clothing)	*The man had a strange hat on.*
hurry up	to do something more quickly	*We haven't got much time, so hurry up!*
join in	to participate, take part	*Ask them if you can play – I'm sure they'll let you join in.*
keep out	to prevent from entering	*Cars should be kept out of the city centre.*
leave out	to not include	*Don't leave your brother out – let him play with you and your friends.*
let down	to disappoint	*You've really let me down.*
lie down	to start lying (on a bed, etc)	*I'm going to go and lie down for a while.*
log off	to disconnect from the Internet/ a website	*Don't forget to log off when you've finished checking your e-mail.*

log on(to)	to connect to the Internet/a website	*You need your password to log on.*
look after	to take care of	*It's hard work looking after three children all day.*
look up	to try to find information in a book, etc	*I had to look the word up in a dictionary.*
make up	to invent an explanation, excuse, etc	*He made up some excuse about the dog eating his homework.*
move in	to start living in a new house, etc	*We're moving in next week.*
pay back	to return money (to someone)	*Did you pay Denise back?*
pick up	to lift something from the floor, a table, etc	*Please pick those toys up and put them away.*
point out	to tell someone important information	*He pointed out that we had two hours of free time before dinner.*
print out	to make a paper copy of something on a computer	*Let me print those photographs out for you.*
pull off	to break by pulling	*I pulled off the arm of my sunglasses by mistake.*
put away	to return something to where it belongs	*He put the notebook away and stood up.*
put back	to return something to where it was	*Can you put the book back when you've finished with it?*
put down	to stop holding	*Emma put her bag down and went upstairs.*
put off	to delay to a later time	*Can we put the meeting off until tomorrow?*
put on	to gain (weight)	*I don't want to put on any more weight!*
put on	to start wearing (a piece of clothing)	*Put your gloves and scarf on – it's cold outside.*
put out	to make something stop burning	*It took three firefighters to put the fire out.*
put up	to put something on a wall (eg a picture)	*The teachers will put a notice up about the new courses.*
read out	to say something out loud which you are reading	*He read the list of names out.*
rip up	to tear into pieces	*Rip up this piece of paper when you've finished reading it.*
rub out	to remove with a rubber	*I can't rub it out because I wrote it in pen.*
run away (from)	to escape by running	*The thief ran away from the police officers.*
run out (of)	to not have any left	*Many hospitals are running out of money.*
save up (for)	to save money (for a specific purpose)	*I'm saving up for a new electric guitar.*
send off (eg football)	to make a player leave a game	*It was a very bad foul and the referee sent the player off.*
set off	to start a journey	*Go to sleep because we're setting off early in the morning.*
set up	to start (a business, organization, etc)	*My dad is going to set up a taxi company.*

share out	to give a part of something to a group of people	The money will be shared out between 30 different environmental organizations.
shut up	to stop talking, stop making a noise	Just shut up a minute and let me tell you what happened!
sit down	to (start to) sit	Please, sit down and make yourselves comfortable.
sort out	to solve a problem	Investigators are still trying to sort out why the accident happened.
speak up	to talk more loudly so someone can hear you	You have to speak up a bit because my gran's a bit deaf.
split up	to end a relationship	Tommy and Liz have just split up. It's very sad!
stand up	to (start to) stand	You have the chair. I don't mind eating standing up.
stay up	to go to bed late	We stayed up until two o'clock last night.
take away	to remove	Have they taken the rubbish away yet?
take back	to return something to the place it came from	I'm going to take my library books back.
take down	to remove (from a high place)	The old man took a large book down from a shelf.
take off	to leave the ground	Let's go and watch the planes taking off while we wait.
take off	to remove (a piece of clothing)	It felt good to finally take my shoes off after a long day.
take over	to take control of (a business, etc)	The shopping centre has been taken over by an American company.
take up	to start (a hobby, sport, etc)	I've taken up stamp collecting and it's really interesting.
throw away	to put something in a rubbish bin	Have you thrown the papers away?
try on	to put on (a piece of clothing) to see how it looks and if it fits	You should try it on to see if it's the right size.
turn down	to lower the volume of	Turn the radio down – I'm trying to work.
turn off	to stop a machine working	Will you turn the television off, please?
turn on	to start a machine working	Will you turn the television on, please?
turn over	to turn something so the other side is towards you	You may turn over your exam papers now.
turn up	to increase the volume of	We asked our teacher to turn the CD up, so that we could hear it.
wake up	to stop being asleep	Wake up! It's nearly ten o'clock!
wash up	to wash plates, cups, cutlery, etc	I can help to cook and wash up.
watch out	to be careful	Watch out – you're going to hit that car!
work out	to find the solution to a problem, etc	We can't work out how to get the Internet connection going.
write down	to write information on a piece of paper	Do you want to write down my phone number?

Prepositional phrases

accident	by accident	*I meant to call Helen, but I called Roger by accident.*
addition	in addition (to)	*In addition to all the food, we took some games to play.*
age	at the age of	*I left home at the age of eighteen.*
air/etc	by air/sea/bus/car/etc	*The best way to get there is by bus.*
back	at the back (of)	*Let's go and sit at the back.*
beginning	in the beginning	*I found Chinese hard to learn in the beginning, but it's easier now.*
board	on board	*The ship left as soon as all the passengers were on board.*
bottom	at the bottom (of)	*What's it like at the bottom of the sea?*
business	on business	*I travel a lot on business.*
cash	in cash	*The woman paid for the car in cash, which was unusual.*
CD/DVD/video	on CD/DVD/video	*I didn't see it at the cinema, so I'm watching it on DVD tonight.*
chance	by chance	*I met Venia by chance in the town centre.*
charge	in charge (of)	*I'd like to speak to the person in charge.*
coast	on the coast	*We used to live on the coast.*
common	in common (with)	*I've got nothing in common with you!*
comparison	in comparison to/with	*Germany is very small in comparison with Russia.*
conclusion	in conclusion	*In conclusion, I believe that television is a positive invention.*
condition	in good/bad condition	*For sale: camping equipment, in good condition.*
contact	in contact (with)	*I'm still in contact with several friends from school.*
corner	in the corner (of)	*In the corner of the room there was a guitar.*
credit card/cheque	by credit card/cheque	*Can I pay by cheque?*
danger	in danger (of)	*That house is in danger of falling down.*
debt	in debt	*It can be very worrying to be in debt.*
diet	on a diet	*I'm on a diet at the moment so I'm not eating any fatty food.*
distance	in the distance	*Is that a car I can see in the distance?*
duty	on/off duty	*My dad's a policeman and he's often on duty at night.*
e-mail/etc	by e-mail/phone/letter	*Get in touch by e-mail and I'll send you my photos.*
end	in the end	*I thought we would get there at three, but in the end we arrived at five.*
end	at the end (of)	*At the end of the film, everyone got married.*
fact	in fact	*Many people think Greece is hot in the winter but, in fact, it sometimes snows.*
fashion/style	in fashion/style	*Those shoes are really in fashion at the moment.*
fashion/style	out of fashion/style	*Things seem to go out of fashion very quickly these days.*
favour	in favour (of)	*Are you in favour of school uniforms?*
first	at first	*I didn't like Mary at first, but then we became friends.*
foot	on foot	*Can we go from the hotel to the beach on foot, or is it better to take a bus?*
front	in front (of)	*Don't worry – you can park in front of our house.*
fun	for fun	*I sing in a band for fun.*
future	in the future	*Will people live on other planets in the future?*
general	in general	*In general, TV programmes are not educational.*
heart	by heart	*I've learnt the song by heart.*
holiday	on holiday	*Isn't it great to finally be on holiday?*

instance	for instance	Many countries, for instance the UK, don't have identity cards.
Internet	on the Internet	You can find a lot of information on the Internet.
last	at last	At last, we've arrived!
law	against the law	Stealing is against the law.
least	at least	It's cold, but at least it's not raining.
love	in love (with)	I'm in love with Chris.
mess	in a mess	Your room is in a mess. Go and tidy it!
middle	in the middle (of)	In the middle of the stage, there was an elephant.
mistake	by mistake	I meant to call Helen, but I called Roger by mistake.
moment	at the moment	I'm busy at the moment.
most	at most	The tickets should cost about €20 at most.
news	on the news	They mentioned the accident on the news.
night	at night	It usually gets dark at night.
opinion	in my opinion	In my opinion, we shouldn't go to school on Saturdays.
order	out of order	This phone is out of order. We'll have to find another one.
own	on your own	Did you go to the cinema on your own?
phone	on the phone	Come in and wait a second – I'm just on the phone.
pressure	under pressure	My dad is under a lot of pressure at work at the moment.
public	in public	Politicians can say things in private that they can't say in public.
purpose	on purpose	I didn't do it on purpose.
radio	on the radio	I first heard that song on the radio.
rent	for rent	Do you have any rooms for rent?
response	in response to	I am writing in response to your letter of 13th July.
risk	at risk	You're at risk of failing the exam if you don't work harder.
sale	for sale	I'm afraid the pictures on the wall aren't for sale.
schedule	on schedule	Our train arrived on schedule.
secret	in secret	We planned a birthday party for Julie in secret.
shape	in shape	It's important to me to stay in shape, so I go to the gym whenever I can.
spite	in spite of	Tina seems to be happy, in spite of her recent problems.
stage	on stage	There were three actors on stage.
strike	on strike	We got a day off school because our teachers were on strike.
tears	in tears	When I found Fiona, she was in tears.
teens/twenties/etc	in your teens/twenties/etc	Life isn't always easy when you're in your teens.
time	for a long time	I haven't seen George for a long time.
time	in time (for)	We arrived at the cinema just in time for the start of the film.
time	on time	Make sure you are here on time tomorrow.
times	at times	I like studying French, but it can be hard work at times.
top	at the top (of)	What was it like at the top of Mount Everest?
top	on top (of)	He sprinkled sugar on top of the cake.
total	in total	In total, we made over €200 for charity.
touch	in touch (with)	I'm still in touch with several friends from school.
trouble	in trouble	We'll be in trouble if the teacher catches us.
TV	on TV	Is there anything on TV tonight?
view	in my view	In my view, we shouldn't go to school on Saturdays.
yourself	by yourself	Did you go to the cinema by yourself?

Word patterns

accuse	accuse sb of	They accused me of stealing some money!
addicted	addicted to	I'm glad I'm not addicted to drugs.
admire	admire sb for	I really admire you for everything you've achieved.
advantage	an advantage of	One advantage of MP3 players is that they're very small.
advert(isement)	an advert(isement) for	Have you seen that really funny advert(isement) for coffee?
advise	advise against	I would advise against studying all night.
afraid	afraid of	I'm afraid of the dark.
agree	agree (with sb) about	I don't agree with you about that.
allergic	allergic to	My mum is allergic to gold, so she can't wear any gold jewellery.
amazed	amazed at/by	We were all amazed at/by the tricks the magician did.
angry	angry (with sb) about	Are you angry with me about something?
apologise	apologise (to sb) for	Simon apologised to me for losing my pen.
apply	apply for	Yiota has applied for a job at the new hotel.
approve	approve of	I don't approve of kids lying to their parents.
argue	argue (with sb) about	I don't want to argue with you about something so unimportant!
argument	an argument (with sb) about	I had an argument with my dad about how much pocket money I get.
arrive	arrive at	Let's have dinner as soon as we arrive at the hotel.
arrive	arrive in	I hope it's not raining when we arrive in Manchester.
ashamed	ashamed of	Aren't you ashamed of what you did?
ask	ask (sb) about	Why don't you ask your dad about the party?
ask	ask for	Ed asked for a pencil, so I lent him one.
aware	aware of	I'm not aware of any flights being cancelled.
begin	begin sth with	Let's begin the lesson with a revision test.
believe	believe in	Do you believe in UFOs?
belong	belong to	Do these belong to you?
blame	blame sth on	I blame the accident on Jake.
blame	blame sb for	You can't blame Susie for what happened.
book	a book (by sb) about	I read a great book by an English writer about travelling around Europe.
bored	bored with	I'm bored with watching this film.
borrow	borrow sth from	You can borrow some money from me, if you like.
buy	buy sth from	Where did you buy your new shoes from?
capable	capable of	Are you capable of holding your breath under water for two minutes?
care	care about	Everyone should care about protecting the environment.
careful	careful with	Please be careful with that vase – it was my grandmother's.
change	change sth (from sth) into	In the story, the witch changes the prince from a man into a frog.
chat	chat (to sb) about	I'll have a chat to Mrs Peters about your marks.
cheat	cheat at/in	You should never cheat at cards. You didn't cheat in the exam, did you?
choose	choose between	I love both my brother and my sister and I can't choose between them.
close	close to	The Town Hall is quite close to my house.
combine	combine sth with	If you combine oxygen with hydrogen you get water.
comment	comment on	The politician refused to comment on the situation.
communicate	communicate with	I communicate with my cousins in Australia by e-mail.
compare	compare sth to/with	I'd like you to compare your composition to/with your partner's composition.
complain	complain (to sb) about	I'm going to complain to the manager about this.
confuse	confuse sth with	I think you've confused me with someone else.
congratulate	congratulate sb on	The coach congratulated us on winning the final.

connect	connect sth to/with	Can you connect this wire to/with this one?
continue	continue with	Continue with your work and I'll be back in a moment.
cope	cope with	I can't cope with all this homework!
covered	covered in/with	My shoes are covered in/with mud.
crazy	crazy about	Marshall is crazy about video games.
criticise	criticise sb for	Don't criticise me for asking questions in class!
cure	a cure for	Will they ever find a cure for this disease?
damage	damage to	Did the storm do a lot of damage to your house?
deal	deal with	I'll deal with that problem tomorrow.
decide	decide on	Have you decided on the music for your party?
depend	depend on	Going to see your cousins this weekend depends on the weather.
describe	describe sth as	'Would you describe him as tall?' the police officer asked.
die	die from/of	You won't die from/of a cold!
difference	a difference between	What's the difference between a crocodile and an alligator?
different	different from/to	This song is very different from/to their last one.
difficult	difficult for	It must be difficult for Peter, having so many sisters.
disappointed	disappointed with	I like that actor, but I was disappointed with his last film.
disconnect	disconnect sth from	I'll disconnect the TV from the wall before I go to bed.
embarrassed	embarrassed about	I'm a bit embarrassed about what I did at the party last night.
enthusiastic	enthusiastic about	John is really enthusiastic about the karaoke competition.
escape	escape from	How did they escape from prison?
explain	explain sth to	Let me explain the rules of the game to you.
familiar	familiar with	We might need a map because I'm not very familiar with the area.
famous	famous for	This area is famous for cheese and pasta.
fan	a fan of	If you're a fan of Tony DeVito, you'll love his latest album.
far	far from	Is the cinema far from here?
fed up	fed up with	I'm fed up with working here.
feel	feel like	What do you feel like doing this weekend?
fight	fight against	The two countries once fought against each other in a war.
fill	fill sth with	She filled the trolley with food.
fond	fond of	I'm really fond of my dog!
forget	forget about	I'd completely forgotten about the party!
forgive	forgive sb for	I'll never forgive you for what you've done!
frightened	frightened of	Are you frightened of flying?
full	full of	The cupboard is full of food.
game	a game against	In a game against a local school I scored four goals.
glance	glance at	I glanced at Clare and I could see that she was upset.
good	good at	What sports are you good at?
guilty	guilty of	He was found guilty of murder.
happen	happen to	What happened to you?
happy	happy about/with	David seemed to be happy about/with his exam results, anyway.
help	help (sb) with	Can I help you with that?
hide	hide sth from sb	You can't hide anything from me!
idea	an idea about	I've got no idea about computers.
increase	an increase in	There's been an increase in traffic in the town centre recently.
influence	an influence on	My uncle has had a strong influence on me.
inform	inform sb about	Please inform a member of staff about any problems you may have.
information	information about	I'd like some information about the local area, please.
insist	insist on	My dad insists on my being home by ten o'clock.
interested	interested in	I'm quite interested in history.
invite	invite sb to	I'm going to invite everyone to my party.
involved	involved in	When did he first become involved in crime?

jealous	jealous of	I'm jealous of Katy because she always has such nice clothes!
joke	a joke about	Trisha told us a joke about two penguins.
keen	keen on	I'm not very keen on spicy food.
kind	kind to	You've been very kind to me. Thank you!
kind	a kind of	Haddock is a kind of fish.
know	know about	Do you know anything about astronomy?
late	late for	Hurry up or we'll be late for school.
laugh	laugh at	Your problems will seem less serious if you can laugh at them.
learn	learn about	We're learning about dinosaurs at school at the moment.
lend	lend sth to	I haven't got any money because I lent €100 to Richard.
letter	a letter (from sb) about	I got a letter from Miranda about her new job.
listen	listen to	In my free time, I like to listen to music.
look	look at	What are those people looking at?
married	married to	My brother is married to a woman called Margo.
nervous	nervous about	I'm really nervous about appearing in the school play.
number	a number of	I've got a number of books about horses.
opinion	an opinion about/of	What's your opinion about/of classical music?
part	take part in	Have you ever taken part in a talent contest?
pay	pay for	We paid for dinner by credit card and left.
picture	a picture of	This is a picture of a family on holiday in Africa.
pleased	pleased with	Are you pleased with your exam results?
popular	popular with	This band is very popular with teenagers.
prepare	prepare for	How do you prepare for a big match?
prevent	prevent sb from	The wall is designed to prevent the animals from leaving.
proud	proud of	I'm sure your parents are very proud of you.
provide	provide sb with	The college provides all the students with books.
punish	punish sb for	You shouldn't punish someone for telling the truth.
question	a question about	Can I ask you a question about the maths test?
ready	ready for	Are you ready for your exam tomorrow?
reason	a reason for	What was the reason for his anger?
receive	receive sth from	At the end of the course, you'll all receive a certificate from the college.
recipe	a recipe for	My mum has got a great recipe for chocolate cake.
recover	recover from	I hope you've recovered from your injury.
refer	refer to	I realised Doug was in charge when one of the others referred to him as 'the boss'.
relationship	a relationship with	Do you have a good relationship with your parents?
rely	rely on	You can always rely on Andrew.
remind	remind sb of	Who does this picture remind you of?
remove	remove sth from	You have to remove this piece of card.
reply	reply to	Don't forget to reply to Kelly's letter, will you?
responsible	responsible for	Who's responsible for cleaning the classroom?
result	result in	Falling out of the tree resulted in me going to hospital!
save	save sth from	We've got to save lots of animals from becoming extinct.
scared	scared of	Hold my hand – there's nothing to be scared of.
send	send sth to sb	I'm going to send some photographs to Irene.
serious	serious about	If you're serious about being a doctor, I'll give you some advice.
share	share sth with	I'll share this bar of chocolate with you.
short	short of	I'm very short of money!
similar	similar to	Horse meat tastes a little similar to beef, or lamb.
smell	smell of	These sweets smell of flowers.
smile	smile at	Smile at the camera!
solution	a solution to	I hope we can find a solution to that problem soon.
sorry	sorry about/for	I'm sorry about/for what I said to Susie.

spend	spend sth on	*What do you spend your pocket money on each week?*
succeed	succeed in	*I really hope you succeed in all your exams.*
suitable	suitable for	*This film is not suitable for children under the age of 15.*
sure	sure about/of	*I'm not sure about/of the answer.*
surprised	surprised at/by	*We were all surprised at/by Tom's decision to give up football.*
talented	talented at	*Cilla is really talented at singing.*
talk	talk (to sb) about	*What were you talking to James about?*
tell	tell sb about	*I've got something to tell you about.*
think	think about	*I'm going to think about that carefully.*
tired	tired of	*I'm tired of helping people and not even getting a 'thank you' for it.*
translate	translate (from sth) into	*The notice had been translated from Japanese into English.*
type	a type of	*How many types of music can you think of?*
wait	wait for	*Are you waiting for a taxi?*
work	work as	*I've always wanted to work as a lawyer.*
work	work for	*Rupert isn't a bad boss to work for.*
worry	worry about	*I'm very worried about Tracy.*
write	write (to sb) about	*Write to your grandma about what you bought with your Christmas money.*
wrong	wrong about	*I think Serena is wrong about Ian – he seems really nice to me.*
wrong	wrong with	*There's something wrong with my watch. What time is it?*

Word formation

able	ability	I admire your ability to speak so many different languages.
	disabled	Lots of disabled people have jobs.
	unable	I'm unable to attend the meeting tomorrow.
act	action	They say that actions speak louder than words.
	actor	I would love to be an actor.
	active	Johnnie is six years old, so he's very active and has a lot of energy.
	inactive	I've been a bit inactive since I got a job in an office.
add	addition	The team is much better with the addition of Simon Jones.
admire	admiration	I'm full of admiration for Jamie.
advice	advise	I would advise you not to get that MP3 player.
	adviser	Phil works as a housing adviser for the local council.
afford	affordable	The homes we sell are very affordable.
agree	agreement	We're all in agreement about this.
	disagree	I'm afraid I disagree.
art	artist	Picasso was a great artist.
	artistic	Ralph has always been artistic and he loves drawing.
assist	assistant	My mum has an assistant at work who helps her.
	assistance	The police officer offered her assistance to the old woman.
athlete	athletic	You need to be very athletic to play volleyball.
	athletics	When we go to the Olympics, I want to see the athletics.
attract	attractive	The south of England is really attractive at this time of year.
	attraction	The old castle is probably the most popular attraction in this area.
back	backwards	Have you ever tried running backwards?
bake	baker	The baker is making a cake for the party.
	bakery	I'll go to the bakery to get some bread.
beg	beggar	I was surprised to see beggars on the streets of London.
begin	began	The lesson began at ten o'clock.
	begun	We'd already begun when Sam arrived.
	beginner	She lost the game, but she is only a beginner.
	beginning	I missed the end of the film, but I saw the beginning.
belief	believe	I don't believe you!
	believable	The film was completely believable.
	unbelievable	That's unbelievable! It can't be true!
bend	bent	I had an accident on my bike and now the front wheel is bent.
boil	boiler	There's a problem with the boiler, so there's no hot water.
	boiling	The pan was full of boiling water.
bore	boring	This game is really boring. Let's do something else.
	bored	The start of the film was okay, but I soon got bored.
boss	bossy	Stop telling me what to do and don't be so bossy all the time!
brave	bravery	The police officer got an award for bravery.
break	broke	I dropped the cup on the floor and it broke.
	broken	You can't use my MP3 player because it's broken.
	breakable	Are these pots breakable?
	unbreakable	This window is made out of unbreakable glass.
care	careful	Be careful!
	careless	I made a lot of silly mistakes because I was careless.
centre	central	They live in central London.
certain	certainly	The weather is certainly getting better, isn't it?
	certainty	'Matt must have left,' George said with certainty.
chemist	chemical	Sodium is a chemical.
	chemistry	I like doing chemistry at school.
child	children	I watched some children playing in the playground.
	childhood	My mum spent her childhood in France.

choose	chose chosen choice	*Sylvia finally chose chocolate ice cream.* *Take the book you have chosen and get it stamped by the librarian.* *You have a choice – you can either have strawberry or chocolate ice cream.*
circle	circular	*Our dining table is circular.*
collect	collection collector	*John has got a great collection of football shirts.* *I sold my old stamps to a collector.*
comedy	comedian	*My favourite comedian is Jim Carrey.*
comfort	comfortable uncomfortable	*That sofa looks very comfortable, doesn't it?* *After four hours on the plane, I was beginning to feel uncomfortable.*
communicate	communication	*This course is designed to improve your communication skills.*
compare	comparison	*You can't draw a comparison between Tim and Alex – they're completely different.*
compose	composition composer	*Please give me your compositions on Thursday.* *Mozart is my favourite composer.*
conclude	conclusion	*I've come to the conclusion that exams are useful.*
confident	confidence	*You need confidence to perform in public.*
confuse	confused confusion	*I'm still confused about what happened.* *There was a lot of confusion when the fire alarm went off.*
connect	connection disconnect	*My connection to the Internet costs about €30 a month.* *You need to disconnect the DVD player from the TV before you connect the PlayStation.*
cook	cooker cookery	*We bought a new gas cooker yesterday.* *Can I borrow your cookery book?*
correct	correction incorrect	*I've made a few corrections to your article.* *I'm afraid that's incorrect.*
courage	courageous	*That was very courageous of you.*
danger	dangerous	*It's dangerous to drive very fast.*
decide	decision	*So, what's your final decision?*
deep	deeply depth	*That's when I fell deeply in love with him.* *What's the depth of the swimming pool?*
deliver	delivery	*There's a van outside – are you expecting a delivery?*
depart	departure	*British Airways announces the departure of flight BA 632 to Moscow.*
destroy	destruction destructive	*We've got to stop the destruction of the local environment.* *Storms can be very destructive.*
direct	direction	*Which direction did he go in?*
divide	division	*I'm good at multiplication, but not division.*
drive	drove driven driver	*I can't believe you drove all the way to Paris.* *Can electric cars be driven on the roads in the UK?* *I asked the taxi driver to slow down.*
educate	education	*Every child should get an education.*
elect	election	*Who are you going to vote for in the election?*
emotion	emotional	*Nigel is quite an emotional person and gets upset very easily.*
employ	employment unemployment employer employee unemployed	*What kind of employment are you looking for, Mr Rogers?* *Unemployment is a really big problem in this area.* *Your employer is responsible for providing training.* *Our boss doesn't always let all the employees know what's happening.* *My uncle has been unemployed for more than five years now.*
energy	energetic	*Jack is really energetic. I can't keep up with him!*
entertain	entertainment	*There isn't much entertainment in the evenings in my town.*
equal	equality unequal	*I believe in equality for women.* *They had 15 people in their team and we only had 12, so it was unequal.*
examine	exam(ination) examiner	*I've got a French exam(ination) tomorrow.* *The examiner was very friendly.*

except	exception	*Everyone, with the exception of James, passed the test.*
excite	excitement exciting excited	*Come to Adventure World for fun and excitement!* *Swimming with dolphins must be really exciting.* *I'm so excited about Georgia's party!*
exhibit	exhibition	*Have you seen the Egyptian exhibition at the museum?*
expense	expensive inexpensive	*It's nice, but isn't it a bit expensive?* *The clothes in that shop are good quality, and quite inexpensive.*
express	expression expressive	*What does the expression 'save someone's bacon' mean?* *French seems to me to be a very expressive language.*
fame	famous	*I'm quite shy, so I don't think I'd like to be famous.*
fascinate	fascination fascinating	*Where did your fascination for cars come from?* *I've always found cars fascinating.*
feel	felt feeling feelings	*I've never felt so happy in my whole life.* *I have a feeling that I've been here before.* *You really hurt my feelings last night.*
fly	flew flown flight	*A bird flew past the window.* *Have you ever flown in such a small plane?* *Our flight leaves at three in the morning.*
fog	foggy	*It was so foggy I couldn't see my feet!*
forgive	forgave forgiven forgiveness	*Colin apologised, so I forgave him.* *I've forgiven you.* *I'm asking for your forgiveness.*
free	freedom	*People often have to fight for their freedom.*
garden	gardener gardening	*My grandfather is an amateur gardener.* *Gardening is a very relaxing pastime.*
hand	handful handle	*I asked my dad for some money and he gave me a handful of coins.* *Put the money in, pull the handle and your chocolate bar comes out here.*
happy	unhappy happiness unhappiness	*You seem a little unhappy. Can I help?* *I don't think that money brings you happiness.* *There's a lot of unhappiness in the world.*
hate	hatred	*Why is there so much hatred between people from these two countries?*
help	helpful unhelpful helpless	*Thank you, you've been very helpful.* *That shop assistant was really unhelpful.* *I felt helpless and didn't know what to do.*
hero	heroic heroine	*The story was all about two heroic young men.* *The heroine of the book finally gets married.*
history	historic historian	*It's a(n) historic building.* *I want to be a(n) historian.*
honest	dishonest honesty	*I don't like people who are dishonest.* *Honesty is a very important quality in a friend.*
identify	identity identical	*She hid her identity by wearing a disguise.* *These two pictures are identical.*
imagine	imagination imaginative	*Theresa has got a lot of imagination.* *Your story was really imaginative.*
inform	informative information	*Your e-mail was very informative – thanks.* *Have they got any more information about the explorers yet?*
instruct	instruction instructor	*Listen carefully to the instructions before you do the exercise.* *She's a driving instructor.*
intelligent	intelligence	*It's not easy to measure the intelligence of chimpanzees.*
intend	intention intentional	*It wasn't my intention to upset you.* *It wasn't intentional! I did it by mistake!*
introduce	introduction	*I didn't read the introduction to the book.*
invade	invasion invader	*Julius Caesar led the Roman invasion of Britain.* *Local people fought against the invaders.*
jog	jogging jogger	*I go jogging every morning.* *The park is full of joggers in the morning.*

judge	judgement	*Nobody was surprised at the judgement – not even the criminal himself.*
lie	liar lying	*You're a liar!* *Lying to your friends is very bad.*
life	live alive	*I used to live in Canada.* *I'm glad I'm alive!*
long	length	*I swam the length of the swimming pool.*
luck	lucky unlucky luckily unluckily	*Do you think you're a lucky person generally?* *We were unlucky to lose the match.* *Luckily, I won the game.* *Unluckily, our car broke down.*
measure	measurement	*They took measurements of the level of pollution in the river.*
medicine	medical	*Is it a serious medical problem?*
memory	memorise memorial	*Do we have to memorise all these irregular verbs?* *There's a memorial to Mr Watkins in the school garden.*
music	musical musician	*Do you have much musical talent?* *It's not easy becoming a professional musician.*
nation	nationality national international	*What's her nationality? Is she French?* *Tomorrow is a national holiday.* *We're an international organisation.*
nature	natural naturally	*It's an area of great natural beauty.* *Is your hair naturally curly?*
noise	noisy noisily	*It's very noisy in here! I can't hear what you're saying.* *Larry came in at four in the morning and noisily took his boots off.*
occupy	occupation	*The form asked for my occupation and I wrote 'Student'.*
office	officer	*A police officer saw the man take the bicycle and started to chase after him.*
	official	*They haven't made an official announcement of the reason for the delay yet.*
	unofficial	*The decision is unofficial until the boss signs the agreement.*
pain	painful painless	*My knee is very painful.* *The operation is painless – it won't hurt at all.*
peace	peaceful peacefully	*You looked very peaceful when you were asleep.* *The dog was sleeping peacefully when it suddenly heard a noise.*
perfect	perfection	*You can make your painting better and better, but perfection is impossible.*
	imperfect	*Don't feel too bad about what you did. We're all imperfect.*
person	personality personal	*Fiona has got a great personality.* *I've got a few personal problems to sort out.*
play	player playful	*One of the players was injured when he scored a goal.* *My baby brother is very playful.*
pollute	pollution polluted	*There are lots of different kinds of pollution.* *Polluted rivers are not safe to swim in.*
predict	prediction predictable unpredictable	*My prediction is that City will win the match 2–0 on Sunday.* *You're so predictable – I knew you were going to say that!* *Be careful! Their dog is quite unpredictable.*
prefer	preference preferable	*I'd like pizza, but that's just my personal preference.* *I think flying is preferable to going there by train.*
prepare	preparation	*The key to a good performance is a lot of preparation.*
prison	prisoner	*The prisoner asked the guard for a blanket.*
recommend	recommendation	*We made a number of recommendations to the manager.*
reduce	reduction	*There's been a small reduction in the price of petrol.*
refer	reference	*I'm applying for a job, so could you write me a reference?*
refuse	refusal	*We were all surprised by Danny's refusal to apologise.*
relate	relative relation relationship	*Are all your relatives coming to the wedding?* *Are all your relations coming to the wedding?* *I have a great relationship with all my teachers.*

retire	retired retirement	*My grandad is retired and has lots of hobbies.* *My dad seems to be looking forward to retirement.*
safe	save unsafe safety	*The man next to me saved me when I almost fell in front of the train.* *Don't go into that old house – it's unsafe.* *Safety at work is very important.*
sail	sailing sailor	*I love sailing and I try to go every summer.* *A sailor helped us put our bags onto the ship.*
science	scientist	*Albert Einstein was a scientist.*
secret	secretly secrecy	*Jim secretly placed the love letter in Andrea's bag.* *I don't like all this secrecy. Why don't we tell Mary the truth?*
sense	sensible sensitive	*It was sensible to bring an umbrella.* *Dave is very sensitive, so don't criticise him.*
serve	service servant	*The service here is terrible!* *What was it like to live in a big house with dozens of servants?*
shoot	shot shooting	*Ronald Reagan was shot when he was President of the USA.* *We go shooting a lot, but we never shoot animals or birds.*
silent	silence silently	*I want absolute silence in the exam.* *The students all worked silently.*
simple	simplify simplicity	*It's very difficult, so I'll simplify it for you.* *Simplicity is important in good written communication.*
sing	sang sung	*I sang in the choir when I was young.* *When my dad was at school, they had a song which was sung every morning.*
	song singer singing	*What's the name of that song you're singing?* *Kylie Minogue is one of my favourite singers.* *I love Katy's singing – she's got a good voice.*
solve	solution	*I hope we can find a solution to this problem soon.*
speak	spoke spoken speaker speech	*I didn't know Len spoke Turkish.* *Can you name four countries where English is spoken?* *I can't hear what the speaker is saying.* *I have to give a speech at school and I'm really nervous.*
succeed	success successful unsuccessful	*What's the secret of your success?* *Work hard and I'm sure you'll be successful.* *I was unsuccessful in changing his mind.*
suggest	suggestion	*Can I make a suggestion?*
sympathy	sympathise sympathetic	*I can sympathise with you because I've been through the same problems.* *Jody was very sympathetic when I told her about my bad luck.*
translate	translation translator	*I haven't read War and Peace in Russian, but I've read a translation.* *You need to work hard to get a job as a translator.*
travel	traveller	*If you're an experienced traveller, you'll know how important it is to be organised.*
true	truth untrue truthful	*Now, I want you to tell me the truth.* *What she said is untrue – I didn't hit her at all!* *To be truthful, I don't really like Liz.*
use	useful useless	*My laptop is really useful – I don't know what I would do without it.* *You've broken the DVD player and now it's useless!*
value	valuable	*Are any of these paintings valuable?*
visit	visitor	*The zoo has about 250,000 visitors a year.*
weigh	weight	*You don't need to lose weight.*